Lyman Hotchkiss Bagg

Four Years at Yale

Lyman Hotchkiss Bagg

Four Years at Yale

ISBN/EAN: 9783743353800

Manufactured in Europe, USA, Canada, Australia, Japa

Cover: Foto ©ninafisch / pixelio.de

Manufactured and distributed by brebook publishing software (www.brebook.com)

Lyman Hotchkiss Bagg

Four Years at Yale

FOUR YEARS AT YALE

By a Graduate of '69

NEW HAVEN, CONN.

CHARLES C. CHATFIELD & CO.

1871

PREFACE.

The erroneous and absurd ideas which very many intelligent people, who have not chanced to experience it, entertain upon the subject of college life, have led me to believe that a minute account of affairs as they exist to-day at one of the chief American colleges would not be without value to the general public, nor without interest to the alumni and undergraduates of other colleges as well as of the one described. Hence, though not without some little diffidence, I venture to offer this compilation of facts, which no one has ever yet taken the trouble to group together, with the hope that it may be of service as a corrector of opinion and of interest as an aid to the memory.

Looking at things from the undergraduate in distinction from the official stand-point, I have given as little attention as possible to those matters which a formal historian would render prominent, and have gone into the smallest details in cases which he would take no notice of. I have accounted no fact too trivial or insignificant to be unworthy of record. I have attached no moral to the most important one. I have simply endeavored to place every scrap of evidence fairly before the reader, leaving him to decide for himself how much of it to use in making up his judgment. I have studiously refrained from urging any idea or theory of my own, and have endeavored, in cases where some expression of opinion seemed necessary, to offer simply the prevailing sentiment of college. Yet, that my position may not be misunderstood, I have added a Concluding Chapter, for the expression of my personal beliefs, and I respectfully ask that no one represent anything in the book as an "opinion" of mine until he has read that chapter. Facts are facts, and because I see fit to describe them in cold blood, without comment of any sort, I do not wish to be quoted either as approving of or as condemning them.

Some of my statements will doubtless be distasteful to many. Some may be called untrue or unfair. Especially will the facts offered in regard to the Society System be likely to arouse ill-will. Now, I have never gone out of my way to pry into society secrets; nor have I attempted any betrayal of them. I have simply repeated the current beliefs and rumors, without pretending to vouch for their correctness. Indeed, as a society man, I know that some of the things reported are not true in fact; but I have taken an outside view of matters, and reported nothing save what a man learns—or at least might easily learn—who never enters a society-hall. My narrations, I think, on the whole, tend to the societies' advantage; and if any fierce partisan blames me for having, in some instances, said too much, let him at least give me the credit for having, in every instance, kept back much which I might have said. As I was left a neutral in senior year, I can hardly be accused of having much prejudice in favor of the senior societies, and if I have treated them with fairness, the fact may perhaps induce some to believe in my ability to take an impersonal, unprejudiced, outside view of the others which make up the system.

I am aware that the arrangement of this book is to some extent arbitrary. I accepted it only as a choice of evils. But I hope that the head-lines placed before each Chapter, and the Index at the end, may in great part compensate for this defect. I know, too, that there are in it many repetitions and some seeming contradictions and inconsistencies. I perceive how easy it will be to mis-quote my work, and to use isolated and disconnected portions of it to the detriment of particular interests of the college, or even of the institution itself. I regret the fact most keenly; yet, after all, such snap-judgments are of less account than deliberate opinions drawn from a full consideration of all the facts, and I firmly believe that anyone who reads this book to the end will have no worse opinion of Yale life from knowing what it really is. If the event proves otherwise, "so much the worse for the facts"; but these ought none the less to be made known. What I ask is, that they should *all* be taken into account; and that hasty conclusions should not be jumped at, from a partial or one-sided glance at the evidence.

Covering as it does a ground never before touched upon, this book must inevitably contain many errors in its facts and state-ments; for, though I have given the largest attention to detailing things known to my own experience, I have of necessity been obliged to trust to hear-say and tradition for many of my assertions. I shall, therefore, most gladly receive any corrections or additions, which may be offered to my notice, either publicly or privately, by those who are able to make them, in order that, should a second edition be called for, it may be made more perfect than the present one. It is equally inevitable that the book, being the production of a young and unpractised writer, must contain many errors of expression, and special literary defects; and I ask of the critics who may happen to notice it, that, as a particular favor, they will, if they condemn my literary execution, be good enough to descend into the details of the matter, and not dismiss it with a few general maledictions. The latter would probably do no one any good, but the former might be a real benefit to me, as I make no pretensions to excellence, and am not yet too old to learn.

One thing more. I have written this book impersonally and published it anonymously. No officer of the college, or member of my class, has had any knowledge of it, or connection with it. Of course every one who knows me will be likely to at once recognize me in these pages, and of course I am perfectly willing thus to be recognized. But one thing I do ask, and that is that those who know me will refrain from dragging my personality before the public. For the one and only thing which it concerns the public to know, in forming its opinion of what I have written, is the thing which I have announced upon the title-page, in saying that I am

A GRADUATE OF '69.

June 17, 1871.

CONTENTS.

INTRODUCTORY CHAPTER.

HISTORICAL AND EXPLANATORY, ... 1

Origin of Yale College—Its Early Wanderings—The First College Hall—Elihu Yale—The Rival Commencements of 1718—Restoration of Harmony—Religious Tests—The Nine Presidents—Relations between the State and the College—Members of the Corporation—Proposed Change in the Charter—Organization of the Faculty—Division of Responsibility—Position of the College Yard—Construction of the Brick Row: South Middle, 1750; Athenæum, 1761; South, 1793; North Middle and Lyceum, 1800; North, 1821; Chapel, 1824; Divinity, 1835—Situation of the Dormitories—The Central Row: Laboratory, 1782; Cabinet, 1819; Treasury, 1832—The High Street Row: Library, 1842; Alumni Hall, 1853; Art Building, 1864—Proposed Removal of the College—Final Adoption of the Reconstruction Plan—The Two New Dormitories — Presidents' Houses — Gymnasium — The Theological School—The Law School—The Medical School—The Sheffield Scientific School—College Men and School Men—The Patrons of the College — Its Financial Condition — Vocabulary of College Words—List of Publications relating to Yale.

PART FIRST.
THE SOCIETY SYSTEM.

CHAPTER I.—FRESHMAN SOCIETIES, ... 51

Development of the Modern System—Kappa Sigma Epsilon—Delta Kappa—Gamma Nu—Sigma Delta—Election of Active and Honorary Members—Catalogues—The Outside Chapters and Statistics of Membership—The Society System in Other Colleges—Badge Pins and Mottoes—Halls and Mode of Renting Them—Electioneering—Initiation—Suppers—Interference of Upper-class Men—Farewell Ceremonies of the Sophomores—Meetings anp

1*

Exercises—"Peanut Bums"—Treatment of Intruders—Officers
and the Campaign Election—Coalitions—System of Electioneering
—Initiation Committees' Supper—Expenses of Membership—
Society Zeal and its Gradual Decline—Significance of Prize Lists—
Notable Members—Comparison of the Societies—Anomalous
Position of Gamma Nu—Initiation Fables and their Origin—
Theory of the Supper Business—Advice to sub-Freshmen.

CHAPTER II.—SOPHOMORE SOCIETIES, . . . 87

Kappa Sigma Theta—Alpha Sigma Phi—Phi Theta Psi—Delta
Beta Xi—The Yale "Banger" and "Tomahawk"—Chapters—
Posters and Song Books—Electioneering and Pledging—Giving
out Elections—Initiation—Ordinary Exercises—Singing—Class
Elections—The Sophomore Type.

CHAPTER III.—JUNIOR SOCIETIES, ... 106

Alpha Delta Phi—Psi Upsilon—Delta Kappa Epsilon—Badges,
Vignettes and Mottoes—Catalogues, Chapters and Membership—
The Death of Old Chapters and the Origin of New Ones—Names
of Prominent Members—General Conventions—Intercourse
between the Chapters—Giving out Elections—Initiation—Meetings
and Exercises—Halls—Corporate Titles—The Course of Politics
in '69 (the Freshman Societies; the Annual Dinner Committee;
the Gamma-Nu-Delta-Phi Embroglio; the Cochs and "Lit."
Editors)—The Effect upon Delta Phi—Agreements concerning the
Freshmen—Real Character of a Coalition—The Division of the
Spoils—The Contested Elections of Members—Duration of Society
Influences—Comparison of the Societies.

CHAPTER IV.—SENIOR SOCIETIES, ... 142

Peculiarities of these Societies—Skull and Bones—Its Badge Pin
and Numeral—Hall and Corporate Title—Origin—Catalogue—
Mode of Giving out Elections—Initiation—Mode of Summoning
Members to the Annual Convention—Attendance upon the Regular
and Special Meetings—Peculiar Customs and Traditions—Scroll
and Key—Its Badge Pin and Vignette—Hall and Corporate Title
—Origin and Growth—Customs and Traditions—Spade and Grave
—Its Origin, Precarious Existence, Change of Name, and Final
Catastrophe—The Societies and the Neutrals—Bull and Stones—
The Coffin of '69—The Tea-Kettle of '53—Crown and Scepter—
Star and Dart—Notable Members of the Existing Societies—Mode
of Packing and Making up a Crowd—Comparison of the Societies
—Their "Policies," Actual and Possible—Failure of their Imitators

in Other Colleges—General Facts about all the Class Societies—Comparison of their Importance in Each Year—General Result of the System.

CHAPTER V.—SOCIETY INSTITUTIONS, . . . 190

Linonia, and Brothers in Unity—Their Origin and Early History—Rivalry in Gaining Members—The Statement of Facts—The Campaign, a Dozen Years Ago—The Rush—Latest Modes of Distributing the Freshmen—Initiation—Meetings and Exercises—Exhibitions—Officers, Politics, and the Campaign Election—Attendance—Management of the Finances—The Society Halls—Catalogues—Libraries—Reading Room—The College Bookstore—The Prize Debates—Annual and Centennial Celebrations—Analysis of the Society Tax of 1869-70—Calliope and Phœnix—Phi Beta Kappa—Its Origin and Peculiar Organization—Names of the Chapters—Meetings and Exercises—Orations and Poems—Qualifications for Membership—An Invasion of Barbarians—The Society Badge Key—Initiation—The Annual Business Meeting—Catalogues—Significance of the Fraternity—Chi Delta Theta—Its Literary Character—The Present Wearers of its Badge.

PART SECOND.
THE STUDENT LIFE.

CHAPTER I.—FRESHMAN YEAR, ... 237

Board and Lodging—Eating Clubs—Their Formation and Characteristics—Names, Mottoes and Devices—The College Club or Commons—The Old Commons Hall System—The Old Buttery—Smoking Out—Stealing—Hazing—Put Out That Light!—Rushing—The Foot-Ball Game—The Painting Disgrace—Gate Lifting—Lamp Smashing—Thanksgiving Jubilee—As it was Known to '69—Its Previous Origin and Growth—Interference of the Faculty—The Last Jubilee—Its Character in the Future—Pow-Wow—The Annual Dinner, and its Predecessor, the Biennial Jubilee—The Freshman Laws of the Last Century—The Old Manner of Lecturing.

CHAPTER II.—SOPHOMORE YEAR, ... 287

Rooming in College—Drawing and Choosing the Rooms—Trading of Choices—Rooming Alone—Packing an Entry—Moving—Rent—Buying and Selling Furniture—Fuel, Water and Light—Sweeps, Regular and Private—Paraphernalia of a Student's Room—Its Self-Invited Visitors—Candy Sam, Hannibal, Fine Day, and

the Rest—The Tricks Sometimes Played upon Them—The College
Police, and the Extent of their Interference—The Charm of Dormi-
tory Life—Sitting on the Fence—Unsuccessful Attempt to Break up
the Practice—Cause of the Failure—Out-door Singing—Origin of
the Practice, and of the Songs—Glee Clubs, Cecilia and Beethoven
—The Latter's Connection with the College Choir—R. S. Willis's
Account of It—And its First Concert—Its Recent Character and
Membership—Concerts and their Profits--Sophomoric Abuse of
Freshmen—Public Sentiment concerning It—Areopagus—Nu Tau
Phi—Omega Lambda Chi—A Mock Initiation—Compromises with
the Faculty—Burning the Coal Yard—Base Ball—Yale against
Harvard—The Record with other College and Professional Clubs
—Places and Times Devoted to the Sport—Entertainment of Vis-
itors—The Burial of Euclid—As Described in 1843—Fifteen Years
Later—Davenport's Lithograph—The Last Celebration of the Rite
—Similar Ceremonies Elsewhere.

CHAPTER III.—JUNIOR YEAR, ... 327
Boating—The Decade Ending in 1853—Organization of the Yale
Navy—Catalogue of Boats—Formation of Permanent Boat Clubs
in 1860—Their Boats—Adoption of the Present System in 1868-70
—Third List of Boats—Riker's and the Boat House of 1859—
Dedication of the Present Boat House—Incorporation of the Navy
—The Boat House Lease—Payment of the Debt by the Commo-
dore of '70—The Annual Commencement Regattas, 1853-58—The
Fall Races, 1859-67—Course of the Champion Flag, 1853-71—The
Regattas on Lake Saltonstall—The Phelps Barge Races and the
Southworth Cup—Irregular Regattas, 1856-65—Uniforms and
Flags—Yale and Harvard—The First Period, 1852-60—The Sec-
ond Period, 1864-70—The Lesser Races of this Period—The Seven
Great University Races—Regatta Day at Worcester—Student Row-
dyism—Blue and Red—Betting—Dress, Training and Trainers—
Attempt to Belittle Yale's Triumph in 1865—The Foulings of 1870,
and the Resulting Complications—Refusal of Harvard to Answer
the Challenge for 1871—The Seven University Crews—Gymnastics
—The Practice of Boating Men—The Favorite Hour for Exercise
—The Annual Exhibition—The Wooden Spoon Presentation—Ori-
gin of the Idea—Mode of Electing the Cochleaureati—Political
Considerations—Initiation, and the Spoon—" Insigne Cochleaurea-
torum"—The Temple Exhibitions—Humbugging an Audience—
Brewster's and Music Halls—The Opening Loads—Philosophical
Orations—Changes in the Exhibition—Its Increased Cost, and How

it was Met—Mode of Distributing Tickets and Reserved Seats—
Character of the Audience — The Promenade Concert—Society
Statistics—Abolition of the Spoon Presentation by '72—Proposed
Substitute for the Exhibition and Concert.

CHAPTER IV.—SENIOR YEAR, ... 424
Journalism—The Yale Literary Magazine—Election of Editors
—Initiation Supper—Chi Delta Theta—Organization and Manage-
ment of the Magazine—Its Printers and Publishers—Mode of So-
liciting Subscriptions—Number of Subscribers—Back Numbers
and Sets—Paying the Printer—The Repudiated Debt of 1858—Collecting Subscriptions—Profit and Loss—Advertisements—The Lit.
Prize Medal—Class and Society Connections of the Winners—
Character of the Medal and the Essay—Typographical Changes—
Editorial Independence in '64—Theory of After Elections—The
Original Literary Ideal—Gradual Growth of the Mirror-of-College-
Life Theory—Contributors—The General Index of 1868—Illustra-
tions and Typography—The Position of Editor—Notable Gradu-
ates of the Lit. Office—Society Statistics of the Editors—Repre-
sentative Character of the Magazine—Its Predecessors : Literary
Cabinet, Athenæum, Crayon, Sitting Room, Student's Companion,
Little Gentleman, Gridiron, Medley — The Yale Review and Yale
Literary Quidnunc—The University Quarterly—Its Mode of Publi-
cation—Organization of the Quarterly Asssociation—Names of the
Colleges Composing It—The Yale Men and Their Work—Editorial
Convention—Finances and Prizes—Credit Due the Publishers—
The Yale Banner, Pot Pourri, and Other Catalogues—Minor Papers
and Feuilletons—The College Courant—Its Humble Origin in 1865
—Change of Name and Management in 1867—Advertisements—
The Undergraduate Department—Society Connections of the Edi-
tors—The New Yale Courant of the Undergraduates—Printers and
Typography—Recent Make-up of the College Courant—Class Pic-
tures—How Procured— How Distributed and Exchanged— The
New Plan—Origin of the Custom—Varieties of Pictures, 1847-71
—Class Seals and Mottoes—Memorabil and Its Collectors—Pres-
entation Day—The Original Formalities—As Celebrated in 1778
and Afterwards—The Modern Poem and Oration—Announcement
of Prizes—The Faculty's Collation—Election of Orator and Poet—
Course of Senior Politics in '69—Society Statistics—General Good
Feeling — Plagiarism— Presentation Afternoon— Class Histories
and Historians—The True Test of College Wit and Humor—Class
Statistics—The Ring and Triangle—Under the Elms—Singing, an

Obsolete Custom — Reading the Histories — Planting the Ivy—
Cheering the College Buildings and Professors—Saying the Last
Farewell—History of the Class Ivies—Incidents and Accidents of
the Day.

CHAPTER V.—Town and Gown, ... 500
Bullyism—Capture of the Bully Club—Election of Bullies—Their
Duties and Privileges—The Fight of Bully against President—Its
Culmination in 1840—Abolishment of Bullyism—Preservation of
the Club—Town and Gown — the Firemen's Riot of 1841—The
"City Guard" and the "Banner"—The Riot of 1854—Preliminary
Hostilities — The Attack — Death of the Rioters' Ringleader —
Frenzy of the Mob—South College to be Bombarded—The Siege
Abandoned—Preparations for the Defence—Coroner's Investigation
—The Popular Verdict—The High street Fracas of 1858—Who
Fired the Fatal Shot?—The Stafford Homicide of 1860—The
Stabbing of a College Officer in 1843 — The Students and the
Peelers—Cause of their Enmity—The Knock-down of 1870—The
City Tradesmen and their College Customers—The Old Sumptuary
Laws—Present Habits in Dress—Disregard of Family or Local
Pretensions—Politics and the Suffrage—The Student in Society—
College Widows—Society and the Mission Schools—Prayer Meet-
ings—The Missionary and other Religious Societies—The Tem-
perance Society—Drinking and Licentiousness—Swearing, Smok-
ing, Chewing, Billiard Playing and Gambling—Cards, Chess, and
Velocipedes — Sailing Excursions — Camping Out on the Thimbles —
Walking, Foot-Racing, Skating and Driving—Obituary Customs—
Post-Graduate Class Meetings—The Class Records—Exercises of
a Class Reunion—Origin of the Class Cup—The First Cup Presentation of '44—Changes in the Custom—Recent Abandonment of
the Ceremony.

Part Third.

THE OFFICIAL CURRICULUM.

CHAPTER I.—Studies, ... 542
The Entrance Examinations—White and Blue Papers—When to
Attend—How to be Prepared—Quantity and Quality—Advanced
Students—Organization of the Class—The Recitation Rooms and
Recitations—Mode of Instruction—Exceptional Pronunciation of
Greek Society-Letters—Optional Work—The Term Examinations
—The Annuals—The Studies Pursued by the Class of '69—Fresh-

man Year—Sophomore Year—Junior Year—Senior Year—Variations and Changes in the Curriculum—The Studies of a Century Ago—Old Systems of Examination.

CHAPTER II.—MARKS, ... 569
Morning Prayers—The Ordinary Ceremonies—Sunday Services —The College Church and its Members—Attending City Churches —The College Choir and Organ—Government by Marks—Schedule of Penalties—"The Course of Discipline"—Monitors and Their Duties—Matriculation—Scholarship by Marks—Time and Mode of Giving out Stands — Making-up Omitted Lessons—Excuses and Church Papers — Leaves of Absence — Letters Home — Official Hieroglyphics—Appealing to the Faculty—Living Regulations and Dead Laws—Origin and Growth of the 'Code—Discipline in the Olden Time—Fines, "Degradation," and "Cuffing"—The Modern Theory of Discipline—The Recent Experiment in Division.

CHAPTER III.—HONORS, ... 590
Appointments for Junior Exhibition and Commencement—How they are Determined and Announced—The Amount of Exertion which they Call Forth—Stand, as Popularly Regarded—"Scholars of the House"—The Berkeley Scholarship—Sheldon Clark, and his Donations—The Bristed Scholarship—Freshman Scholarships : Woolsey, Hurlbut and Runk—DeForest Scholarship for Modern Languages—Beneficiary Funds—The Harmer Foundation—The DeForest Fund—Premiums for Translation and Latin Composition —Miscellaneous Clark Awards—Prizes in Astronomy and Mathematics—Declamation Prizes : Old and New Modes of Awarding Them—Prizes for English Composition—Prize Poems—New Mode of Awarding the Composition Prizes—"Honorary Mentions" for the Seniors—The Townsend Premiums, and the DeForest Medal —Speaking for the Prize—Statistics of the DeForest Men—Total Prize and Scholarship Funds of the College—General Effects of the Honor System.

CHAPTER IV.—MANNERS, ... 620
Skinning—Ordinary Methods—Blackboard Work—Conics and Chemistry in '69—At Term Examination—Stealing the Papers— Hands and Feet — Skinning-Machines — Indexing a Subject—A Unique Fraud Detected—Swapping the Papers—The Yale and Williams Chemists of '68—At Annual—The Type and Pencil Game—Watch-Chrystals and Eye-Glasses—Pocket Skinning in '67

and '55—Calculations for Cramming—Robbing the Printers—
Attempted Seizure of the Puckle Paper of '69—How a Baffled
Thief at last Succeeded—Working up a Case—Inner and Outer
Rings—Cheating on Make-ups—Accidental Erasures—Ponying—
Composition Frauds—How Marks are Got Rid of—Precautions
and Penalties—College Sentiment in Regard to Deceiving the
Faculty—Behavior in the Recitation Rooms—At Lectures—In the
Chapel—How Faculty and Students Address and Refer to Each
Other —Farewell Cheers for the Instructors — Absence of the
Rebellious Spirit—Insolent Tricks Discountenanced—The Faculty
Personally Respected.

CHAPTER V.—SHOWS, ... 659

Junior Exhibition—Time and Place of Holding It—Its Recent
Transformation — Managers and Invitation Notes — The Exer-
cises and their Value — The Promenade Concert — Commence-
ment—Rules for the Attendance of the Seniors—The Procession
—Arrangement of the Audience — The Speakers and the Lis-
teners — Conferring the Degrees — The Dinner and the Evening
— Recent Changes in the Show — Its Celebration in the Olden
Time—Gunpowder, Rum and Riot—The Official Calendar—The
Society of the Alumni—Concio ad Clerum—The Obituary Rec-
ord — The General Statement — The Annual Catalogue — The
Triennial Catalogue—The Alumni Associations in the Cities.

CONCLUDING CHAPTER.

A MATTER OF OPINION, ... 686

Caution to the Reader—Two Kinds of Preparation for College—
The Best Fitting-Schools — The Society System — Its General
Fairness—A Word for the Reformers—The Abuse of Freshmen
—A Disgraceful Puzzle for Moralists—Modern Languages and
Optional Studies — A " Practical" Argument for Classical Dis-
cipline — The Last American Stronghold of the Humanists —
Procrusteanism and Common Sense—The Claims of the Muscle
Men—And of the Supporters of all Honorable Customs—Who
Best Enjoy College Life ?—The Real Value of the Training—
Pecuniary Needs of the College—The Rewards of Doing Much
from Little—Unselfish Devotion of the College Officers—A Cry
from Macedonia.

FOUR YEARS AT YALE.

INTRODUCTORY CHAPTER.

HISTORICAL AND EXPLANATORY.

Origin of Yale College—Its Early Wanderings—The First College Hall—Elihu Yale—The Rival Commencements of 1718—Restoration of Harmony—Religious Tests—The Nine Presidents—Relations between the State and the College—Members of the Corporation—Proposed Change in the Charter—Organization of the Faculty—Division of Responsibility—Position of the College Yard—Construction of the Brick Row: South Middle, 1750; Athenæum, 1761; South, 1793; North Middle and Lyceum, 1800; North, 1821; Chapel, 1824; Divinity, 1835—Situation of the Dormitories—The Central Row: Laboratory, 1782; Cabinet, 1819; Treasury, 1832—The High Street Row: Library, 1842; Alumni Hall, 1853; Art Building, 1864—Proposed Removal of the College—Final Adoption of the Reconstruction Plan—The Two New Dormitories—Presidents' Houses—Gymnasium—The Theological School—The Law School—The Medical School—The Sheffield Scientific School—College Men and School Men—The Patrons of the College—Its Financial Condition—Vocabulary of College Words—List of Publications relating to Yale.

Yale College is situated in the city of New Haven, in the State of Connecticut. It dates back its origin to the very beginning of the eighteenth century. Fifty years before that, the project of establishing such an institution had been discussed, only to be finally pronounced impracticable, both on account of the poorness of the colony, and of the superior claims of Harvard upon the patronage of all friends of learning throughout New England. But, as the century drew near its end, the old plan was revived and became the great topic of interest among clergy and laity, until, at last, ten of the principal ministers of Connecticut, representing as many different towns, were nominated and appointed by general consent to act as trustees and managers of the embryo college. They first met and formed a society for the prosecution of their project, at New Haven, sometime in the year 1700; and at a subsequent meeting, the same year, at Branford, each of the trustees brought a number of books and presented them to the association, using words to this effect as he laid them on the table: "I give these books for the founding of a college in this colony." ' This act of depositing the books has ever since been considered the beginning of the college. The entire donation consisted of about forty folio volumes, valued at thirty pounds sterling. As doubts were entertained as to whether the trustees could legally hold lands, and the new institution be supported wholly by private contributions, application was made to the Colonial Assembly, which—October 9, 1701—duly ratified a charter which some Boston gentlemen had drawn up at the request of the trustees, and voted an annual allowance of sixty pounds sterling in support of the " collegiate school." The first meeting under the charter was held at Saybrook, November 11, 1701, when the trustees chose one of their own number, Rev. Abraham Pierson of Killingworth, as first rector, and decided that he should open the "school" at Saybrook, if he could be done without too much inconvenience. The first student was Jacob Hemingway — afterwards for many years the minister at East Haven—who studied alone with the rector from March till September, 1702, at which latter time the number of students was increased to eight. One of these, John Hart, who had passed three years at Harvard, graduated alone in 1703, but "the first student" did not graduate until the year following, when his class numbered three in all. The first Commencement was held in September, 1702, at Saybrook, where four young gentlemen who had been graduated at Harvard, and one who had been privately educated, received the degree of Master of Arts, and one (Nathanael Chauncey) received the degree of Bachelor. At this time a tutor was added to the corps of instructors. For five years, or until the death of the rector, March 5, 1707, the students resided with him at Killingworth, while the Commencements were held at Saybrook, privately, at the house of one of the trustees. Then, Rev. Samuel Andrews of Milford was chosen temporary rector, and for about nine years the Seniors resided with him, while the under-classes remained, under the charge of two tutors, at Saybrook, where the Commencements still continued to be held. Dissatisfaction having arisen among them at this state of things, the trustees, at a meeting in April, 1716, voted a leave of absence until the next Commencement, for such as preferred to study elsewhere. A majority of the students accordingly went to Wethersfield, some to Hartford, some to East Guilford, and a few remained at Saybrook. The senior class still continued to reside with the rector, and so, for the rest of the year, the " collegiate school" was scattered about in half a dozen different towns of the colony. In several of them, meanwhile, subscriptions began to be raised as an inducement to secure its permanent location. The largest—£700 sterling—was made by the citizens of New Haven, and thither—at a meeting held there October 17, 1716, adjourned from one held at the Saybrook Commencement, a month before, when the matter had been discussed but not fully decided—the trustees voted to remove it. At the same time they appointed a committee to attend to the building of a large and commodious college and a rector's house (there being in the treasury about £1000 sterling, derived from private subscriptions and legislative gifts); elected two tutors; and summoned them, the rector, and the scattered students, to New Haven. Thirteen attended during the year, while fourteen remained at Wethersfield, and four at Saybrook;—the latter, who comprised the entire senior class, coming up to New Haven to get their degrees at the Commencement of 1717.

"The college house was raised October 8, 1717, and within a year after was so far finished as to be fit for the commodious reception of the students. It was 170 feet long, 22 feet wide, and three stories high; made a handsome appearance, and contained nearly 50 studies, besides the hall, library, and kitchen; and it cost about £1000 sterling." It stood near the corner of the present college yard, in front of where the Athenæum and South College now stand, and was demolished in 1782. The same year in which the "school" was removed to New Haven, it received several valuable donations in books, goods and money,—the chief donor being Elihu Yale of London, governor of the East India Company. Accordingly, on the morning of the first public Commencement,— September 10, 1718,—the trustees, with requisite formalities, named the new building "Yale College," in honor of the man by whose generosity they had been enabled to complete the edifice. The patron of the institution was born at New Haven, April 5, 1648, where his father had come with the earliest settlers, ten years before, and he died, July 8, 1721. He was buried in the church yard at Wrexham, the capital of Denbighshire, in North Wales,—a town which had long been the residence of his ancient and wealthy family. Going to England at the age of ten, he received his education there, and in 1678 went to the East Indies. Here he remained twenty years longer, serving for much of the time as governor of Fort St. George on the coast of Coromandel, accumulating a very large property of his own, and marrying a wealthy lady— widow of his predecessor in office—by whom he had three daughters. He was elected governor of the East India Company, on his return to London; and there, hearing that a college had been started in his colonial birth-place which he left half a century before, he made it those valuable presents which first brought it on a respectable foundation. He seems to have been an affable, good humored man, of ready generosity, with no possible thought of the future glory and immortality accruing to his name in consequence of his careless gifts to the little collegiate school in the far-off colony of Connecticut.

At this first public Commencement, eight men were graduated, and besides their "disputations," in one of the city churches, and other exercises, the governor of the colony " was pleased to grace and crown the whole solemnity with an elegant Latin oration, wherein he congratulated the present happy state of the college in being fixed at New Haven, and enriched by so many noble benefactions ; and particularly celebrated the great generosity of Governor Yale, with much respect and honor." " All which being ended, the gentlemen re-turned to the college hall, where they were entertained with a splendid dinner ; and the ladies at the same time were also entertained in the library. After which we sung the first four verses of the sixty-fifth Psalm, and so the day ended. Everything was managed with so much order and splendor, that the fame of it extremely disheartened the opposers, and made opposition fall before it." That there was opposition is shown by the fact that, on the same day, another Commencement was held at Wethersfield, where five men were graduated. These, however, were shortly afterwards presented with regular diplomas by the authorities at New Haven, and were entered in the catalogue with the rest of their class; and the remaining students at Wethersfield were again ordered to come to the former town. In the following October, the Colonial Assembly repeated the request, as the last of its measures "to quiet the minds of people and introduce a general harmony into public affairs,"—its other decrees being: "that a State House should be built at Hartford to compensate for the college at New Haven; that £25 sterling should be given to Saybrook for the use of the school, to compensate for the removal of the college; and that the governor and council should, at the request of the trustees, give such orders as they should think proper for the removal of the library from Saybrook to New Haven." This last was quite a necessary precaution, for in December, 1718, when the trustees wished to remove the books, a large crowd of men collected in and about the house where they were stored, bent upon forcible opposition to the plan. No attention being paid to the sheriff's warrant,—issued by order of the governor and council, who, with the trustees, were present in person,—he was obliged to break open the door and, with his attendants, to wrest the library from the grasp of its guardians. Bridges were torn down and other hindrances made to prevent the return to New Haven, and while on the way the wagons were broken into by night, and to some extent robbed of their contents. In the strife and tumult, about 160 volumes and many valuable papers were lost, but the rest, — more than 1000 volumes,

—after a week's journey, reached New Haven in safety, and were stored in the college library. "After this unhappy struggle, the spirits of men began by degrees to subside, and a general harmony was gradually introduced among the trustees and the colony in general." The "up-river" ministers, who had appealed to the Legislature to interfere in their behalf, and had tried in other ways besides those mentioned to prevent the establishment of the school at New Haven, now yielded to the inevitable, became reconciled to the action of the majority, and were henceforth firm friends of the college.

The second rector, Rev. Timothy Cutler, was chosen March 19, 1719,—a dozen years after the death of his predecessor,—and by vote of the trustees, October 17, 1722, was "excused from all further service," on account of having "agreed to leave the communion of the Connecticut churches and go over to England for Episcopal ordination." Two other clergymen and one of the college tutors joined with him in this schism, which created the greatest alarm and excitement throughout the colony, and led to the establishment of a "religious test,"—all officers of the college being thenceforth obliged to assent to the "Saybrook Platform" of 1708, before entering upon their duties. Other proofs of orthodoxy were afterwards added to this, but in 1823 the whole system of tests was formally abrogated, after having been in effect obsolete for several years. Rector Cutler's dismissal was followed by an interval of four years, in which each of the trustees in turn lived at the college for a month's time and fulfilled the duties of rector,—Mr. Andrews, for twelve years temporary rector, officiating at all the Commencements, save that of 1723, when Mr. Woodbridge, one of the reconciled "up-river" trustees, was allowed to preside. The other, who had been the head of the opposition school at Wethersfield, Rev. Elisha Williams, was in 1726 inducted into office as third rector, having been chosen to the post a year before that. With his accession, the regular life of the college may be considered to have begun, — the confusion and disorder and uncertainty which had characterized its first quarter century's existence being then shaken off. On account of ill-health, he resigned his office in 1739, and Rev. Thomas Clap of Windham became his successor,—serving for twenty-seven years, or until July, 1766. In the century since then, there have been five presidents: Naphtali Daggett of '48, until 1777; Ezra Stiles of '46, until 1795; Timothy Dwight of '69, until 1817; Jeremiah Day of '95, until 1846; and Theodore Dwight Woolsey of '20, until 1871. Their four predecessors were all graduates of Harvard, as were also three tutors and nine of the ten clergymen who founded the "collegiate school" in 1700. Eighty years later, when the last Harvard man withdrew from the board of trustees, there had been fifty-six individuals connected with it, of whom one-half were Harvard graduates.

At the time when the college was founded, there were not above 15,000 inhabitants in the entire colony, and the annuity granted with the original charter was, under the circumstances, a more liberal gift than the Legislature has ever since bestowed upon the institution. The charter underwent minor amendments and amplifications in 1723, but in 1745 a new and more elaborate draft of the document was made, in eleven sections, setting forth with great exactness the powers and duties of the college officers. The names "rector," and "trustees," "founders," "undertakers" or "governors," then gave place to the style, "president and fellows of Yale

College," which title for the governing body has ever since been retained. The name " Yale College," originally applied simply to the college building, was then also first formally bestowed upon the entire institution, which up to that time had been known, officially, only as the " collegiate school." The annual grant was regularly paid until 1755, when, on account of high taxation, change in the currency, etc., it began to be withheld; and, ten years later, a dispute arising in the Legislature as to whether the college had any claim upon it for the annuity or arrearages on the same, "the president and fellows" settled the controversy by a written abandonment of all such claims. In return for this, the Assembly shortly afterwards voted them £245 sterling, towards the building of a chapel. Besides this and the annuity, it had, during the first half of the century, by various grants of land and money, given the college upwards of £2000 sterling. In 1763 certain persons presented a memorial to the Assembly, calling upon it to enquire into the affairs of the college, rectify possible abuses, etc., by means of a " commission of visitation," which it could legally do, under the common law, on account of having "founded" the college, by its grants and patronage. But the arguments of President Clap, in behalf of the independence of the college and its chartered rights, proved so conclusively the powerlessness of the Assembly to interfere therewith, that the idea of anyone save the ten associated clergymen having "founded" the college was speedily abandoned, and the memorialists were dismissed without having any action taken concerning their petition. This decision greatly reässured the friends of the college; and the point in dispute has never since been raised. But the college and its president, for this and other reasons, grew excessively unpopular; the students were encouraged to resist authority ; and in the summer of r766, when all show of subordination was at an end, the tutors as well as the president resigned, and the undergraduates dispersed to their homes.

The feeling that the Assembly ought in some way to share in the management of the college was still cherished, and all sorts of reports derogatory of the corporation—its want of progressiveness, its sectarian character, the abuses of its government, and so on—were freely circulated. At length, in 1778, shortly after the accession of President Stiles, the corporation, which had all along looked with favor upon some official connection of the State with the college, met a committee from the Assembly to discuss the matter. From the plans proposed then and afterwards nothing resulted, until 1792, when another committee, appointed the year before by the Assembly, made a report on the existing state of the college, and of the special facilities accorded them for making the most minute and thorough investigations of its affairs, which greatly pleased that body. Accordingly, the balance of the uncollected "war taxes" due the State (its war debt having been assumed by the United States) was appropriated to the support of the college, with certain reservations as to time and mode of payment ; and from this grant upwards of $40,000 was ultimately derived. As a condition of the gift, the governor, lieutenant-governor, and six senior assistants in the council were to become, by virtue of their offices, "fellows" or members of the corporation of Yale, with full powers except as to the filling up of vacancies in the clerical portion of that body. James Hillhouse, treasurer of the college, was the person chiefly instrumental in the passage of this act, whose conditions were readily accepted by the existing corporation, and which—with the unimportant change of "six senior assistants in the council" to "six senior senators," which change was rendered necessary by the new constitution of the State—has remained in force until the present time. This reunion originally created a very general satisfaction among all parties, and removed all feelings of distrust and jealousy from the minds of civilians; but for a long time past it has had little practical effect upon the management of the institution. Except the governor and lieutenant governor, the civilians who, by virtue of being State officers, are "members of the corporation," seldom take any interest in its affairs or attend its meetings, and the real managers are the eleven other "fellows," — the president of the college, who is one by virtue of his office, and the ten Congregational clergymen of Connecticut, who elect their own successors. These are thirty years old or upwards, and are usually chosen from different towns of the State, and are for the most part graduates of the college. They are not of necessity Congregational clergymen, nor even residents of Connecticut; nor yet is there any rule requiring the president of the college to be a clergyman. But since, from the foundation of the institution, all the presidents and trustees have been Congregational clergymen belonging in the State, it is a generally received opinion that they are forced to be such by the organic law. The regular annual meeting of the corporation is held at Commencement time; and for the rest of the year, except in cases of special importance, it is supposed to act through its executive committee.

The question, so much discussed of late, in regard to the alumni having a direct influence in the affairs of the college, originated in the proposition of President Woolsey — in the *New Englander* for October, 1866 — that the places of the six ex-officio State senators should be filled by as many alumni, chosen by general vote at the annual meeting. At the Commencement meeting of 1869 a committee was appointed to enquire into the feasibility of the plan ; and this committee, a year later, reported that it would be feasible in case the Legislature and the corporation should both give consent ; and it recommended the order of making elections, in case the change were adopted. As to whether or not the same should be adopted, it was about equally divided in opinion, and so made no report. The matter was discussed at length, and it was voted not to attempt making the change. Some resolutions which were offered, looking to the formation of a sort of an Alumni Council, to serve as a medium between the graduates and the corporation, but to be entirely distinct from and independent of the latter, were also voted down. At the Commencement dinner, two or three speakers—in behalf of "Young Yale," or the graduates of the past fifteen years — denounced this display of old-fogyism ; and ever since then the contest has been going on in the public prints. Some writers insist that the clergymen as well as State senators should resign, and allow the alumni to elect the entire board ; some ask only for the resignation of the senators ; and some favor the idea of an advisory council. But everyone clamors for alumni representation in the management of the college, and the institution will be likely to suffer serious injury if in some form or another this representation is not granted.

The general policy of the college, however, is shaped more by the faculty than by the corporation,—the latter apparently doing little more than to confirm the recommendations of the former. The faculty consisted simply of the president and two or three tutors, until the year 1755, when the first professorship—that of Sacred

Theology — was founded. The next — that of Mathematics and Natural Philosophy and Astronomy — was founded in 1770, and divided in 1836. Then came the professorships of Ecclesiastical History, 1777 ; of Law, 1801 ; of Chemistry, Mineralogy and Geology, 1804, afterwards divided into a half dozen branches ; of Hebrew, Greek and Latin, 1805, divided in 1831; of Rhetoric and English Literature, in 1813 ; of Ethics and Metaphysics, in 1846 ; of Modern Languages, in 1863 ; and, finally, of History, in 1865. These are exclusive of the twenty or more chairs set up in the various professional schools, since the opening of the century. The list of "faculty and instructors" of the entire university now numbers upwards of sixty names, but the faculty of the college, or academical department, which is the only one here treated of, consists of the president, twelve professors, and half that number of tutors. This body convenes in " faculty meeting," at the room of the president, every Wednesday afternoon, when notes are compared, the results of the week discussed, penalties inflicted or remitted, and the general interests of the college talked over, as well as these special details of instruction and government. At these " executive sessions" of the active rulers of college, are originated and perfected most of the measures which ultimately affect its welfare, as " enactments of the corporation." On the grave and reverend shoulders of this latter body, also, is sometimes thrown the odium of hostility to reforms which the faculty are not really in favor of, but which they simply profess their inability to make " without the consent of the corporation" — a consent they take no pains to secure. For example, when asked to do away with the absurd rule forbidding a student to take his meals at a public house, without pretending to seriously defend the rule, they say that the corporation

divided into two recitation, and two college officers', rooms ; the second was divided into two more recitation rooms (with small chambers connected with them, in which slept the students who used the public rooms as their studies) and two dormitories ; and the first was divided into dormitories only. Most of these were occupied by indigent Freshmen, and the recitation rooms were devoted to the freshman class alone. In the summer of 1870 the inside of the building was again torn out, and its entire space equally divided into four freshman recitation rooms, two on each floor, six long windows being allotted to each room. The rear entrance, closed in 1824, was reopened, and an unbroken partition was placed between the two rooms entered from that direction and the two entered from the front. In the old times, the society libraries, as well as the philosophical apparatus of the college, were stored in the building, and the tower was largely used as an observatory. More recently it had been rather neglected, owing to the better facilities afforded by the revolving tower of iron and the telescope at the Sheffield Hall, and to the fact that the growth of trees had narrowed the field of view. In November of last year the latter defect was remedied by the erection of à revolving tower of wood, upon the top of the previous tower. From this elevated observatory an extensive view of New Haven can be secured, and the field of view for astronomical work is entirely unobstructed. With all these changes and improvements the Athenæum naturally presents the most patched-up and unsightly outward appearance of any building on the college grounds.

South College was the third one of the row, and its corner stone, laid with appropriate speeches and ceremonies, and supposed to rest beneath the north-eastern angle of the building, is said to bear this inscription :

"Ezra Stiles, Coll. Yal. Præses. Primvm Lapidem posvit, Acad. Cond. 93, Apr. 15, 1793." It was completed July 17, following, and was named "Union Hall" in commemoration of the union of State and church in the college corporation. Rutherford Trowbridge was the builder. When the erection of South was commenced, "a close fence of panneled boards, painted red and relieved by cross stripes of white, surrounded the college yard, which extended no further than to the north end of South Middle. Beyond was a grotesque group, generally of the most undesirable establishments, among which were a barn, a barber's shop, several coarse taverns or boarding houses, a poorhouse and house of correction, and the public jail with its prison yard ; the jail being used alike for criminals, for maniacs and debtors. Being very near the college, the moans of innocent prisoners, the cries of felons, and the shrill screams and wild laughter of the insane, were sometimes mingled with the sacred songs of praise and with the voice of prayer, rising from the academic edifices." But, in 1800, the corporation had by purchase secured the removal of many of these objectionable neighbors, and so decided upon the erection of two new buildings, both of which were finished in 1803. The first of them, North Middle, was named "Berkeley Hall," in honor of Bishop Berkeley, and the other, "the Connecticut Lyceum,"—which title, abbreviated to Lyceum, it still retains. It somewhat resembles the Athenæum, though built in better proportion, having a front of 46 and a depth of 56 feet, and the gables of its roof being at right angles to each other. It is three stories high, and is supplied with a tower in which are the college bell and clock. The room of the bell ringer, upon the second floor, is the only one used as a dormitory, though upon the third floor are two office rooms for the faculty, in connection with the two recitation rooms into which the long room stretching across the building, and serving first for a library and then for a "rhetorical chamber," was divided in 1851. At that time the whole interior of the building was rearranged, and gas and furnace heat were first introduced into both it and the Chapel. The senior recitation room on the second floor became the sophomore mathematical chamber, and the two junior rooms on the same floor were enlarged. On the ground floor, the president's lecture room was formed by joining two smaller rooms and shutting up the rear entrance to the building, while the two remaining sophomore rooms were enlarged. North College was finished in the fall of 1821, or within a year from the time the corporation voted to build it, and was never endowed with any fancy name. A similar length of time was employed in constructing the Chapel, which was dedicated November 17, 1824. It has a front of 56 and a depth of 72 feet, and, including the galleries, is three stories in hight, the upper story, above the main audience room, containing a dozen dormitories. Above these is the attic, whither the library was transferred from the Lyceum. The steeple of the building is about 120 feet in hight. Divinity College, the last on the row, was built in 1835, and had to be torn down during the summer of 1870, to make way for the new stone dormitory.

The four dormitory buildings or colleges — South, South Middle, North Middle and North—are all of the same general appearance and description, as was the fifth—Divinity—before its demolition. Each is about 100 feet long by 40 feet wide, and four stories high. Each has 54 windows and two doors on each side, and eight windows at each end, — except South Middle, whose 16 "corner rooms" have each one window less than those of the other colleges. Each has two halls or "entries" running through it, and each entry gives access to 16 rooms, four on a floor,—there being 32 rooms or "chambers" in each college. "A chamber" usually comprises — in addition to the main sitting room, into which the entrance door from the hall directly opens—two bed rooms, a coal closet, a clothes press or wardrobe, a wash room, etc. ; in all, five or six apartments. The number, size and arrangement of these varies somewhat in the different colleges. Each college is equally divided into "corner" and "middle" rooms, and of course into "front" and "back" rooms, and any particular chamber in a college is indicated by reference to these two facts, in connection with the position of the entry, and the number of the floor. A single series of numbers is employed to designate all the college rooms. It extends from south to north, and from the front lower to the back upper room of each entry. There are of course 128 rooms in the four colleges, and these are numbered continuously, without reference to the three intermediate buildings. Hence "No. 1" is "South, south entry, first floor, front, corner room ;" while "No. 128" is North, north entry, fourth floor, back, corner room." The rooms corresponding to 1 S. are 33 S. M., 65 N. M. and 97 N. ; and those to 128 N. are 96 N. M., 64 S. M., 32 S. ; and so on for the others. The 32 rooms in old Divinity were numbered on continuously to 160 ; the old Athenæum rooms extended from 161 to 173 ; the Lyceum rooms from 174 to 185 ; and the Chapel rooms from 186 to 195 — the highest number reached. After the destruction of Divinity and the erection of the new Farnam College, however, the 49 rooms in the latter were numbered from 129 to 177 ; the Lyceum rooms from 178 to 185 ; and the Chapel rooms remain as before. The four recitation

rooms in the remodeled Athenæum are now lettered instead of numbered. Each of the colleges has an attic and
—except North—a cellar, which are used for purposes
of storage. Each entry of the three colleges possessed
of cellars is supplied with water closets, which improvements were added in the fall of 1870. North is the only
college having a slate roof, the others being shingled.

Of the half dozen buildings in the rear of the
brick row, the oldest is the Laboratory, built in 1782,
for a dining hall and kitchen, and standing behind the
Athenæum. It is of brick, painted yellowish white, one
story and a half high, 90 feet long and 30 feet wide,
with an irregular addition upon the west side. It originally measured 60 by 30 feet,—the size of the present lecture room. In this the seats are very close
together and rise rapidly, so that a class of a hundred
persons can sit in full view of the lecturer. The room
is arched, and its greatest elevation is eighteen feet.
There are two or three other rooms and offices, and a
cellar extends underneath the whole. Since the fall of
1870 one of the college janitors, with his family, has occupied a portion of the premises. The building has
been put to its present use since 1819, when the Cabinet was erected, and the kitchen and dining hall transferred thither. This edifice, covered with yellowish
stucco, is 86 feet long and 45 feet broad, and stands behind South Middle and the Lyceum. Besides the basement, where the cooking was formerly done, and the
attic, it comprises two full stories ; the upper one being
devoted to the mineralogical cabinet, as at first, and the
lower one—which served as the dining hall, until the
abolition of Commons in 1843—containing two sophomore recitation rooms, and the " philosophical chamber,"
which is the largest lecture room upon the college
grounds. Directly behind the Chapel is another stuc-

coed building, bluish brown in color, now called the Treasury, but originally Trumbull Gallery. Its measurements are 65 by 35 feet, and it is two stories in hight. It was built in 1832, to receive the historical paintings of Colonel Trumbull, which that artist had presented to the college the year before, on the condition that the proceeds of their exhibition should go for the benefit of indigent students ; though admission to the gallery was ultimately made free to all. The upper story of the building was divided into two large apartments, lighted from above, in one of which were the Trumbull paintings, in the other, portraits of various college benefactors, and miscellaneous pictures. Below were offices for the treasurer and steward, a recitation room for the Theologues, etc. The steward's office is now used as a dormitory by an indigent student who has charge of the key-box. In 1868, all the paintings having been removed to the Art Building, the vacated apartments were changed into three offices, for the college treasurer, pastor and president, in the latter of which all the faculty meetings are now held. The rooms below are packed with "specimens" which cannot be displayed in the over-crowded Cabinet. At the time of the change, windows were let in to the sides of the second story, thereby removing from the building its former tomb-like appearance. Perhaps it was purposely built to resemble a mausoleum, for, at his own request, the remains of Colonel Trumbull and his wife were buried and now rest beneath it.

The first one of the college structures making any pretensions to architectural beauty was the Library, begun in 1842. The absolute necessity of providing some safe place for the books, which, after the transfers already noted, were then lying in the attic of the Chapel, as well as for the society libraries in the Athenæum, induced a few friends of the college to start a subscription for the erection of a fire-proof building. After $13,000 had been raised, it was thought impolitic to press the subscription further, on account of "hard times"; but, with the consent of the subscribers, the corporation voted to begin the work at once, upon a liberal scale, and trust to the future to finish it. Accordingly they were enabled, within a year's time, by expending all their money, to put up the walls and roof, and fit up a single apartment for the temporary reception of the books. The inside was finally completed and arranged in 1846–47, but the ornamental turrets without have remained unfinished to the present time. Situated exactly in the center of the High street side of the college yard, "the whole pile extends its front, including the buttresses above the base, 151 feet. The front of the main building, measured in the same way, is 51 feet; and its depth from front to rear is 95 feet. The front of each of the extreme wings is 30 feet and the depth 67 feet. The connecting wings are each 26 by 40 feet between the walls; and the extreme hight of the four chief towers is 91 feet. The main building, designed to contain the college library, includes only one room, the interior measurement of which is 41 by 83 feet. It resembles in form a Gothic chapel, with its nave and aisles; the hight of the nave is 59 feet, its breadth 17 feet. Between the clustered pillars of the nave are alcoves, fourteen in number, and each ten by twelve feet in extent. A gallery extends on all sides of the room and contains the same number of alcoves. The ceiling is finished with groined arches." Each of the extreme wings is a copy of this central room, and is supplied with smaller alcoves and gallery. The northern one is occupied by "Brothers," the southern by "Linonia." The usual entrance to the main building is through the northern connecting wing, which serves as a librarian's office, and general consulting room. The southern connecting wing was originally occupied by " Calliope," but is now used for the storing of pamphlets, duplicates, and works which are seldom referred to. In 1860, the wings were connected by an inner passage-way, but as the iron doors are always locked, the different apartments of the building are in effect as isolated as ever. Its walls are of red sandstone, from the quarries at Portland, on the Connecticut ; and its entire cost was about $30,000. Exclusive of the 35,000 books in the society and department libraries, the college now possesses about 60,000 volumes and 20,000 pamphlets. Beginning with the 40 folios which founded the college in 1700, the library had increased to 26,000 volumes in 1743, when the first catalogue was published, and to 12,500, a century later. A good many books were lost, at times when the college was temporarily disbanded, so that by the catalogue of 1791 there were only 2700, although there had been 4000 in 1766.

In line with the Library, in the north west angle of the college yard, corner of Elm and High streets, stands Alumni Hall ; like it, built of red sandstone, and, like it, and the Treasury, roofed with tin. The need of some larger hall than any then existing, becoming imperative with the introduction of " biennials," President Woolsey drew up a plan of a two-storied building, having a large hall below for general college purposes and two smaller ones above, for the societies of "Linonia" and "Brothers," which promised to bear a share of the expense. The plan was modified, so as to allow a third upper hall, for "Calliope," and the building was completed in 1853, — by which time the third society was dead, and the money it had advanced was refunded to its executors. The structure measures 100 by 52 feet, and two towers, 75 feet high, stand beside its principal entrance. Within these, winding staircases lead to the society halls, which are also accessible in the rear by a third stairway, situated within the central projection, 40 feet wide, which juts out 12 feet on the High street side of the building, and corresponds to the towers on the front side. This projection also gives a place for a small gallery overlooking the main hall. The latter is said to be the largest one in the country, having occupied-rooms above unsupported by anything save the outer walls. Perhaps it was well that the experiment was never put to the crucial test by the constant use of the central (Calliope) hall above; for at the time of holding the " sanitary fair" in February, 1864, when the upper rooms were all crowded, a portion of the floor perceptibly " settled," and care had to be taken to distribute the spectators more equally throughout the building. The roof is not visible from below, and the cornices, in the form of battlements, which surround it and the towers, are constructed of wood, instead of stone as was originally planned. In the main hall, where examinations, alumni meetings, etc., are held, are hung the coats-of-arms of all the States, and the portraits of various benefactors, graduates and officers of the college. The cost of the building was a little more than $27,000, of which the college paid $16,000, the Linonia society $5800, and the Brothers $5500.

Corresponding to this structure, in the south west angle of the yard, corner of Chapel and High streets, stands the Art Building, the handsomest edifice which the college or the city can boast of. Its corner stone—containing a copper box, wherein were deposited various mementos of the occasion ; coins, medals, pamphlets and newspapers—was laid, with due ceremony, November 16, 1864 ; the roofs were put on by the close of the following year ; and the entire work was accepted by the corporation as "finished," just before the Commencement of 1866 ; though it was a year later before the "opening reception" was held and the public admitted to the galleries. "The general shape of the building is this : the south wing, fronting on Chapel street, is a building 34 by 80 feet in size, exclusive of projections ; the north wing is a building 36 by 76 feet in size, exclusive of projections, and stands considerably in advance of the other wing on the college grounds. The two are connected by an intermediate building, 44 by 80 feet in size. The general form is that of the letter·H, in which the right-hand stroke together with the cross stroke are somewhat dropped. The exterior is much broken in outline, but is extremely plain in its details. With the exception of the Chapel street entrance, it can scarcely be said to have any ornaments, everything that is seen being for some constructive purpose. The north wing, however, has an addition in the form of a tower, which forms the entrance from the college grounds, and connects with the main hall by a corridor covered with a lean-to roof. At the angles of the wings are small turrets, serving as ventilators, which, together with the larger tower, are still unfinished. On the Chapel street side is a projection, which forms a porch on the first story, and a small room in the second story, and is terminated with a gable roof. The two wing buildings are covered with hipped roofs, the upper halves of which are of iron and glass. The connecting building is covered with a four-pitched roof. The whole building is very massive, both in its materials and effects. The base-course and basement walls under ground are of North Haven stone, the facing of all the exterior walls is of Belleville (N. J.) sandstone, and the water-tables, sills, lintels, labels, etc., are of Connecticut river sandstone. The arches are of alternate Belleville and Cleveland stone. The columns of the front porch are of Gloucester (Mass.) granite, and the capitals are carved with original designs after natural foliage, in Cleveland stone. The roof is slated. The timber throughout is of Pennsylvania white pine. The floors are of oak and black walnut, and the inside finish of the halls and stairs is of chestnut. The architecture is in the style advocated by the 'rationalistic school,' whose aim is to give prominent expression to the constructive features of buildings, and to revive the system of decoration in use in the 13th century." Underneath the whole building is a basement, 12 feet high, divided into lecture rooms, modeling rooms, etc., besides the halls and stairways, and fuel and furnace rooms. Its outer entrance is beside the tower. The first story is 16 feet high, and is divided into studios, professor's and curator's rooms, and a lecture room 80 feet square, from which, if desired, three studios can be formed by the erection of screens. "The second story hall, reached by a broad stairway, is 14 feet wide, 44 feet long and 15 feet high, and from it all the exhibition rooms can be entered. At the end of the hall are the entrances to the two large sky-light galleries, and on the side are two entrances to the long room for engravings and photographs. This room is of the same size as the hall, and also connects the two large galleries. The north gallery measures 22 by 72 feet, is 21 feet high to the highest point of the curved ceiling, and 32 feet high to the peak of the skylight. The walls upon which the pictures are hung are 16 feet in hight, three feet of which are occupied by the wainscoting. At one end of this room is an oriel window, projecting beyond the wall of the building, and affording an excellent view of the college grounds. Near by is a private door, connecting with a small room in the tower, to which access can also be had by means of a corridor under the lean-to roof. The tower affords access to the roof and attic, which latter is a large room, thus far unoccupied. The south gallery measures 30 by 76 feet, and is similar in every way to the other, except that it is 35 feet in hight to the peak of the skylight. Opening out of this gallery, and over the front entrance, is a small room affording an excellent view of the street. The front window of this room goes down to the floor and opens upon a stone balcony." The building has thus far cost about $200,000, or more than twice what was estimated at the outset; but, fortunately for the college, the donor —Augustus R. Street, of the class of 1812—continued to add to his original appropriation of $80,000, as the necessity of the work required, and provided in his will for its ultimate completion. He died June 12, 1866, and his entire gifts to the college amount to upwards of $280,000,—by far the largest sum ever received by the institution from any single source. He did not desire that his chief monument should be called by his name, however, but simply entitled it "Yale School of the Fine Arts," and this name, with the date "A. D. 1864," is inscribed upon the large slab at the base of the oriel window. Since his death, a marble tablet in commemoration of his gift, has been let into the wall of the lower hall, near the entrance. The architect of the Art Building was P. B. Wight of New York, and the masons were Perkins & Chatfield, who also did the masonry for the Library and Alumni Hall.

Besides the fourteen buildings already described, the only others within the yard, while '69 was in college, were the two wooden dwelling-houses, — situated between the Library and Art Building, and facing on High street,—one of which is carried on as a boarding house

under the direction of the college authorities. For a
quarter of a century, the need of new dormitory buildings had been recognized and talked about, until in
1868 it was decided to begin active measures for the reconstruction of the college yard, and ground for a new
dormitory was staked out, in front of South Middle and
the Lyceum. It was to be one link in a chain of buildings which were ultimately to surround the square, and
so—after the demolition of the eight "factories" and
the three inferior structures behind them—enclose a
large open rectangle within. But the ground had
hardly been staked out and the general plan of reconstruction made public, when a cry was raised in the
newspapers that the beauty of the college green—the
pride of the city—would be ruined thereby ; and the
champions of the elms exhorted the authorities to put
up their murderous axes and spare those noble trees.
The work, begun after twenty years' deliberation, was
accordingly postponed once more, and an extensive discussion was for several months carried on, in regard to
the advisability of removing the site of the college to
the outskirts of the city. The result of it was, that,
after the fullest consideration of all the points involved,
it was decided by the authorities that while, on the
whole, the removal would be advantageous to the institution, the state of its finances rendered any such removal practically impossible. In accordance with this
decision—which may be accepted as final—the original
plan of reconstruction was reverted to, after a year's delay, and on Monday morning, August 2, 1869, ground
was quietly broken for the building which is expected
to introduce "a new dormitory system" at Yale. Only
three elms were cut down to give room for it, and the
appearance of the yard, as seen from Chapel street, is
not materially altered by its presence. It sets back 20

feet from College street, and 100 feet from Elm, thus leaving room for the proposed Memorial Chapel upon the corner, and of course stands in front of North College and the open space between it and Divinity's former site. Exclusive of projections, it measures 174 by 37 feet, and is four stories in hight, besides a light basement and Mansard slated roof, which is surmounted by a pair of turrets, also slated. The walls are of brick, laid in cement, and trimmed with dark blue stone from the Hudson river, as well as the common Portland free stone, while the slabs above the entrances are of Westchester (N. Y.) marble, and the pillars which support them are of polished granite. The entrances are approached from the inner side of the college yard and are three in number, corresponding to the number of stairways which are situated in these projections, which are rounded on the College street side and angular upon the inner front. There are 49 studies or parlors in the building, each measuring 13 by 16 feet, and all but nine of them are supplied with a pair of bedrooms—each of which has a window of its own— and clothes' closets. The nine rooms without these appendages are situated in the stairways, and serve mostly as offices for members of the faculty. In the basement, to which there are two entrances from the street front, the janitor lives with his family. The furnace and water closets are also situated there. All the rooms are heated by steam and lighted by gas, and are said to be more perfectly ventilated than those of any other building in New Haven. They were first occupied on the opening of the fall term of 1870. Twelve months later it is hoped that the finishing touches will have been given to the 'Durfee College, the excavation for which was begun upon the afternoon of the second day of May, 1870. This is the largest structure in the

Connected with the college are four professional "schools" or "departments," of which it naturally happens that the oldest is the Theological. The college itself was founded by ministers, for training young men for the ministry ; theology was one of the chief undergraduate studies ; and the first professorship established was that of Divinity, in 1755. The first three incumbents of the office—the third of whom also served at the same time as president of the college—were in the habit of "conducting a number of resident graduates through a course of theological studies such as was considered in those times a competent preparation for the pastoral office," and when the fourth was installed, in 1817, "the instruction of theological students was distinctly included among his duties." In 1822, the department was formally organized by the corporation, in response to a petition from fifteen would-be Theologues. It now numbers a half-dozen professors and about fifty students, and in all upwards of 800 students have been connected with it. Its annual session of eight months extends from September to May, when a public anniversary is held. The latter feature was introduced in 1867, or rather revived then after being omitted for a dozen years or more. Then, too, for the first time the corporation conferred the degree of D.B. (Bachelor of Divinity) upon those who had completed the three years' course. Divinity College was erected for the Theologues, in 1835, and no rent was charged those who occupied its dormitories. Some of its rooms were put to public service for the holding of lectures and recitations, and these were likewise held in various apartments of the other buildings, at such seasons and hours as found them vacated by their regular occupants.

All these drawbacks, however, have recently been

put an end to by the completion of a new building, whose corner stone was laid September 22, 1869,—ground having been broken, July 13, previous. It stands on the north-west corner of College and Elm streets, measuring 164 feet on the former by 43 feet on the latter, and setting back about a dozen feet from both. The dimensions of its lot—which is enclosed by an ornamented iron fence—are 195 by 110 feet, and space is thus afforded for the additions which it is proposed hereafter to make to the building. Its wings are five stories—and 75 feet—in hight ; the middle portion has only four stories. It is warmed throughout by steam and lighted by gas, and fire-places are also provided in all the rooms. There are about 50 of these dormitories, besides lecture, reading and library rooms, corridors, janitor's office, bath rooms, water-closets, etc. The walls are of brick, red and black, trimmed with Nova Scotia stone, and the roofs are of slate, surmounted by an iron railing. The architect was Richard M. Hunt of New York, and the entire cost of the structure was $130,000. . The original plan of the building contemplated the erection on Elm street of a small but tasteful chapel, and in February of the present year Francis Marquand of Southport offered to supply the necessary funds ($25,000) for its erection. Work was shortly afterwards begun upon it, and it is expected that the building will be ready for use at the opening of the new year in September. By the enterprise of the ladies belonging to some of the city churches, all the dormitories were comfortably and even elegantly fitted up with carpets, bed, bedding, and every necessary article of furniture. A few of the parlors have two bedrooms attached to them, but in general provision is made for each student to have a parlor and bedroom by himself. There is no charge for rent, tuition, or the use of libra-

3*

ries ; and those who require it receive a dollar a week towards the expense of board, and have their washing done free of charge. They also receive $100 a year from the income of scholarships and other funds, and an additional $100 a year in case they are the beneficiaries of the American Educational Society. " In general it may be said, that sufficient aid will be provided for every young man who gives promise of usefulness in the ministry, to enable him, in connection with his own efforts, to complete a course of theological study." The endowed scholarships bear respectively the names of James Hillhouse, William Leffingwell, George E. Dunham, Normand Smith, E. E. Salisbury, Thomas R. Trowbridge, Charles Atwater, Richard Borden, Samuel Holmes, Roland Mather, Noah Porter, John DeForest, J. R. Beadle, and David Root.

The Law School grew out of the main college in much the same way as the one just described. In 1801 a professor of Law was appointed ; not for the purpose of training undergraduates for the bar, but rather of giving lectures to them on the general principles of law and government, — a practice which is still kept up. He resigned his office at the expiration of nine years. The next incumbent did not begin his duties until 1826, when he opened a private class for law students, which has since been recognized as the beginning of the present school. In all, about 1400 students have been connected with it, of whom 280 have been admitted to the degree of LL.B. (Bachelor of Laws), which was first conferred in 1848. The regular course occupies two years, and the year corresponds with that of the college, except that it is divided into two terms instead of three. Those who before entering the department, have taken the degree of A. B., Ph.B., or B.S., at any college, receive their degree after an attendance of three terms; members of the bar, after an attendance of two terms; all others, after the full course of four terms. The faculty consists of the president, a professor and three lecturers or instructors. The rooms of the school are in the Leffingwell Building, corner of Church and Court streets. Its special library numbers about 2000 volumes. "At present the department is not only without funds of its own, but is in debt to the general fund of the college."

The Medical Institution, though third in the order of development, was the first of the professional schools to get into active operation. As early as 1806 the propriety of establishing a course of lectures for the benefit of medical students was discussed by the corporation, but it was thought best to secure the assistance of the State Medical Society, before taking any action. Accordingly, four years later, that society joined with the corporation in applying for a change of charter, and the present "school" was founded. Its organization was completed in the fall of 1812, and a year later the first course of lectures was delivered. The faculty consists of the president and eight professors, while a like number of doctors chosen by the State Medical Society —of which the president thereof is always one—are additional members of the examining board. The degree of M.D. (Doctor of Medicine) has been conferred on 800 individuals,—about a third of the whole number ever connected with the school. For the past few years it has had about 30 students; in 1822 it had three times that number. Every candidate for a degree must have studied medicine for two years,—or for three years if not a college graduate,—and must have attended two full courses of medical lectures, at least one of them at Yale. In 1814 the Legislature appropriated to the school $20,000 of a $50,000 bonus, which the State received from the Phœnix bank of Hartford for its charter. With these and other funds contributed by individuals—of which the largest single gift was $5000—was purchased, of James Hillhouse who built it, the square stone edifice on Grove street, at the foot of College, now occupied by the Scientific School. It was sold to Mr. Sheffield for the latter purpose in 1859, and with the proceeds was erected the present Medical College on York street. This is a stucco building, 53 feet square and three stories high, containing a commodious lecture room, lighted from the top, an extensive anatomical museum, dissecting rooms, offices, etc. "The remaining property of the institution, invested principally in bank stocks, yields an income of about $1000 annually, which is inadequate even to its current and necessary miscellaneous expenses."

Youngest but most important of the departments is that of Philosophy and the Arts, or as it commonly termed, the Sheffield Scientific School. Preparations were made for commencing it in 1846, but the first students were received at the beginning of the following academic year. For a long time before this, Prof. Silliman, Sr., had been in the habit of instructing a private class of young men, who desired a more thorough and extended course in natural science than was furnished in the regular curriculum. Such special students were allowed the privilege of the libraries, cabinets, etc., though not officially recognized as members of the institution. At the Commencement of 1847, the corporation voted to establish a "Department of Philosophy and the Arts," under the direction of two professors, one of whom—B. Silliman, Jr.—had for five years been privately conducting a special class in chemistry; and the old president's house, vacated the year before, was fitted up as a laboratory for their use. There were eleven students the first year, six of whom were college graduates. Of the eight who completed the course, six were given the degree of Ph.B. (Bachelor of Philosophy) in 1852, and count as the earliest graduates of the school, in which three of them are now professors. In 1852 a professor of Civil Engineering was appointed, and began his instructions, in the attic of the Chapel, with 26 students. Two years afterwards, his classes were associated with the chemical students under the name of "Yale Scientific School," in which they have since formed a distinct "section." The end of ten years found the new department possessed of a half-dozen professors and instructors, but, as from the very first, almost entirely without endowment. At this crisis, Joseph E. Sheffield, who had been the school's best patron, came forward with an offer to provide a building and permanent fund. He accordingly bought the old Medical College, at the head of College street, had it refitted, added two large wings, provided a large amount of apparatus, and gave a fund of $50,000 for the maintenance of three professorships. The building was taken possession of in the summer of 1860. Five years later, it was enlarged by the addition of a three-story structure to connect the wings, two towers, and other improvements. The front tower is 90 feet high and 16 feet square, contains a belfry-clock with four dials, and is surmounted by a revolving turret in which an equatorial telescope is placed. The north-western tower, of the same dimensions and 50 feet high, was built for the reception of a meridian circle. The extreme length of the edifice, measured from this tower to the east side, is 117 feet, and the extreme depth is 112 feet. The original building of stone and the additions of brick are alike covered with brownish stucco. In purchasing and refitting this structure and endowing the school—to both of which by vote of the corporation in 1860 his name was applied—Mr. Sheffield has expended upwards of $175,000. His own residence, entered from Hillhouse avenue, closely adjoins the premises.

Connecticut's share — 180,000 acres — of the Congressional land-grant of 1863 was ultimately transferred to the school, which now enjoys the income of the $135,000 derived from the sale of it. In return for this, forty free State-scholarships were established, and the governor, lieutenant-governor, the three senior senators and the secretary of the State board of education, were constituted a "board of visitation" on the part of the State. For their benefit an annual report is prepared and printed,—the first one being issued in 1866. The governing board or faculty consists of the president, a dozen professors, and half as many other instructors. For the past few years the number of students has been about 140, and 27 graduated in the class of '69. The regular course, for the degree of Ph.B., is three years in length,—the last two years being divided into seven distinct departments or "sections," and each man choosing for himself which of them he will follow. An additional year in the Engineering Section secures the degree of C. E. (Civil Engineer), which was first conferred in 1867. The anniversary exercises are held in Sheffield Hall, on the Monday before the college Commencement, though the degrees are not conferred until the latter occasion. Besides the three regular classes of undergraduates, there is a fourth class of "special students, not candidates for a degree," and an advanced class, composed of graduates of the school, the college, and other similar institutions. The "second section" of the Department of Philosophy and the Arts— in which, if anywhere, lie the germs of a future university—has been rather overshadowed by the rapid growth of the first or Scientific School section. No regular courses of study have as yet been provided for it, but the Bachelor candidates for its degree, Ph.D. (Doctor of Philosophy), must read for two years at New Haven, under the direction of the faculty, and at the end of that time pass a satisfactory examination in at least two distinct branches of learning. During the past ten years, seventeen persons have received this degree, though it was not conferred upon any one in 1864 and '65.

Sheffield Hall being entirely taken up with recitation and lecture rooms, laboratories, cabinets, library and reading rooms, professors' studies, observatories, corridors, etc., the students have all been obliged to occupy rooms out in town, but a large brick block in the vicinity, which supplies lodging rooms for quite a large number of them, serves as a sort of headquarters and rendezvous, and in some slight way supplies the want of a regular dormitory building. Before the demolishment of Divinity College had been decided upon, it was proposed to surrender to them its 32 dormitories, which the Theologues were to have no further use for, after the opening of the new Divinity building; but had the plan been carried out, it is not likely that their introduction into the college yard would have introduced them to the acquaintance of the regular college students. The latter have thus far been wont, as it were, to look down upon them, as being in a sense their inferiors. Without any open show of hostility, a sort of keep-your-distance air of the college men towards the students of the school effectively repels the latter. Both frequently meet together at the boat house and gymnasium, and less often in the lecture room, but they do not mingle, and few acquaintanceships are formed. Occasionally it happens that a member of the school " runs with " a particular college class, for two or three years, and becomes in a measure identified with it, but the fact only renders it the more evident that there is no general association between the two species of undergraduates. A sentiment analogous to "class feeling" clearly separates them from each other. In the three other departments the students are older than those in college, and the latter naturally have nothing to do with them. The students in Law and Medicine are seldom known or thought of at all, any more than townies; but the Theologues are the traditional objects of a sort of good-natured derision. To speak of them as monsters of vice and iniquity, has been a favorite practice from time immemorial.

The funds by which the college has been supported have been derived almost exclusively from individuals. The entire gifts of every sort made by the Commonwealth of Connecticut in the course of 170 years, have only amounted to $100,000, of which the $20,000 bestowed on the Medical School was expended by State commissioners, and not controlled by the corporation at all. The last gift—of $7000, made in 1831—was of money received by the State as a bonus for a bank charter, and almost all the previous donations had been of a similar character,—made from unexpended resources, and not requiring a special appropriation from the State treasury. Undoubtedly the annuity granted to the institution during its first half century was the most valuable State aid it has ever received. The income of the $135,000 accruing to the Scientific School from the sale of public lands under the Congressional act of 1863, completes the sum total of public benefactions conferred upon the institution. Private generosity alone has kept it alive, though the bequest of $10,000 for the library, received in 1834, by the will of Alfred E. Perkins of '30, was by far the largest individual gift recorded, up to that time. Recently there have been many others of equal or larger amounts, of which those of Joseph E. Sheffield ($175,000, for the Scientific School), and Augustus R. Street ($280,000, for the Art School, a professorship of Modern Languages, and a Theological professorship) have been already noted. Next to them in importance is the gift made by George Peabody in 1866,—$150,000, for a Museum of Natural History. The conditions of this bequest are that not more than $100,000 shall be expended in the erection of the first section of a fire-proof building; that $20,000 shall be left to accumulate to at least five times that amount, when it shall be expended in completing the building; and that $30,000 shall be permanently invested for the support of the Museum. A dormitory fund of $100,000 from Bradford M. C. Durfee, a non-graduate of '67; a similar fund of $40,000 from Henry Farnam; a chapel fund of $36,000 from Joseph Battell; a $30,000 pastor's professorship from Simeon E. Chittenden; a gift of $25,000 to the Theologues from William A. Buckingham, and fourteen other gifts of not less than $5000 each, comprised the most important additions to the college property in the eight years following 1860. More recently a fund of $50,000 has been given by William Phelps, the annual income of which is to be spent by the college under the direction of his son, William W. Phelps of '60, during the latter's life time, and is finally to fall wholly into the control of the authorities. For the Scientific School, too, about $125,000 has been raised in sums of varying amounts, and among other things the professorship of Sanscrit has thereby been placed upon the respectable foundation of $50,000. In February of the present year Francis Marquand presented the $25,000 already mentioned for the construction of a chapel for the Theologues. Every one of these large gifts being for a specific purpose, the availability of the general fund of the college has been diminished rather than increased by their reception. It now amounts to but $300,000—a sum whose income is far too small to meet the every day necessities of the college, the total professorship endowments of which are only $125,000. In 1831, when poverty was bringing the college to death's door, a desperate attempt to lift it from bankruptcy resulted in the raising of a $100,000 fund, from 600 separate subscribers, in amounts varying from $5000 to $4 each. In 1853, another crisis was averted by the raising of a similar fund of $150,000. And now, for a third time, the necessity seems imperative of making a combined effort to increase the general fund. Had this been managed in the past with anything but the shrewdest and closest economy, the college would have been dead and buried, years ago. Perhaps the very fact that it has been made to " go so far" has induced the prevalent belief in its practical inexhaustibleness ; for of all the grand presents lately made to Yale, the largest addition to its general fund, the largest real increase to its available riches, was the $5000 legacy given by the late Chief Justice Thomas S. Williams, of Hartford and the class of '94.

Though most of the peculiar college words and phrases employed in this book are explained wherever they occur, the following vocabulary may be of interest on its own account and useful for purposes of reference : *Alma mater*, the college as related to its graduates. *Alumnus*, a graduate, though the word is more frequently used in the plural, *alumni*. *Annual*, the examination held at the close of every year. *Appointment*, position upon the faculty's honor-roll of scholarship.

These appointments are announced at the close of the first junior and last senior terms. *Average*, the lowest mark ("2") that will "pass" a man in his studies. *Banger*, a heavy club-cane, mostly carried by Sophomores. "*Banner*," the annual society list and college directory. *Berkeley*, the name of a scholarship. *Biennial*, the examination formerly held at the end of sophomore and senior years. *Blind-house*, a secret-society hall, so called by the townies only. *Blow-out*, a supper, spread, convivial entertainment, especially a society celebration. *Bones man*, a member of the Skull and Bones senior society. *Bristed*, the name of a scholarship. *Bully*, good, excellent. *Bum*, a spree, society supper, or convivial entertainment of any sort, innocent or otherwise. Used also as a verb; whence is derived *bummer*, a fast young man, a fellow who *bums*. *Buzz*, to interview and "sound" a man. *Campaign*, the annual strife between the freshman societies for new members. *Chapel*, religious services which must be attended in that building. *Cheek*, brazen audacity. Used also as a verb. *Chum*, a roommate or particular friend. Sometimes called *chummy*. *Chum* is used also as a verb. *Church paper*, an official blank, certifying that the person signing it has attended Sunday service in one of the city churches. *Class*, a body of students who enter upon their studies the same year, and pursue them together to the end. The first year it is called the *freshman*, the second year the *sophomore*, the third the *junior*, and the fourth the *senior* class. *Upper-class*, and *under-class* are terms of various application, according to the position of the person using them. A Freshman is always an *under-class* man, and a Senior is always an *upper-class* man. The Juniors and Sophomores are to the former *upper-class* men also, but to the latter, they as well as the Fresh are *under-class* men. In general, however, by *upper-class* the two higher classes are referred to, and by *under-class* the two lower ones. *Class election*, an after-choice to a secret society by one's own classmates, who themselves enjoyed the greater honor of being chosen by the class above them. *Coalition*, a political compact between two or more societies for controlling the elective honors of a class. *Coal yard*, the college privy. So named because the two structures used to be connected. *Coch* (abbreviated from *Cochleaureatus*), a member of the committee who awarded the Wooden Spoon. *Commons*, the college boarding house. *Condition*, requirement to make up an unsatisfactory examination. Used also as a verb. *Cram*, to prepare for examination on a subject, rather than to really master it. *Crowd*, a common synonym for clique, coterie, or set, especially with reference to society connections. *Curric* (abbreviated from *curriculum*), the established course of studies. *Cut*, to absent one's self from a college exercise. *Dead*, complete, perfect ; as a *dead* rush, a *dead* flunk. *DeForest*, the gold medal of that name. *Dig*, a close, mechanical student. Used also as a .verb. Used also as an abbreviation for *dignity*. *Digger*, a member of the Spade and Grave senior society. *Dog*, style, splurge. To *put on dog*, is to make a flashy display, to cut a swell. *Drop*, to fall into a lower class. *Ear*, dignity, hauteur, self-importance. A man somewhat offended or indignant is said to be *on his ear*, or *eary*. *Egress*, the official name of an exit from a college exercise. *Electioneer*, to argue the claims of a society, for the purpose of gaining new members. *Entry*, a hall or stairway in a college dormitory. *Excuse paper*, an official blank upon which all excuses for failure at college exercises are required to be written. *Faculty*, the active college authorities. *Fizzle*, partial failure on recitation. *Flunk*, an entire failure. Both these words are also used as verbs. *Fraud*, a humbug, an imposition, a sell. *Freshman* (often abbreviated to *Fresh*), a collegian in his first year. *Giglamps* and *goggles*, eye-glasses. *Grad*, abbreviation for . *graduate*. Not common. *Grind*, a hard and unpleasant task, an imposition, a swindle. As a verb, to give close application to a study, especially to a distasteful one. *Grip*, a society's secret mode of clasping hands. *Grub*, food, meals, board. A very common word, both as noun and verb. *Gum game*, a trick, a swindle. *Gym*, abbreviation for *gymnasium*. *Hang out*, to occupy a room, to reside. *Hash*, is sometimes used in a sense similar to *grub*, though as a noun only. *Healthy* and *heavy*, are used as sarcastically complimentary epithets. *Hewgag*, a what-d'ye-call-it, a thingumbob. *Honorary member*, a person elected to a society after his own class has ceased to control it. All society men, as soon as their class withdraws from the active management of a society, are also termed *honorary members* of it. *Hoop it up*, to hurry. Perhaps derived from the driver's ejaculation, *houp la !* *Hunky*, good, excellent, bully. *Joe*, the college privy. *Junior* (sometimes abbreviated to *Jun* or *June* by the necessities of verse), a collegian in his third year. *Keys man*, a member of the Scroll and Key senior society. *Lab* (abbreviated from *laboratory*), a word formerly used to indicate a student in chemistry. *Lalligag*, to fool about, get the better of, "come it over," a man. *Lay*, a trick of policy, a little game. *Light out*, to hurry away, make one's self scarce. *Lippus*, a man of defective vision. "*Lit.*," the "*Yale Literary Magazine.*" *Load*, a practical joke, a sell. *Lunkhead*, a stupid, slow-witted fellow. *Make up*, to recite an omitted lesson. *Medic*, a medical student. Rarely used. *Memorabil* (abbreviated from *memorabilia*), any keepsake to remind one of college life, especially printed matter of every sort. *Muffin*, an unskilful player at base-ball. *Neutral,* a person who belongs to no society, especially to no junior society ; though the qualifying word to denote in what year he was a neutral is usually prefixed when any year save the present is intended. *Nobby,* stylish, fashionable, well-dressed. Applied to young men only. *Owl,* to prolong an evening call until a late hour is to *owl* the person called upon. *Pack,* to organize or to join with "a crowd," with a view of securing some desired honor, especially a senior-society election. The crowd thus made up is itself called a *pack.* *Peeler,* a city policeman. *Pick-up,* a street-walker, of the less disreputable sort. *Pill,* a silly, disagreeable fellow ; a prig ; a scrub. Recently the word has been used as a verb, in the sense of dress, and to *pill up* signifies to put on one's good clothes, to fix up, to rig out. *Pledge,* to bind a man to join a society, and promise him an election to it. *Plug,* a silk hat, of the stove-pipe or chimney-pot order. Also called *beaver, tile* and *roof.* *Pony,* a translation of a classic text. As a verb, to make use of such translations in reading out a lesson. *Poppycock,* a silly pretence, foolishness, nonsense. *Poster,* a representation of a society's emblems, displayed in a room to indicate the connections of its occupant. Also, any sort of printed handbill. "*Pot,*" abbreviation of "*Pot-Pourri,*" the annual society catalogue and college directory. *Prex,* the president. *Prof,* abbreviation for *professor.* *Rag,* to overcome and entirely use up an opponent or rival. *Reckless,* superlatively fine, in the very extreme of fashion. *Red hot,* excellent, perfect, magnificent. Sometimes abbreviated to *hot,* and usually used with some tinge of sarcasm. *Roomer,* a word used by landladies to designate a lodger or occupant of a room who takes his meals elsewhere. *Roots,* tricks. Used only in the phrase, to "come the *roots* over" a person, that is, to get the better of him by some trick or deceit.

Rope in, to join one's self to a set or party uninvited, to attach any one to the same unceremoniously or without his consent. *Rum*, good, excellent, bully. *Run*, to direct, conduct, manage. Also to chaff, make sport of. Also to stand as a candidate for office. To *run with* signifies to keep the company of, to become identified with. *Rush*, a perfect recitation. Also a pushing, scrambling street-fight between two classes, or rather a trial of their strength in shoving through and breaking up each other's ranks. Used as a verb, chiefly in the former sense. *Russellite*, a member of Gen. Russell's military school. *Rusticate*, to suspend a man from college exercises; because during the period of his suspension he is supposed to stay in the country, cramming in private. *Scientif*, a student in the Scientific School. *Scrub*, a poorly dressed, badly appearing, socially disagreeable man. *Seed*, is used with about the same meaning, though more nearly equivalent to *pill*. *Senior* (sometimes abbreviated to *Sen* or *Sene* by the necessities of verse), a collegian in his fourth year. *Shad-eater* (or simply *shad*), a member of the State Legislature. *Shake up*, to make haste. To "*shake up* a song," or "a tune," is to sing ; and the imperative, *shake it up !* signifies, wide awake, there ! bestir yourself ! *Shebang*, rooms, place of abode. Also a theatrical or other entertainment in a public hall. *Sheepskin*, the college diploma, or A.B. degree. *Shekels*, money. *Shenannigan*, chaff, foolery, nonsense ; especially when advanced to cover some scheme or little game. *Sick*, bad, inferior, disgusting, contemptible. *Sing*, an informal concert, a singing of college songs. *Sit on*, to silence, thwart, crush, annihilate. *Skin*, to use unfair means for gaining knowledge in recitation or examination. *Slathers*, an abundance, quantities, lots. *Sleep over*, to arise from bed too late for a college exercise. *Sling*, to put on, exhibit, display.

Smear, food, hash, grub; especially a society spread or supper. This word was introduced by '69, and has been very popular in later classes. It is sometimes also used as a verb. *Snabby* or *snab*, stylish, tasteful, good looking (applied chiefly to young women, who thence themselves come to be referred to as *the snab*). Also, good, perfect, excellent. *Soft thing*, an easy place, a pleasant position, a sure chance. To have a *soft thing* on, or the *dead wood* on, any object, is to hold the " inside track," the best opportunity for gaining it. *Softy*, *spooney*, and *spoops* or *spoopsey*, are all used as synonyms for a silly, insignificant fellow. *Sophomore* (often abbreviated to *Soph*), a collegian in his second year. *Sour on*, to become disgusted with, turn one's back upon, repudiate. *Spoon Man*, the recipient of the Wooden Spoon. *Sport the oak*, to keep one's door locked against visitors. An English term of recent introduction. *Spread*, an informal supper or treat, especially if given to upper-class men. *Stand*, rank in scholarship. *Stick*, a loutish fellow, a pill. As a verb, the word signifies to secure the pledge of a man's money or services in support of objects to which he really does not wish to give them. *Stones man*, a senior-society neutral. *Stoughton-bottle*, a thick-headed, blundering fellow; a stick; a pill. *Sub*, a sub-division at examination time. *Sub-Freshman*, a prospective collegian during the last year of his preparatory course. *Supe*, a toady, a boot-licker. Used also as a verb. *Sweep*, a servant who takes care of the dormitories. *Swing out*, to display any personal adornment, especially a society badge, for the first time. *Theologue*, a theological student. *Thin*, transparent. A sell or joke whose point is suspected or seen in advance is said to be *too thin*. *Townsend*, the name of a high literary prize. *Towny*, a resident of the city, especially a young man who might be mistaken for a collegian.

Triennial, the triennial catalogue of graduates. Also the triennial class-meeting. Also the triennial class record. *Tute,* abbreviation for *tutor.* Not common. *University,* the picked boat-crew of six who row against Harvard. Also the picked base-ball nine. *Wharf rat,* a young waterside Arab. *Wooden man,* an impassive, methodical, cold-blooded fellow; a stick; a Stoughton-bottle. *Wooden Spoon,* the prize conferred at the end of junior year upon "the most popular man in the class." *Wood up,* to rap with the knuckles, in mock approbation of a recitation-room joke. *Woolsey,* the name of the first freshman scholarship. *Worst,* latest, newest. A general sarcastic superlative, made popular by '71. Anything, from a new hat to a society election or long lesson, is called the *worst yet,* the *very worst,* or the *worst we've seen. Yalensian,* a Yale man. Used also as an adjective. This word, though much affected by college writers and often seen in print, is never heard of in conversation, and has not been employed in the present work.

The following publications—comprising all the important works relating to the subject—have been of use in the preparation of this book, and their perusal is recommended to all those who are interested in the history and present condition of the college. New Haven is the place of publication, when not otherwise specified. President Clap's "Annals of Yale College"; 16mo, pp. 124; printed by Hotchkiss & Mecom, 1766. Baldwin's "Annals of Yale College"; 8vo, pp. 214; Hezekiah Howe, 1831: second edition, pp. 343; B. & W. Noyes, 1838. "Sketches of Yale College," by a member of that institution [E. P. Belden of '44]; 16mo, pp. 192; New York: Saxton & Miles, 1843; "embellished with more than thirty engravings." "Reminiscences of

Scenes and Characters in College," by a graduate of
'21 [Rev. John Mitchell]; 12mo, pp. 229; A. H.
Maltby, 1847 ; stereotyped by J. H. Benham. Professor
Kingsley's "Historical Sketch," 8vo, pp. 48 ; Boston :
Perkins, Marvin & Co., 1836 [reprinted from the *Amer-
ican Quarterly Register*].   President Woolsey's "Histor-
ical Discourse"; 8vo, pp. 128 ; printed by B. L. Ham-
len, 1850. B. H. Hall's "College Words and Customs";
12mo, pp. 508 ; Cambridge : John Bartlett, 1856. Avery
Allyn's "Ritual of Freemasonry"; 12mo, pp. 302 ;
Boston : John Marsh & Co., 1831. Professor Porter's
"American Colleges and the American Public"; 12mo,
pp. 285 ; C. C. Chatfield & Co., 1870. Garretson's
"Carmina Yalensia"; 8vo, pp. 88 ; New York : Taintor
Bros., 1867. Elliot's "Songs of Yale"; 12mo, pp. 126 ;
C. C. Chatfield & Co., 1870. Waite's "Carmina Col-
legensia"; 8vo, pp. 254 ; Boston : O. Ditson & Co.,
1868. "Yale Literary Magazine," monthly, 1836–71.
"Yale Banner," annual, 1841–70. "College Courant,"
weekly, 1865–71. "New Englander," quarterly, 1843–
71. "American Journal of Science and Arts," semi-
annual, quarterly, bi-monthly, monthly, 1818–71. "University Quarterly," 1860–61.

PART FIRST.

THE SOCIETY SYSTEM.

CHAPTER I.

FRESHMAN SOCIETIES.

Development of the Modern System — Kappa Sigma Epsilon —
Delta Kappa—Gamma Nu—Sigma Delta—Election of Active
and Honorary Members—Catalogues—The Outside Chapters
and Statistics of Membership — The Society System in Other
Colleges—Badge Pins and Mottoes—Halls and Mode of Renting
Them — Electioneering — Initiation — Suppers—Interference of
Upper-class Men—Farewell Ceremonies of the Sophomores—
Meetings and Exercises—"Peanut Bums"—Treatment of Intruders—Officers and the Campaign Election—Coalitions—System
of Electioneering—Initiation Committees' Supper—Expenses of
Membership — Society Zeal and its Gradual Decline — Significance of Prize Lists—Notable Members—Comparisons of the
Societies—Anomalous Position of Gamma Nu—Initiation Fables and their Origin—Theory of the Supper Business—Advice
to sub-Freshmen.

The secret-society system has come to be so important a part of undergraduate life at Yale, that, for a just
comprehension of the latter, a full understanding of the
former is an essential prerequisite. The sub-Freshman
is pledged to his society months before he approaches
the college walls, and the graduate keeps up his senior-
year connections long after he has left those walls behind him. The present system is a comparatively new

one, dating back its establishment but little more than
a generation, yet it is easy to see in it the natural outgrowth of the scheme which preceded it. This may
be said to have originated in 1753, with the establishment of "Linonia," an open society, shared in by all
classes of undergraduates, and at present the oldest
institution of the kind existing in this or any other
American college. Fifteen years later, a secession from
Linonia resulted in the establishment of another similar
society called the "Brothers in Unity." In 1780, was
founded the Connecticut Alpha of "Phi Beta Kappa,"
a secret society, confining its membership to the senior
class. In 1821, came "Chi Delta Theta," secret, in the
senior and junior classes. All of these societies, though
greatly changed as to their scope and object, are still
extant, and will be described at length hereafter. In
their original form they have been gradually superseded
by the modern system, which began in 1832 when a
strictly senior society called "Skull and Bones" was
established. In a few years later there were junior societies, then sophomore, and in 1840 a freshman society
ventured to appear; so that at present there are two or
more secret societies in each of the four academical
classes. The "order of development" being thus traced
out,—from which it would seem likely that the societies
of each lower class were modeled to a certain extent
upon those in the class above, — the different societies
may be described in the order in which the undergraduate becomes acquainted with them: it being premised
that those of the three lower classes resemble Phi Beta
Kappa in being "Greek-letter societies," that is, in
taking their names from the initial letters of a phrase
in Greek, which has been adopted as a secret motto or
watchword of the society. This at least is the theory,
though in practice it sometimes happens that a harmo-

nious combination of letters is first selected for the name, and the motto afterwards fitted to them.

"Kappa Sigma Epsilon," the oldest freshman society, was founded in July, 1840, by a dozen members of the class of '44, of whom Senator O. S. Ferry of Connecticut is perhaps as well known as any. A like number from the class of '49, among whom was Charles G. Came of the Boston *Journal*, established "Delta Kappa" in November, 1845 ; while "Gamma Nu," a non-secret society, was started about ten years later by nine members of the class of '59, including Prof. A. W. Wright of Williams College and Rev. J. H. Twichell of Hartford. There was also a fourth society, called "Sigma Delta," which died in 1860 at the age of eleven. The first of these is always spoken of as "Sigma Eps"; the second as "Delta Kap" or less often "D K"; the third is usually named in full, except when contemptuously referred to as "Gammy." At the outset, Sigma Eps, having the field to itself, was a select society, restricting its membership to about twenty, picked during the first term from each successive freshman class. Delta Kap also partly maintained this character for a year or two, but the rivalry between the two societies for the possession of the "best men" soon became so great as virtually to do away with the plan of individual election, and the practice, now in vogue, was introduced, whereby each society endeavors to gain the largest number of members, — irrespective of merit or want of it on their part, — and the one which succeeds is said to "win the campaign" of the year. The victory always lies between Sigma Eps and Delta Kap, which in a class, say, of one hundred and fifty Freshmen, usually secure about sixty each, while Gamma Nu has to be content with half that number. Delta Kap has now won five out of six successive campaigns, and its last two victories have been quite decisive ones. In the class of '73 Delta Kap had 88 members, Sigma Eps 36, and Gamma Nu 30; and in the class of '74 the corresponding figures were 72, 49 and 29. Though the form of a unanimous election is gone through with, and a single negative vote is sufficient to reject, no Freshman ever *is* rejected by these societies, and every Freshman is expected to join one of them. Thus it happens that a "neutral" or non-society Freshman is of late years very rarely heard of. Men who enter college after freshman year are usually secured as honorary members of these societies, and figure in the catalogues and prize lists the same as regular active members. Occasionally, when such a late-entered upper-class man has distinguished himself in some way, two or more societies make efforts to obtain him ; but as a rule there is little rivalry in this respect. It sometimes happens, on the other hand, though not often, that an upper-class man who attempts to gain admission to these societies is rejected. It has been customary, furthermore, to elect as honorary members some of those who were freshman neutrals in the early years when the societies were select, and who afterwards in college or elsewhere distinguished themselves. Generally, though not always, their consent was obtained beforehand, but they were seldom initiated, as are the honorary members from the upper classes in college. Nevertheless their names usually appear undistinguished from the others in the catalogues, and it hence becomes difficult to discover therefrom the number of regular active members of these societies in all the earlier classes. A very few honorary members are also elected who are indicated as such in the catalogues, because of their never having been connected either with any class represented in the society, or even with the college itself. Such members are ranked with the class which elected them.

These catalogues are published every five or six years ; the last one of Sigma Eps being put forth in the summer of 1865 by the class of '68. This is an octavo pamphlet of sixty-four pages, embellished on the outside with the society emblem, and contains the full names and residences of the members, arranged in classes, with an alphabetical index at the end. A "reference table" at the beginning explains the meaning of the Greek-letter symbols attached to many of the names. These signify the various college "prizes," "honors," and "offices," gained by particular members. Sigma Eps at Yale, calling itself the "Kappa" chapter, estabtablished a branch "Alpha" chapter at Amherst, which ran through the four classes from '53 to '57, and died with a total membership of thirty-two. The "Delta" chapter at the Troy Rensselaer Polytechnic Institute, was started with a dozen men in 1864, and lasted a little more than a year. The "Sigma" chapter, founded at Dartmouth in the class of '57, and numbering in its first ten years some two hundred members, still exists in a flourishing condition. According to the catalogue alluded to, the total membership of the society at Yale in twenty-five classes was 1011, and of all the chapters combined at that date, 1260. Delta Kap has had six branches outside of Yale, two of which survive. Calling itself the "Alpha" chapter, it named the others, in the order of their establishment, from the successive letters of the Greek alphabet. According to the last catalogue, published at Yale in 1866 by the class of '69, the "Gamma" chapter of Amherst, begun in the class of '52, showed a membership of 403, the "Zeta" chapter of Dartmouth, begun in the class of '64, a membership of 151, which with Yale's 997 members in twenty-one classes, gave a total of 1553, or about two hundred more than Sigma Eps at that time,- allowance being made for a hundred increase in the latter's figures of the year before. The " Eta" chapter was established at Center College, Danville, Ky., in 1867. The war broke up three southern chapters, and destroyed all record of their membership. These were: the " Beta," started at the North Carolina University, in 1850; the " Delta" at the Virginia University, in 1851 ; and the " Epsilon" at the Mississippi University, in 1853. The Gamma chapter of Amherst died in the fall of 1870, the faculty forbidding the class of '74 to be initiated. Gamma Nu has never published any catalogue, but from the lists printed in the Yale *Banner*, its first ten classes appear to number 296 members in all, 40 being the largest number belonging to any single class (that of '63). A society of the same name and character was established at Brown University eight or ten years ago, and in 1864 some attempt was made to bring about a formal connection between the two, but nothing resulted and the societies are quite independent of each other. In August, 1854, the Sigma Delta men of '57 issued a catalogue of their society, comprising twenty-two pages and a steel-plate frontispiece of the society badge, with which was connected the motto, *Ingenium labore perfectum*. In college esteem the society occupied a position not unlike that since held by Gamma Nu. After its disruption many of its upper-class members were elected into the other two freshman societies. Sigma Delta had chapters at New York University and Amherst, the latter of which died but two years ago. The very general failure of these branch chapters is chiefly due to the different society systems which prevail at most of the other colleges. There, "the junior societies," as Yale men call them, are composed of members of all the four classes, and a man's active connection with his society continues till the day he graduates.

Hence, the most desirable Freshmen being "picked" by "the junior societies" very early in the course, have little to gain in joining a distinctively freshman society also, and, if they do join it, their interest in the more worthy organization naturally tends to the disadvantage of the other. At Dartmouth, however, as "the junior societies" elect no members before sophomore year, Sigma Eps and Delta Kap have the freshman field all to themselves, and are able to maintain a creditable existence. The tie which binds the different chapters together is a very slight one, as the active membership lasts only a year,—a year in which individual visits between different colleges are least likely to happen,—and a man's zeal in the cause is seldom prolonged beyond this. The occasional interchange of compliments by the corresponding secretaries, the transaction of a little common business, the entertainment of a very rare visitor, these comprise the sum of the relations between the chapters.

The badge pins worn by all the members constitute one of the most distinctive features of these societies. That of Sigma Eps somewhat resembles a Greek cross, except that there are five bars instead of four, between each of which comes the point of a star, the center consisting of a shield of black enamel, bearing the letters "$K \Sigma E$" and "Yale." This last gives place to "Dart" for the Dartmouth chapter, and to corresponding changes for other colleges. Aside from the black shield, there is no relief to the gold surface of the rest of the pin, which, as to size, is perhaps an inch in diameter. A fasces, a caduceus, an anchor, a torch, and an olive-branch are the emblems engraved upon the five projecting bars. The original badge of this society, in use for ten years or more, was a golden anchor, twined about by the two serpents and surmounted by the winged hat of Mercury. The motto, *Sæpe agendo bene agere discere*, is generally found in connection with Sigma Eps cuts and posters. The Delta Kap pin is a crescent, three-quarters of an inch in diameter, of black enamel edged with roughened gold, having in its broadest part a white shield, whereon lie a crossed dagger and key, a star in either horn, and below them the symbols "*Δ*" and "*K*." This is considered the handsomest badge at Yale. It was formerly of plain gold, with three small crescents engraved upon the shield, in place of the dagger and key. *Semper crescens*, is the open motto of this society. The badge of Gamma Nu, in size a trifle smaller than the above, consists of a five-pointed star bearing the symbols "*Γ N*," surrounded by a circular band, with a wreath ornament upon the lower part, and "Yale" inscribed upon a scroll above; the body of the pin being gold, the inscriptions and scroll work of black enamel. Its original badge, in use up to 1862, was in the shape of a book, upon the cover of which figured an open hand, with the letters "*Γ*" "*N*" at the sides, "*Δήλως*" above, and "Yale" below. The motto of the society is *Δήλως καὶ ἀδελφικῶς ἀθλοῦμεν*, and its name in full is *Γυμνάσιον Νοόν*. The last badge of Sigma Delta was diamond shaped, and represented a book labeled "Yale," surmounted by a coronet. An upright oval, wherein a star cast its rays upon an enwreathed "*Σ Δ*," was the pattern previously employed. These badges are worn constantly, from the time a member is initiated until the society is given over to the succeeding class. The usual position is the left side of the vest, at the collar or near the watch-chain, though the pin is sometimes attached to the neck-tie or shirt-bosom, and once in a while a Freshman is seen displaying his badge upon the outer collar of his coat,—a practice not at all uncommon at other colleges. A small gold letter indicative of the chapter,—"*K*" for Sigma Eps, "*A*" for Delta Kap,—connected to the main badge by a chain, is often to be noticed upon a Freshman's waistcoat. Their note-paper and envelopes are also embellished with the society insignia, in gold or colors ; and the same in the form of elaborate steel-plate or lithographic "posters," often handsomely framed, are displayed upon the walls of their rooms —where they are apt to hang undisturbed until graduation day itself.

The halls of the lower-class college societies are in the upper stories of buildings in different parts of the town, rented of their owners for the purpose, at an annual cost of from one hundred and fifty to two hundred and fifty dollars. A graduate member or other responsible person is persuaded to take out a two or three years' lease of a hall for a society, and so long as he is responsible the society is generally honorable enough to pay the rents promptly, and give him no trouble in the matter. By the time the lease has expired the society has become pretty well established in its hall, cannot easily be ejected without actual violence, which the owner or agent does not like to evoke, for fear of incurring ill will, and often keeps possession of its hall for many years without lease or written agreement of any kind with its owner. It usually pays its rent with tolerable regularity, and in cases when it does get two or three quarters behind hand, a little judicious threatening and a few hints at ejectment are apt to bring about an early settlement ; so that real-estate holders seldom lose money in these transactions. Yet it is worthy of notice that "strict business men" thus entrust to irresponsible "societies"— endowed with no legal existence as such, composed of careless college boys, who are not individually liable for society debts— considerable sums of money, well knowing that the only security for its payment lies in so intangible a thing as traditional society integrity. The three freshman halls are situated on Chapel street, the main thoroughfare of the city; that of Sigma Eps being in Collins Building, a short distance below State street, and distant half a mile from the colleges; that of Delta Kap being at No. 334, near Church street, half as far away; that of Gamma Nu being in Lyon Building, midway between the other two. Sigma Eps for many years occupied a hall in Brewster Building, southeast corner of State and Chapel streets, and close beside the railway station, and moved into its present abode in the fall of 1870; Delta Kap spent eighteen years in Austin Building, opposite its present quarters, which it took possession of in 1864; and Gamma Nu, after subsisting in the college recitation rooms and elsewhere, became established where it now is in 1863. Its hall is commodious and well furnished, but, though more attractive than the old hall of Sigma Eps, is inferior in size and elegance to the halls now possessed by the other two societies. Each of these contains a stage for theatrical purposes, though Delta Kap is the only freshman hall whose entrance is guarded with double doors of iron.

When "the candidate for admission to the freshman class in Yale College" draws near to New Haven, for the purpose of attending the dread entrance examination, he is usually accosted with the utmost politeness by a jaunty young gentleman, resplendent with mystic insignia, who, after some introductory commonplaces, "presumes he may be intending to enter Yale?" "Yes." "Perhaps he has heard of some remarkable societies existing in that neighborhood?" If he has, and says at once that he's "pledged" to this or that society, our affable friend congratulates him on the wisdom of his choice, if it be *his* society, or quickly turns the subject if it happens to be its opponent, and in either case soon bids him good day. But if he wants information on the subject, the jaunty young gentleman is most happy to supply it. "He chances to have in his pocket a prize list, recently published by the college authorities, which shows exactly how the thing now stands." This list of course places one society far ahead of the rest in the matter of "honors," and other desirable things ; which society our friend at length confesses he had the honor of belonging to last year, and thinks he has still enough influence there to secure the unanimous election of his new acquaintance, if he decides to work for it. " Will he pledge to accept the election, in case he is so lucky as to get it for him?" Perhaps the sub-Freshman says Yes, forthwith. More likely, he "wants to think about it," and would rather " wait till he gets to the city, and looks around for himself, a little." But no, that would be useless. His time will then be taken up with other things. Besides, this list contains all the facts. Hasn't President Woolsey authorized it? Presume *his* word isn't doubted? Oh, dear, no! Well, the whole ground is gone over, and some sort of a pledge is at last exacted. " If you won't pledge to Sigma Eps, you'll at least promise not to go to Gamma Nu?" Yes, sub-Fresh will promise that. "And you won't pledge to Delta Kap till you talk with me again?" "No." And so they part. This is supposed to happen before the train or boat reaches the station or landing. By that time our Sigma Eps partisan—for as such we now recognize him — is in the midst of his argument with another "candidate." They are just preparing to alight, when other Sigma Eps men surround them. At a sign from the first, one takes his valise, another his umbrella, a third his bundle. "This way if you please, Mr. ——."

And before the sub-Fresh has time to protest, he is rolling along in a hack, and his new found friends are en-
quiring the number of his boarding house, or the name
of the hotel he wishes to go to? Very likely they treat
him to dinner or supper, but at any rate they are very
attentive to his wants and do not leave him until he is
"pledged." Sometimes the transfer to the hack is not
so easily accomplished, for the runners of another society may scent the prey, rush for it, and bear it off in
triumph. There are plenty of representatives from all
three societies hanging about the railroad station on
the arrival of the important trains, and rarely does a
sub-Freshman run the gauntlet of their eyes without detection. They jump upon the platforms of the moving
cars, they fight the brakemen, they incommode the
travelers, they defy the policemen,—but they *will* offer
the advantages of "the best freshman society" to every
individual "candidate." And they do. "Pledged" is
the magic word, and the only one, that secures the new
comer an immunity from their attentions. Amusing
mistakes often happen in these contests. A quiet Senior, or resident graduate, mistaken by a society runner
for a sub-Freshman, may "play off verdant," allow
himself to be electioneered, accept a free ride to the
hotel, and possibly a supper, and at last, carelessly displaying a senior-society pin upon his shirt-front, inform
his terror stricken entertainers that he "belonged to
Delta Kap about four years ago," and wish them a very
good evening.   .

Within a week from the commencement of the term,
about every Freshman has been pledged, and preparations are being made for the "initiation." The term
opens on Thursday, and the traditional time of initiation
is Friday night of the following week. As the darkness
approaches, the discordant blasts of tin horns and the

rattle of bangers upon the pavement admonish the expectant Freshmen that the hour of their trial is rapidly drawing near. Each one has received during the day a black-edged envelope, covering a black-edged card or sheet of paper, bearing the society badge and this fearful summons: " Freshman [or " Mr."] So and So : You will be waited upon at your room this evening, and be presented for initiation into the dark and awful mysteries of the —— fraternity. Per order." The half of a card of fantastic design and peculiarly notched edge is also enclosed, and the Freshman is instructed to surrender himself only to the personage who presents him with the other half of that particular card, which will be identified by the "matching" of the edges,—no two cards of the many given out having been notched exactly alike. Sometime between the hours of seven and ten our Freshman is called for, identifies the card presented to him, and gives himself up to his conductor, who may very likely have a companion, wearing a mask, like himself, or otherwise disguised. Perhaps they visit some eating house where the Freshman treats to an oyster supper ; or perhaps he promises to give the supper on the following evening ; or perhaps he doesn't care to treat at all. Possibly he has been blindfolded from the time he left his room, and has had a tin horn blown close to his ear occasionally, on the way, though this is unusual. But at length they draw near some public building, from within which proceed sounds as of pandemonium itself. The Freshman is blindfolded for a minute or two, is shoved forward, hears a door open and close behind him with a bang, and opens his eyes to find himself in pitch darkness. However, he at once perceives that he is not alone, but in the midst of other Freshmen, like him " waiting their turn." The noise meanwhile seems louder and louder, and when an inner door opens and a name is called, it becomes almost deafening. Soon our Fresh is wanted. A red devil in the passage way, assisted by a living skeleton, redolent of phosphorus, quickly blindfolds him, and he is hurried upward. When he has reached an elevation apparently of several hundred feet, a new element in the continual din assures him that he is at last in the inquisitorial hall. But just as he begins a reply to the last nonsensical question put by an attendant fiend, some one jostles against him, and down, down, down he falls until he strikes—a blanket, held in readiness for him. Then up he flies into the air again, amid admiring shrieks of " Go it, Freshie !" " Well done, Sub !" " *Shake* him up !" until a new candidate demands the attention of the tossers. Then he is officiously told to rest himself in a chair, the seat of which lets him into a pail of water, beneath, though a large sponge probably saves him from an actual wetting ; his head and hands are thrust through a pillory, and he is reviled in that awkward position ; he is rolled in an exaggerated squirrel wheel ; a noose is thrown around his neck, and he is dragged beneath the guillotine, when the bandage is pulled from his eyes, and he glares upon the glittering knife of block-tin, which falls within a foot of his throat, and cannot possibly go further. Being thus executed, he is thrust into a coffin, which is hammered upon with such energy that he is at length recalled to life, pulled out again, and made to wear his coat with the inside outwards. This is the sign that his initiation is over, and he can now stand by and enjoy the fun. Ranging himself with the turn-coated classmates whom he finds have preceded him, he looks upon a motley throng of struggling Sophomores, arrayed in every variety of hideous and fantastic disguise, shouting, screaming, horn-blowing, and putting the Freshmen through the various stages of the ceremony, which in his own case has just been completed, while Juniors and Seniors stand by as passive spectators of the sport. A lithographic sketch by W. H. Davenport, for a time in the class of '60, gives a very correct idea of this grotesque initiation scene.

Formerly, Sigma Eps and Delta Kap held the initiation in common, hiring for the purpose a public hall, and admitting to the show a select number of visitors, not connected with the societies or with college. The doors were securely guarded by policemen, and no one without society badge or admission ticket could pass the entrance. These tickets were embellished on the one side with some terrific representation of Freshmen seething in fiend-tended cauldrons, or being rended in pieces by animate skeletons, or undergoing some similar torture ; while the other side bore the badges of the two societies, inter-locked or else connected with the clasped hands, and the names of the sophomore committee men. Though no longer of any special utility, these cards are still issued, separately, by the societies, and bear but a single badge and committee, though the same cut is employed by both. This cut afterwards figures in the *Pot Pourri*, in connection with the names of both committees. At these quasi-public initiations, more elaborate processes could be gone through with than those already described. The Freshmen could be raised to any required hight, in a coffin-shaped box, the bottom of which dropping out would allow him to tumble into the awaiting blanket ; or a blank charge from two or three muskets could be fired over his head at the instant when he fell through a trap door into the inevitable blanket prepared below ; or the same trap could be made to do service as a grave into which his encoffined form might be lowered ; or he could be given a "cradle ride," in a vehicle, much like a reversed hen-

coop mounted on wheels, which might be dragged
swiftly across the stage over the rough clumps of wood
carefully placed in its way:—things which have not been
possible since 1865, when the college authorities decreed
that each society must initiate in its own hall, in the
presence of no one but its own members.

Each Sophomore has a particular Freshman assigned
to him for initiation, and usually selects some former
friend or acquaintance, or a man whom he himself
pledged, or one whom he thinks likely to " treat" liberally, or in lack of these is content with any Freshman
whatever.   As the Freshmen usually outnumber the
Sophomores, a few of the former are assigned to Juniors,
members of last year's initiation committee perhaps,
who are very glad to seize the opportunity thus offered
for a possible "supper."   But many of the upper class
men—for Seniors as well as Juniors engage in the disgraceful business—who have no Freshmen assigned to
them, seize if they can upon those allotted to others,
and get from them a supper.   Perhaps two or three
Freshmen are brought together in a college room, and
put through a mock initiation : made to box or fence
with one another, dance blindfolded on a table, sing,
answer nonsensical questions, pass a mock examination
in their lessons before a pretended professor, and so on ;
but the supper is the main thing, after all.   There are
always many Freshmen absent from the evening recitation of initiation night—most of whom are keeping close
to their own rooms by order of their sophomore owners,
or are lying secreted in the rooms of the upper-class
men who have " stolen" them,—and there is always a
scuffle on the dismissal of that recitation, in which some
Freshmen are "gobbled up" and spirited away.   Late
in the evening the upper-class men present themselves
at the initiation halls with their charges, and attempt to

" get through" the latter with a light initiation or none at all. This attempt the Sophomores resist, and a fierce commotion ensues. The Freshman is dragged about by the contending parties, and perhaps has his clothes torn in the struggle. If the Sophs finally get him, he is put through, the whole extent of the ceremony ; otherwise, his friends get his coat turned, and that is the end of it. It is not always in return for a treat simply that this is done. An upper-class man or even a Sophomore, may have a brother or friend whom he wishes to get through, or the mere excitement of the thing and a pure love of mischief may furnish the only motives for the action. Spite of every precaution against it, it is not very difficult in the confusion and hubbub to slide a Freshman through unnoticed, and it is every year accomplished in many cases. But when " detected in the act," the guardians of the Freshman are usually obliged to surrender him to his "rightful owners." In 1866, on account of a rumor that the faculty would attempt to abolish the initiation entirely, Delta Kap had a secret one, the night before the usual time, in which none but the Sophomores participated. Since then both societies, by varying the nights of the ceremony and conducting it in comparative quiet, have endeavored to keep it from the knowledge of upper-class men and the faculty, but without a very marked success. The institution has plainly seen its best—or its worst— days, yet will doubtless continue to exist for some time to come ; for such things die hard in college.

The ceremony concluded, the newly initiated are pledged to observe the secrets of their society, ordered to assemble at the hall early on the following evening, and dismissed,—though not until several have been called upon to "make speeches," which are greeted with uproarious mock-applause, and sarcastic cries of

"Well done, Freshie!" "Good for you!" and so on. Next day the Freshmen pay their initiation fees, which vary from five dollars to twice that, in different societies and different years; swing out their badges, most of which are lent them by the Sophomores until their own can be engraved upon the back with their names and that of their class; and at the appointed hour approach their society hall, which they find entirely transformed in appearance since the previous night. The Sophomores are now stretched out upon the carpeted floor, in the center of the hall, smoking, laughing, and singing, while the Freshmen occupy the seats about them. The president orders the reading of the constitution, whereto the new members affix their names. A farewell poem and oration are pronounced, or possibly a play is acted. Then a new president is elected by the Freshmen, a few parting words of explanation and advice are offered by the retiring sophomore president, hearty cheers are given for him, for the society, and for the new members (which the latter feebly reciprocate—not having yet learned to cheer effectively), and the Sophomores, striking up a farewell song, for the last time march forth in a body from the hall. The final chant of Delta Kap consists in an indefinite repetition of the words: "Oh Delta Kappa Kappa Kap, Oh Delta Kappa Kappa," to the tune of "Yankee Doodle." Reaching the street in front of their hall, the ex-members combine in giving a tremendous "three-times-three" cheer for their society, and disband forever. Previous to the exercises of the second night, a few who had not answered to their names at the roll-call of the night before are sometimes shaken a little in the blanket, as are also, though more rarely, the few who join the society after their own class controls it. The initiation of honorary members is only a formal ceremony. In the days of joint-initiation, the members of each society, at its close, marched off with their Freshmen to their respective halls, and there, as now, pledged them to secrecy, and dismissed them until the following night. The ceremony which takes place at Gamma Nu on initiation night corresponds to that of the second night in the other societies, though the members are formally summoned and escorted to the hall by Sophomores. There are no treats or suppers in connection with this society.

The Freshmen, left to themselves, elect their remaining officers,—a half dozen or more in number,—make arrangements for their next society meeting, and adjourn,—having first engaged the janitor, recommended them by their predecessors, who keeps the hall in order, and locks its doors. A duplicate set of keys, however, is kept in possession of the president. The meetings of the societies are held every Saturday evening, opening about eight o'clock and lasting two or three hours. The exercises are of a literary character and consist of debates, declamations, and orations, the reading of essays and selected passages and the society "papers," which are made up of miscellaneous writings prepared by regularly elected editors. The paper of Sigma Eps is called the *Star*, that of Delta Kap the *Crescent*. A critique upon the proceedings of that or the previous meeting is generally the last thing offered. The appointments for the various duties are announced by the president one, two or three weeks in advance, and the order of exercises of the following week is read at the close of each meeting. Full programmes of the exercises and appointments of each evening, written out by the secretary upon blank forms printed for the purpose, are posted about the halls. Fines are exacted for failure to fulfil appointments, or for absence at roll-call, which is made both at the opening and the close of the meeting; and a neglect to pay fines or taxes may deprive a member of the right of suffrage. Once or twice in a year a " prize debate" is instituted, before old society men—members of the faculty if possible—as judges. Printed programmes are provided, and neither these nor the names of the prize takers are kept secret from the outside world. These semi-public debates were started by the Delta Kap men of '70, though less extensive prize trials had been known of in previous years in both societies. There is considerable singing of society songs at the meetings, with accompaniment on the piano forte,—one of which instruments is owned or rented by every college society,—and nearly every class feels bound to add a song or two to the collection, if not to print a new edition of the song book. Delta Kap no longer pretends to keep its song book secret, and with Sigma Eps the concealment is only nominal, but as the Freshmen disband at a comparatively early hour, they rarely sing their songs upon the street. A group of upper-class men may sometimes strike up a freshman-society song, though not usually in the day time.

For the first few weeks succeeding initiation, a good number of Sophomores drop in at the meetings, " to see how the Freshies are getting along," but after that only a few upper-class men will be found there, except there be some special attraction, as a contested election of officers, or a play, or a " peanut-bum." When the society, in the persons of its active or honorary members, has come off with honors in some college contest (or without them—it makes little difference), the event is celebrated in this wise at the next succeeding meeting: After the close of the literary exercises, a sack containing one or two bushels of peanuts is emptied upon the floor, and an indiscriminate scramble is made for them by the upper-class guests and their freshman entertainers. Then cigars are distributed, and perhaps in extraordinary cases fruit also, while lemonade may supersede the customary ice water—for stronger beverages are unknown in a freshman society. Smoking is also forbidden during the exercises, and card-playing at any time is a thing unheard of. Gamma Nu holds once a term what is called a "jubilee," on which occasions upper-class men and other honorary members address the society. These and all its literary exercises are open to all in college who choose to attend them, though the business of the society is transacted in the presence of none but members. In rare cases a Senior or even a Junior will invite to his freshman hall a classmate who belonged to a rival society. This causes much indignation among the Freshmen, and when they discover any such visitor, he is apt to be expelled without much ceremony. Even upper-class men regard the practice as rather dishonorable. It happens on initiation nights oftener than at other times, when, on account of the disguises and the confusion, an interloper is more likely to escape detection ; though if he *is* detected then, his chances for an easy escape are proportionately lessened. It might be a serious matter for anyone not a college man to be caught trespassing in a freshman-society hall. A few years ago a person, believed to be a reporter for a city paper, was found at the Sigma Eps initiation, and so thoroughly " put through" that he will not be likely to repeat his visit. It is possible that the public is indebted to this gentleman for many of the fabulous accounts of college doings, which have been so widely circulated by the newspapers.

The society officers are elected twice a term. The office of president is accounted a high honor, especially that of final or "campaign" president of each class,

the members of all schools of any importance are "pledged" months before they approach New Haven, and it is only the ones fitted under private tutors or in distant parts of the country, who have to be met and argued with in the manner already·described,—though these doubtless form in the aggregate a majority of the whole number. As the time of the entrance examination approaches, not only do the freshman-society runners infest the trains and the New Haven depot, as already stated, but they are. also regularly stationed at important railway centers, as New York, Springfield and New London, and there lie in wait for the unpledged "candidates." The expenses of a campaign conducted in this manner are of course considerable, and are borne for the most part by the society, though not unfrequently the campaign president or even members of the initiation committee individually pay out considerable sums of money for "the cause." Shortly after initiation night, the two committees join in giving an elaborate supper, to which are invited the committees of the year before, and perhaps also those in the senior class—what there are left of them. Ornamented bills-of-fare bearing the insignia of the two societies and the names of those partaking of the feast, are sometimes provided.   For this supper sometimes the society pays, sometimes the individual committee men ; and sometimes the latter agree in consideration of the supper to present no bills for electioneering expenses incurred in the society's behalf. There is a dispute as to the theory of the thing, but in practice it amounts to this, that if any money is left in the treasury after the regular debts of the society have been paid, the committee are pretty certain to have it, for their supper ; otherwise their claim amounts to little. The last supper was given by the committees of '71. Those of '72 set a better precedent, and as those of '73 followed it, perhaps the custom will not be again revived.

Each class gives the society free from debt to its successor, and generally leaves behind some substantial token of remembrance in the form of an improvement to the hall or other addition to the society property. A large amount of money, even, was left in the Delta Kap treasury by the Sophs of '72. Aside from the fines, which avail but little, taxes, to the amount of ten or fifteen dollars in all, are levied upon the members, at various times during the year, to meet the current expenses; and the initiation fees derived from the succeeding class are expended in advance for the same purpose. Directly and indirectly, a man's freshman society will cost him on the average from thirty-five to forty dollars. In the case of Gamma Nu, where there are no outside and unnecessary expenses, these figures may be somewhat reduced, but from the fewness of its members the share of each in its regular expenses must be proportionately greater than in the other societies. When Freshmen find no traces of their initiation fees in the society treasury, they are often a little indignant, imagine themselves the victims of "another swindle," and put ready confidence in current rumors that all their money is expended upon a supper for the initiation committee or for the society in general. As already shown, however, the greater part of the money is invested for the permanent benefit of the society, for which their predecessors of course claim the credit.

At first the Freshman cares a good deal for his society. He is punctual at the meetings, fulfills his appointments, pays his fines and taxes promptly, and above all is very zealous about keeping its "secrets." He scorns and detests those upper-class men who talk over his society affairs so freely with outsiders, and vows to himself that *he* will never be guilty of such baseness in future years. Gradually his interest lessens. He gets a pledge to a junior society—or tries to—and begins to "wonder how the sophomore-society elections are coming out." He grows inclined to think his taxes oppressive, and to vote that the society expenditures be hereafter met by future initiation fees. If he belongs to a faction far in the minority, perhaps he absents himself from most of the meetings, and gives the majority leave "to run their own society." The third term comes, with its many special excitements, and the regular routine is sadly broken up. Delta Kap for the first time nails down its foot-lights and brings out a play or two. The campaign elections are decided, and the fight over the unpledged sub-Freshmen begins in earnest. The new year opens, and the Sophomore—who has probably experienced a sea change for the worse in his notions of morality—initiates his Freshman, and "gets a supper" from him if he can. He still takes a little interest in his old society, but doesn't scruple to relate outside anything notable which he sees occurring there. By the time he becomes a Junior or Senior, he hardly thinks of his society at all, save when he tries to "get a supper" of a Freshman in its name, or is invited to a play or "peanut bum." A dozen years after graduation, he would hesitate before he could tell you the name of it. A graduate rarely enters the society unless specially invited, or sent by the faculty as its representative. It is esteemed dishonorable for an upper-class man to electioneer or pledge for a freshman society, and such pledges count for little in the college code. He may say to a friend or relative: "I account my society the best one, and advise you to go there," but nothing more. So, likewise, public sentiment condemns an upper-class man who allows freshman-society considerations to effect his choice of candidates for office, or to prejudice in any way his action or opinion.

The prize lists issued by each society as electioneering arguments do not really conflict with one another, though each makes its own society appear ahead in the matter of honors, and, taken by itself, conclusively proves it to be in those respects "the best." The inference drawn by Freshmen from the apparently contradictory statements, that all the figures are unreliable, is a mistaken one in fact, though practically about correct, since the figures as arranged are the means of as much deception as if really in themselves untrue. Taking the three lists of 1866, as fairly representing how the "art of putting things" is usually practised by these societies, we find that Sigma Eps ignores Gamma Nu altogether, and compares itself "with its rival Delta Kap" in respect to those classes of honors which have, during the last few years, turned the scale in its own favor. Delta Kap, on the other hand, reprints the summaries of the two catalogues, and thus makes out its total membership and number of honors to be ahead of its rival. It shows how that it has had more of the Cochleaureati and the senior-society men of the past few years than all the other societies combined, and has "received eight out of fourteen Wooden Spoons." It also exhibits itself ahead in the matter of "Editors of the Yale *Lit.*," "class orators and poets," "DeForest-medal men" and "Commodores of the Navy,"—taken for a long series of years. An examination of opposing lists may show that of late years it has been behind in these respects. The Gamma Nu list, calling itself, with a certain amount of truth, "the only complete and authentic record published," does not display its badge, as the other lists do, or otherwise indicate its origin. Like Sigma Eps, it confines most of its statistics to the four classes in college, and, unlike it, compares the honors taken by all three societies. The result is of course in its own favor. A peculiarity of this list is the indication in the "summary" of the "cash value" of the honors. As Gamma Nu takes most of the scholarships, which are the only "honors" whose "cash value" is of any consequence, the reason of this is obvious. The highest elective, and all but the highest literary, honors — and these are accounted of more importance than any others — are thus reduced to nothing in the "summary of cash values;" while a single important scholarship makes a greater display of dollars and cents than could all the other honors of college combined. Another peculiarity of the list is the publication of "the elective political honors of the past year, that is, the officers of Linonia and Brothers." Formerly, without doubt, these offices might fairly be included among the honors; but for some years past the "elections" have gone by default, and an "office" in one of these defunct institutions has been quite as commonly considered a disgrace as an honor to the holder. The present list, in its "grand total of the four classes," gives Gamma Nu 109 honors with a cash value of $2400; Sigma Eps 72, valued at $680; and Delta Kap 62, valued at $316. Each society of course possesses "strong points" of·its own, and the effectiveness of a prize list depends upon the skill with which they are brought into prominence, and made to overshadow its shortcomings in those respects wherein a rival list as evidently has the advantage. Of the verbal arguments employed by the partisans of these societies no description is possible, but nothing more absurd and preposterous than much which is said in favor or against them can well be imagined. Perhaps the claim which excites the most general derision is that soberly advanced by Gamma Nu men, to account for their want of success in securing Freshmen, that "the number of their members is designedly limited." On the whole, the opposing arguments and prize lists may be said to prove almost nothing, and to do little more than confuse the "candidate" who attempts to compare them and make out their significance.

In the college faculty Sigma Eps and Delta Kap are each represented by a half-dozen professors, and Gamma Nu by two or three tutors. Among other names to be noticed in the Sigma Eps catalogue are those of Henry T. Blake of '48, patron of the Wooden Spoon ; William D. Bishop of '49, founder of a prize debate fund in Linonia ; Champion Bissell and Frederic B. Perkins of '50 ; George W. Smalley of '53, London correspondent of the *Tribune;* Sidney E. Morse of '56, publisher of the N. Y. *Observer;* and many professors at other colleges, tutors at Yale, lawyers, doctors and clergymen. Among Delta Kap men may be mentioned Charles D. Gardette of '50 ; Homer B. Sprague, and William M. Stewart, U. S. Senator from Nevada, of '52 ; Andrew D. White, president of Cornell University, Charlton T. Lewis, of the *Evening Post*, and Edmund C. Stedman, of '53 ; Rev. William H. H. Murray of '62, with the usual proportion of Yale tutors and outside professors, a general or two upon either side during the late war, and others. From the comparatively recent establishment of Gamma Nu, it naturally happens that few well known names can be found upon its lists.

The attempt to indicate the relative position of these societies is rendered the more difficult by the anomalous character of the youngest one, which calls for an extended explanation. Gamma Nu was started as an *open* society, in direct defiance of the established order of things, and its founders, suffering the fate of all reformers, were despised, derided and abused. Every possible attempt was made to crush the " Gamma Nuisance" and to bring its supporters to naught ; but spite of persecution and obloquy—or perhaps because of them—the society slowly gained ground, and finally fought its way into recognition as a college institution. Attempts are no longer made to break it up, or to debar its members from the elective honors of the college; yet a trace of the old proscriptive spirit still manifests itself both in the ill-defined prejudice against "Gamma Nu men" which always prevails among the members of the other societies, and in the instinctive consciousness on the part of the former that they are "looked down upon" by their rivals. The name is still a sort of reproach, and a general sigh of "Too bad!" goes up when the fact is known that some "good fellow" has "pledged to Gamma Nu." Yet some "good fellows," and some of the very best men, in every class, do go there—as also do some of the very poorest. Two quite opposite motives draw members thither: the one, a manly contempt for the silly mummeries and greedy extortions attendant upon the secret societies; the other, a childish dread of the pictured terrors of initiation. But as time passes on, and the one influenced by the former consideration finds that these evident faults as compared to offsetting advantages are small, and the one influenced by the latter finds that they are little more than inventions,—both are apt to repent of their action. Probably few men ever joined the society who were not afterwards, in their own hearts, a trifle ashamed of it. The natural result is a fierce attempt by zeal in its behalf to cover up the disappointment. Gamma Nu men fulfil their society duties more faithfully than do others, electioneer more persistently, attend to its interests more noticeably when they become upper-class men, and so on. They are, in short, harder workers, and, in proportion to their numbers, they secure a far larger share of the substantial college awards. But by everything they do they show the consciousness of the hated social inferiority, against which they so pluckily and hopelessly contend. Among upper-class men, Sigma Eps may deride Delta Kap, and it passes for a joke ; Delta Kap may insinuate that Sigma Eps as a Junior blackballs all but his own men, and nothing but laughter results ; but when the attempt is made thus to jest about Gamma Nu, it falls flat. For there is a sort of sneaking feeling that upper-class Gamma Nu men *do* work for their freshman society on occasion, and facetious references to the belief may "hit" some one awkwardly. A man may be retailing the most fearful slanders concerning either the secret societies without thinking who are his auditors, but the moment he has said anything against Gamma Nu he instinctively glances through them for fear lest some one be ● hurt."

The faculty have sometimes favored this society as against the others, by giving notice that those who join the latter diminish their chances of receiving pecuniary assistance as indigent students. The principle, too, which excites sympathy for " the under dog in the fight" has drawn to the fold many of its best men. A few of the weaklings—those who at the first secretly admired the worst features of the other societies, but were afraid to join them—often leave Gamma Nu, and sometimes even join one of its rivals,—where, like all traitors, they are received joyfully, and despised heartily ; while on the other hand no Sigma Eps or Delta Kap man ever yet deserted his society for a rival one. · Yet almost universally the fact is as stated, that the consciousness of being under the ban of college opinion causes the Gamma Nu men to make more of their society than do any of the others. Much of the prejudice against it is undoubtedly due to this, that it cannot lay claim to the respect always given to consistent action. Its members are as ready as anyone to join the upper-class secret societies, so that the pretence of their being any "principle" involved in its anti-secret character is of course absurd.　Such a society is only possible in freshman year, for no man who understands the drift of things in college could ever be persuaded to join it.　In a broadly general way, Gamma Nu may be called the society of hard working scholarship, Sigma Eps of careless literary excellence, and Delta Kap of good fellowship and sociability ; though the characters here assigned as distinctive of the two last are not so marked, perhaps, as that indicated for the first, and their social standing in the college world is one of absolute equality.　Judged by its success, Delta Kap is at present "the best society," and in it an average man is likely to enjoy himself more and improve his opportunities less than in either of the others.　The exact reverse in both these respects is true of Gamma Nu ; while Sigma Eps occupies an intermediate position—very much nearer the former than the latter.　The scheme of exercises in the three societies is, as already stated, essentially identical ; the influence which each exerts in inclining a man to make the most of his chances, is the thing in which they differ. As to their "secrecy," it can hardly be said to amount to more than this, that while Gamma Nu transacts only part of its business with closed doors, the other two societies keep theirs shut against outsiders altogether. The transactions themselves, after freshman year at least, are known to all who care to enquire about them. It has been said that "some very poor men go to Gamma Nu," and of course the same hold true of the other societies ; but there is this important difference, that while, from the smallness of its membership, a man must in the first case be thrown in close contact with those whom he dislikes, and be thought of as their companion, it happens in the case of the other societies that their numbers allows the formation of congenial cliques with whom alone a man directly associates or is associated in the popular mind. Thus the names of these two societies become connected almost entirely with their best representatives, and the poorer ones are in some way overlooked ; so that in speaking of an upper-class "pill," the habit is common to say, "Gamma Nu man, I suppose?" and if the reply is, " No, I believe he belonged to Sigma Eps," or "to Delta Kap," to add, " Well, he should have been one if he was n't."

The initiation, as it has been described, may perhaps appear somewhat formidable, and it may be well to add a few negative statements concerning it, and also to explain away the absurd fictions founded upon it, which are annually current in the newspapers. In the first place, there is nothing dangerous about the ceremony, and no one ever comes to serious bodily harm. In exceedingly rare cases, from accident or carelessness, a slight bruise or so may be inflicted, but as for the broken arms and legs which excite so much editorial indignation, they are simply the myths of imaginative reporters and nothing more. In 1869 a report, started by an obscure city paper called the *Lever*, was copied all over the country, to the effect that " at the Delta Kap initiation one Freshman had both bones of the forearm broken short off near the elbow, and several others were carried away in carriages in an insensible condition." Of this so plausibly circumstantial a story the sole basis was a carriage or two ; for the carriages were really before the hall, and in them two or three Freshmen were hurried off to the awaiting suppers,—their conductors fearing to walk them thither lest they be "gobbled up" on the way. The theory of the initiation is to try the Freshman's nerves in every way, to scare him thoroughly,

but not to hurt him.   There is nothing specially unpleasant about being tossed in a blanket, and Freshmen often
toss one another for the mere fun of the thing.   But a
blindfolded man, in a pandemonium of noises, and an
atmosphere of tobacco smoke, flying up and down
through illimitable space, needs all his wits about him
if he would keep cool and reason himself into a feeling
of security.   No one has any right to enter college until
he is old enough to go through these imaginary terrors
without any great amount of flinching, but in the rare
instances when a very young Freshman shows signs of
faintness, at any point in the ceremony, the bandage is
at once pulled from his eyes and he is declared initiated :
a proceeding which is pretty certain to restore him forthwith.   Nor is it true that drunken men control the proceedings.   A Sophomore or two may be present who
have plainly imbibed too freely at their suppers, but
they are closely watched by their sober companions, and
prevented from putting Freshmen through any process
outside the regular programme.   The stories of Freshmen being forced to lie down with corpses, in the basement of the State House, or being really buried in
grave yards, or in the pit where the subjects from the
dissecting room are finally thrown, have no grain of
truth in them beyond the fact that the regular initiation
has sometimes been held in the State House basement,
and sometimes in the hall of the old Medical College.
A mask or wax-figure in a coffin may really be mistaken
for a corpse by a bewildered Freshman, and the lower-
ing of his encased form through a trap door may perhaps startle him.   There the imagined horror ends.
The many other fearful rumors, which prevail among
the uninitiated and find their way into print, when traced
to their source will be found to have no more groundwork of reality than the fables whose genesis has just
been indicated.

On another point there seems to be a great misapprehension in the public prints. According to newspaper authority the suppers are bribes, and the initiation a thing devised solely to punish those who do not "treat." It has been already shown that the one thing does not depend upon the other, that men are " put through" without any regard to their liberality in the way of feasting their conductors, and that nothing enrages the Sophomores more than to have upper-class men who have been " treated" by Freshmen try to "get them through," solely on that account. Freshmen also, to avoid being " stolen" by the wrong men, often pay their conductors in advance the price of the supper they propose to furnish, and by some accident or confusion it may in rare cases happen that they do not share in the treat they have paid for. This must be the foundation of the tales of Sophomores extorting money from Freshmen, under penalty of initiating them with severity, and quietly putting it in their own pockets. This supper business, which is really the worst feature of these societies, is evidently bad enough in itself, without these imaginary embellishments. It is, however, patterned after the treats connected with entrance to the upper-class societies. But there, entertainers and entertained are fewer, and more select, and to a great extent personally known to each other, and the elected are supposed to show their gratitude for the honor conferred upon them by their superiors: while here, except in a few rare cases, both parties to the supper are unacquainted, and either enemies to one another or likely to become so ; everything about the affair is constrained and unnatural ; and, without the pretence of sociability—still worse, *with* the pretence—the enjoyment is simply an animal one. In its essence, the principle which induces a man to give the expected supper in freshman year—that is, the active desire to appear liberal or the passive one not to appear mean—hardly differs from that which influences him on similar occasions for the two years following; yet the "accidents" (as the logicians say) which surround its display in the former case are much more repulsive and disgraceful than in the latter.

Undoubtedly the initiation and its attendant customs put an unusual amount of power into the hands of the Sophomores, which those of them who, as compared with the rest, are unscrupulous oftentimes abuse; yet as Freshmen have hardly acquired any distinct personality or made any individual enemies up to the time they are initiated, the private revenges which particular Sophomores take this occasion to wreak are not common. On the whole, then, a fair-minded man who fully understands the thing looks upon the initiation as a ceremony silly, childish and perhaps a trifle disreputable, but certainly not cruel, nor malicious, nor barbarous; while as for the suppers, he either wishes that most of the upper-class men who swallow them might choke in the process, or, if a believer in the decency of human nature, resolutely refuses to think of them at all.

To the boy fitting for Yale, this much of advice can fairly be given: Pledge early to one of these three societies. Choose the one where your friends will be with you, or the one which your upper-class friends recommend. If you enter college alone and unacquainted, and have no preference in the matter, either decide upon your society in advance, by the simple expedient of drawing lots or throwing dice, or else pledge to the first society for which you are electioneered. You can gain nothing by delay. You can learn nothing from partisan arguments or prize lists. You can accomplish nothing by personal inspection. Pledge at once, and your troubles will be over. Attempt to find out "the best," and you will be pretty certain to take up with the worst.

CHAPTER II.

Kappa Sigma Theta—Alpha Sigma Phi—Phi Theta Psi — Delta
Beta Xi—The Yale " Banger" and " Tomahawk"—Chapters—
Posters and Song Books—Electioneering and Pledging—Giving
out Elections—Initiation—Ordinary Exercises—Singing—Class
Elections—The Sophomore Type.

Tradition has it that in the old days of Bully Clubs
and town-and-gown disturbances, there were sophomore
societies whose members were distinguished by the
peculiar shape of the clubs which they carried as
badges.   Sometimes the societies grew out of the debating associations of freshman year, which each class
established for itself.   Like them, they seem to have
been without name or formal organization.   Apparently,
the first regular sophomore society originated in the
class of '41, and started into being in July, 1838, though
a freshman debating club perhaps served as the nucleus
which drew its members together.   It was called " Kappa
Sigma Theta,"—though, as is the case of Sigma Eps,
the " Kappa " was popularly unrecognized, — and its
badge was a small rectangular gold plate on which,
above the society letters, the enwreathed. helmet-crested
head of Minerva was engraved.   The surface of the pin
was glazed over, to prevent the engraving from become-
ing rubbed and worn.   Besides its secret motto, *Κοινῆς
Σοφίας Θέα*, it had several open ones: *Tu nihil invita
dices faciesve Minerva, Τὸ τοῦ ἀνθρώπου μέτρον ἐστίν ἡ
φρήν*, and, *Coronat scientia cultores suos*,—of which the
first was the commonest.   The story goes that, as the

sophomore year of '41 drew to its close, some members
of the society proposed that, instead of disbanding the
organization, it should be turned over to the incoming
Sophs of '42, in consideration of a supper given by
them.   The respectable portion of the society opposed
the plan, and when the others took advantage of their
absence and carried it through, they themselves destroyed
the society plate and records.   Sigma Theta, however,
thenceforth existed as a regular sophomore society, and
though a rival sprung up a few years later, it continued
to flourish until the sophomore year of '57, when ten or
a dozen of the ablest men of that class, most or all of
whom belonged to Sigma Theta or its rival, formed a
sort of select club, which was apparently intended to
last through the course and not to conflict with any of
the existing societies.   Its badge resembled the original
one of Sigma Eps, and a room in Townsend's Block,
opposite the colleges, served as its place of meeting, but
the club never figured in the *Banner*, and its name, if it
had any, has not been preserved.   Though no mention
was ever made of it in any of the college prints, the
existence of the club caused a great uproar throughout
college, especially among the Sophomores, and sophomore-society men.   Its members were said to be traitors
to the regular societies which they belonged to, and enemies of the whole system, and so were expelled from
the former as a punishment for their crime.   Few of
them ever got into the junior societies except by honorary elections, and though several of them become senior-society men, more doubtless would have been elected
except for the unfortunate club.   But the expulsion of
its best men from Sigma Theta, was that society's death
blow, for the internal dissensions which resulted therefrom were never harmonized, and things went on from
bad to worse until in 1858, when no more members could

be induced to join it, the society definitely gave up the ghost.

As already remarked, Sigma Theta was not left many years without a rival, for the same class and some of the same men who founded Delta Kap established in 1846 the " Alpha Sigma Phi,"—whose name in its abbreviated form of Sigma Phi is not to be confounded with a society so designated which exists in other colleges. Its badge in shape was an upright rectangle, almost a square, a trifle less than an inch in diameter ; its device was an open book, in white, displaying several hieroglyphic characters, and crowned by a pen ; below were the letters "*A Σ Φ*" in gold,—the pen and the framework being of the same material, and the ground a shield of black enamel. The wood-cut vignette of the society was identical with its badge, except that the framework surrounding the shield gave place in the former to a rectangular wreath of oak leaves. Neither badge nor vignette ever underwent the slightest change. Its open motto was, *Causa latet, vis est notissima*, and its secret one, Ἀρρησία, Σοφία, Φιλία. Sigma Phi survived its rival Sigma Theta only a half-dozen years, and in 1864 came to a rather inglorious end. The trouble arose in this wise : About half of the Sigma Phi Sophomores of '66 were pledged to the junior society of Psi U, and half to its rival DKE. Each faction wished that a majority of the elections given to the Freshmen of '67 should be received by those who were pledged to its own junior society, and hence a fearful strife arose. The final result of it was that each faction in turn "expelled" the other from the society, gave out elections to its own Freshmen, and initiated them without taking them to the hall. This had in the meantime been closed, for the faculty, influenced by the notoriously disreputable character of the society, took advantage of

the disorganized condition of things to order its summary abolishment.   The Sophomores were forbidden to
give out any elections, and the Freshmen to receive any,
or to wear the Sigma Phi badge.   Irregular elections
were nevertheless given out in the manner stated, and
the Freshmen evaded the other prohibition by wearing
badges from which the "$A \, \Sigma \, \Phi$" had been erased, or
displaying the unmutilated badge only in places where it
could be done "in safety."   This state of things could
not long continue.   The elections had been given out in
the middle of the summer term, and, with the opening
of the new college year, the Psi U pledged men of '67,
who had received elections to Sigma Phi, set about the
establishment of a new sophomore society.   The consent of the faculty was at length obtained on the conditions that the society should not bear the name, or
adopt the badge, or occupy the hall, or in any way become the successor, of the late Sigma Phi ; that it
should give attention to literary exercises, and should
elect some member of the faculty an honorary member.
In obedience to these conditions was organized, in October, 1864, " Phi Theta Psi,"—called, of course, Theta
Psi, simply,—with a badge shaped like that of Sigma
Phi, but having as a device, upon a black enamel groundwork, a golden raven perched upon a white closed book,
below the letters " $\Phi \, \Theta \, \Psi$."   A month or two after
Theta Psi's appearance, under the same conditions, the
DKE faction were allowed to establish " Delta Beta
Xi,"— called Beta Xi, or rarely DBX,— with a badge
and wood-cut vignette identical with those of Sigma Phi,
except that the letters "$\Delta \, B \, \Xi$" superseded the original "$A \, \Sigma \, \Phi$."   Even now, Beta Xi men often wear
pins bearing the old letters.   Sigma Phi was the only
society ever abolished by the faculty, and its two successors are probably the last which they will ever con-

sent to have established. Prof. Thacher of '35 was the honorary member chosen by Theta Psi from among the faculty ; Prof. Northrop of '57, the one chosen by Beta Xi.

A feature of the two earlier sophomore societies, of which no trace remains in those now existing, was the publication of annual "feuilletons," or printed attacks upon one another and the college world in general. Sigma Theta's "paper" was called the Yale *Banger*, apparently to burlesque the Yale *Banner*, and displayed a heavy club-cane, or "banger" in its heading,—this species of walking stick being esteemed by tradition the Sophomore's peculiar property. At the head of the *Banger's* first page was displayed the vignette of Sigma Theta, with its list of members ; then followed lists of the other societies, accompanied in each case by bur-lesque badges and mottoes, Sigma Phi of course getting its full share of notice. The remaining three pages comprised personal and political gossip, poetry, adver-tisements, and notices, of a more or less scurrilous character. The paper was issued in the fall term of the six years 1845–50, and the spring term of '52. Its rival, the *Tomahawk* of Sigma Phi, followed it by a month or two, but, appearing first in 1847, issued only five numbers in all. This paper displayed but two cuts : the one, at the head of the first page, a distortion of the Sigma Theta badge, accompanied by an abusive article regarding that society ; the other, at the head of the editorial column on the second page, a genuine Sigma Phi badge, accompanied by a list of members. This paper had nothing to say of the upper-class societies, but bestowed its derision solely upon Sigma Theta and its freshman inferiors, and though its general character was not unlike that of the *Banger*, its tone was yet a trifle more disreputable. So far as appears at this day, the *Banger's* ridicule of all the upper-class societies, was impartial and without discrimination, and when it is borne in mind that the Sophomores responsible for it were all desirous of joining these societies in the future, they deserve some credit for their independence, whatever may be thought of their taste. This cannot be said of the *Tomahawk*, whose conductors never ventured upon dangerous ground. The only other society paper was the *Battery*, issued by the Delta Kap Freshmen, in February, 1850, which, by the aid of a sanguinary woodcut and hardly less dreadful letterpress, was enabled to "use up" most effectually its rivals and oppressors.

A society called "Kappa Delta Phi" which was started at the Wesleyan University of Middletown, Conn., at about the same time that Sigma Theta appeared at Yale, and which had also adopted Minerva's head as its badge, was persuaded to change its name and become a chapter of Sigma Theta ; but it shortly afterwards underwent another change, and became the Xi chapter of Psi U, under which name it exists at the parent day. Another chapter of Sigma Theta was extant at Amherst College in Massachusetts, in 1852, when it issued a sheet called the Amherst *Scorpion,* which was a worthy counterpart of the Yale *Banger*, published by the parent chapter. If any additional chapters ever existed, they long ago died or became absorbed in some stronger fraternity. Sigma Phi established a chapter called the " Delta " at Marietta College in Ohio, where it still flourishes, though not as a distinctively sophomore society. It of course has been independent of Yale since the death of the original " Alpha " chapter in 1864. The " Beta " was established at Amherst in 1847, but was abolished by the faculty, after a few months' existence. The "Gamma " was established at Princeton in 1854, and had a somewhat longer life, though the general decree against all such societies finally killed it. Beta Xi calls itself the "Alpha" and Theta Psi the "Phi," but, as neither have yet established any outside branches, these chapter titles have no special significance. The reasons given in the case of the freshman societies show equally well why the chapter system will be apt to fail in sophomore year also. There is, besides, as will be shown hereafter, less *to* these societies than there is to those of the other years; they are little more than tenders of the junior organizations; and the interest in them, considered apart from the junior societies they represent, is very small indeed. No Yale sophomore society has ever yet published a catalogue of its members.

The steel-plate poster of Theta Psi represents the sun rising over the waves, and supporting the letters "Φ Θ Ψ" amid its rays; above the shield on which this is pictured rests the raven upon his book; below it is a bull dog's head; while upon the scroll-work surrounding the design rests a band bearing the motto, *Amici, usque ad aras*, and the letters, "J. C." The wood-cut vignettes, of which there have been two or three varieties, are of the same general design. The Beta Xi poster reproduces the design of the pin, and amid the ornamental scroll-work which sets off the central shield are the words, "Alpha," "Yale," the date "1864," and the letters "C. L. V. E. N.," initials of the old Sigma Phi motto before given, which, through printed in full at the head of the *Tomahawk*, is not in these days generally known outside the society, except in the version, "College laws violated every night." In smaller characters, the old letters "Α Σ Φ" and date "1846" are also displayed upon the design. The Beta Xi song book also contains all the old Sigma Phi songs, and the name was apparently chosen so as to be interchangeable with the latter. In every way this society makes prominent its parentage and represents itself as the "legitimate successor" of the old one. Theta Psi, on the other hand, though the eldest child, and holding undisputed the proud position of "oldest sophomore society," makes no claim for the succession, but prefers to keep its ultimate ancestry in the background, and in its songs greets without much respect "the bones of the dead, defunct and euchered Sigma Phi." Each society possesses a few Sigma Phi relics,—Beta Xi a larger proportion,—though what little portable property of any value the old society held at the time of its death was probably seized upon by its indignant creditors. The Theta Psi hall is [was] in the Cutler Building, corner of Chapel and Church streets, a quarter of a mile from the colleges, and a rod or two from the hall of Delta Kap. Beta Xi hall is in Townsend's Block, corner of Chapel and College streets, directly opposite the college yard itself. Both halls have been occupied since the societies were established, and are quite elegantly fitted up. That of Beta Xi is considerably the larger, and has the advantage—disadvantage, some say—in the matter of locality. Each hall is guarded without by a heavy iron door, and supplied with a well-equipped stage within—as a sophomore society without theatricals would be an absurdity difficult for a college man to conceive of soberly. Since the above was written, Theta Psi has deserted Cutler Corner and moved into the old Diggers' hall in Lyon Building, which, after refitting at an expense of $1,000, it "opened" with a grand celebration on February 25, 1870. It now claims to have the most handsomely furnished hall in college.

When the Freshmen have been in college about a month or two, it begins to be generally known among them that certain of their number are being pledged by the upper-class men to join their societies. These chosen ones are soon perceived to be "their most prominent men," and as the line between the pledged and unpledged becomes more sharply drawn, the latter are seized with an irresistible inclination to get their names also enrolled among the elect. Sometimes the sophomore societies act with nominal independence in this matter ; more often in their real characters as tenders to the organizations of junior year. These latter, by means of committees, make haste to pledge all the Freshmen who at first view are desirable, and each of them having thus formed a nucleus of pledged men as a working force, is content to entrust to them in some measure the making up of "its crowd." Thereafter the upper-class committee and the pledged Freshmen act in concert. If the latter, by secret ballot, unanimously recommend a class-mate, the former will probably pledge him ; or if, on the other hand, they strongly object to a man recommended them by the committee, he will probably not be pledged. The committee or the society which it acts for are of course not bound in either case to do as indicated, but it is not often that they venture to set aside the wishes of the pledged men, either to reject a man recommended by, or to take one unpopular with, the latter. Each man as soon as pledged of course has the right to vote upon all names afterwards recommended, so that those latest chosen undergo a closer scrutiny as to their qualifications than do the components of the original nucleus. For the first two years after the present sophomore societies were started, neither of them pledged independently. The Freshmen who pledged to DKE were assured of elections to Beta Xi, while those who pledged to Psi U — and Delta Phi also, though to a lesser extent—implied that their chances for Theta Psi were "good," though they were promised nothing. Then followed a year when none of these societies gave pledges; but since that time the sophomore societies have had regular pledging committees, and though most of those pledged to Theta Psi are also pledged to Psi U by the Juniors, and those to Beta Xi to DKE, it happens that in many cases the distinction is not observed. A man rarely refuses a pledge to a sophomore society, and the reason for the cases in which it is done is the pecuniary one solely.

About a month after the third term begins, rumors prevail among the Freshmen that the sophomore elections are soon to be given out. Though most of the men are definitely "pledged" in advance, there is always enough uncertainty as to the fact of their actual election to make the best of them feel a trifle anxious, as the time draws nigh for the official announcement of their fate; while those who are not pledged hope against hope that when the hour actually comes, "something will turn up" to place their names among the elect. Both societies generally agree upon the same night, which is usually that of Friday, for the giving out of elections—though there is no settled rule about the matter, either way. On the appointed evening, the sophomore, junior and senior members assemble at the society hall, and at a late hour, not much before midnight, sally forth in a body upon their errand, marching by classes in the order named, the president or some other official, distinguished by a dark-lantern, leading the way, upon the "route" marked out in advance. Arriving at the rooms of the nearest Freshman, the procession halts, and sings a society song or two; then the Sophomore appointed for the purpose goes up to the room and says something to this effect: "Mr. So and So, I have the honor [or "the pleasure," or simply "I offer"] of offering you an election to the So and So fraternity.

Do you accept?" Of course the Freshman says Yes, upon which the Soph congratulates him, and the whole party file in and do the same, each individual shaking him heartily by the hand. Congratulations over, the society men at once fall to discussing the provided " spread " of fruits, cake, and wine, and having partaken of the entertainment and lit fresh cigars, they assemble outside again, sing another song, and perhaps cheer a little, and proceed on their way to the next stopping place, where the ceremony is again repeated. If, as is usually the case, several pledged Freshmen are assembled at a single room, instead of one, a corresponding number of Sophomores go up to give them their elections, for each Sophomore has a particular Freshman assigned him to whom he is to offer the honor.

This theoretical manner of proceeding, however, is not apt to be observed after the first few elections have been given out. It generally happens that before the men deputed for the purpose have had time to offer any formal words, the crowd at their heels fill the room, and attack the eatables, without wasting time in hand-shaking or congratulation. A few are generally found who will secretly lug off a bottle of champagne or handful of cigars for future consumption. The procession grows more and more hilarious, and its songs hoarser and huskier as to utterance, until towards the last it is little better than a disorderly crowd, whose members are apt to laugh when some one smashes a street lamp with a banana, or tosses an orange through on open window; and when it has given out its final election, it lingers longingly about the concluding " treat," and perhaps is at length obliged to drag away by main force a few of its tipsiest members, who drowsily insist on "making a night of it," then and there. The disorder and rowdyism are due almost exclusively to members of the two upper

classes ; were the Sophomores left to themselves, discipline would be maintained. The elected Freshmen of
the same or different societies meet together over the
remains of their spreads, and "celebrate" their good
fortune more or less uproariously, so that it is very near
daylight when the last of them are once more quiet in
their beds. Sometimes an expectant Fresh hears the
society move by his house without stopping, and goes to
bed in despair, only to be aroused on its return trip and
suddenly made happy by receiving the pledged election.
Sometimes an over-confident one prepares a treat for
guests who never call. Sometimes an irate landlord,
roused from sleep by the tramp of a disorganized host
through his dwelling, and lashed into a frenzy by their
discordant melodies, ejects from the house the Freshman lodger upon whom the honor has been bestowed,
and writes off to his parents how their son has fallen
into evil ways, and become the habitual entertainer of
midnight revelers. Generally, however, the boarding
house keepers, knowing the character of the thing, and
remembering that it comes only one night in a year,
recognize it as a necessary evil, and submit to the infliction with as good grace as may be.

As the treat, formerly a trifling and impromptu affair,
has gradually grown in importance, the custom comes
more and more into vogue of offering it in the dining
room of a hotel or restaurant, whither the half dozen
or so who combine in paying for it go to receive their
elections, in place of having them at their rooms. This
proceeding of course prevents any unpleasantness with
the private landlords. The Freshmen are generally ad-
vised in an unofficial manner as to the evening when
they may expect elections, and in case a pledged man is
not to receive an election, he usually receives a hint to
that effect beforehand. A card, bearing on one side the

society vignette, on the other the names of the men elected, is given to each man, so that after one election has been given out, the whole are in a measure made public, for the receiver of the card may contrive to hurry off and show it to the men named upon it, in advance of the procession which formally presents it to them. The names are usually printed, but in cases where elections were contested until the moment of issuing them, they are written with ink instead.

An interval of two or three weeks elapses before initiation takes place. Both societies may adopt the same evening,—usually that of Friday or Wednesday,—though about this there is the same indefiniteness, as about the times of giving out elections. The Freshmen having paid an initiation fee of from fifteen to twenty-five dollars,—to one of their own number, appointed collector by the Sophomores, and on account of his trouble excused from paying any fee for himself,—are directed, by a printed note addressed to each, to assemble at some particular room occupied by a Sophomore, at an early hour of the appointed evening. Here they are perhaps supplied with cigars, and left by themselves, to smoke and talk over the prospect before them, until summoned for initiation. They are generally led away alphabetically, from time to time, in parties of a half dozen or so, until in the course of an hour or more all have been put through the ceremony. What this is to consist of greatly exercises the freshman mind, and rumors that it is merely a formal rite are contradicted by other rumors that it is a thing considerably more unpleasant than the freshman initiation itself. The latter are the ones most credited by the Freshmen, while college belief in general rather favors the former. This much at least is certain, that the initiation is confined entirely to the society halls, and if some strange noises do that night emanate therefrom, the Freshmen come out of the ordeal not perceptibly injured, and the city newspapers print no facts or fancies concerning it. All the upper-class members are present at the initiation, and at the play which follows it, and at the supper which comes after the play. In old times this initiation supper was partaken of in the dining room of some hotel, and the bills of fare were embellished with the society vignette and motto, but the present societies have always held their suppers in or near their halls. It is rarely that any drink stronger than wine is provided at these suppers, though upper-class men may smuggle in a few bottles of more fiery beverage for their own private use, and after the newly initiated members have been dismissed, stay behind and "celebrate" by themselves. Next morning the Freshmen swing out their square pins with great pride, not unmingled with pity, in many cases, for friends who were less fortunate than themselves. The freshman-society pins are still worn, however. In some cases the two are displayed side by side upon the vest, though more often the freshman pin is attached to the vest, and the sophomore badge to the shirt bosom, by the man who sports them both. In sophomore year, when the freshman pin has been discarded, the badge is oftener worn upon the shirt bosom, than in freshman year, and when attached to the vest is usually worn lower down than in that latter year.

The meetings of the sophomore societies are held each Saturday evening, from about ten o'clock till midnight, or a little past. Theta Psi generally sings as it marches up Chapel street to the colleges, and gives forth an additional song or two from the corner of the college fence before it disbands. Beta Xi also sings its songs upon that corner, at the close of its meetings. It sometimes happens that the two societies, reaching the fence at about the same time, take up positions at a short distance from one another and "sing with responsive strains,"—each society after offering one of its songs, pausing long enough to let the other sing out one of *its* own, before proceeding with the next. Perhaps, after having sung themselves out, both societies give cheers for each other, and so disperse. Similarly, when the two processions engaged in giving out elections chance to pass near one another, songs and cheers may be exchanged. On the other hand, less creditably and good naturedly, each society has on some occasions tried by singing to drown the voices of the other. These society songs, without being of a very high order of composition, are yet possessed of a sort of jovial melody, well adapted to the capacity of the miscellaneous voices accustomed to render them. In several of the Theta Psi songs, the "caw!" of the raven is introduced with fantastic effect. Though the present tense is retained in this paragraph, the state of things described no longer really exists, since, within a year, all society singing has been forbidden by the college authorities ; while of their own accord the Sophomores have substituted Friday night, for the traditional Saturday night, as the time for holding their meetings. For a while, after that singing had been brought under the ban, each society used to march in a body to the college corner, and there shout the names of its three Greek letters, with one sharp and united cry, as a signal for breaking up. But this practice was also forbidden.

Though the songs were thus publicly sung upon the street, the song books are kept secret with great care, and never shown to outsiders by active members. Nor do these often mention or refer to their societies in private except to other members, and hence outsiders rarely speak to a Sophomore concerning his or a rival

society.   Among upper-class men of course this carefulness does not prevail, but on the whole the sophomore
societies are, except those of senior year, more secret
than any others,—for in the sophomore class little is
known of their doings except by their members, while
in the junior class the proceedings of the junior societies
are generally understood by nearly everyone.   Seniors
or even Juniors do not hesitate to talk over in public the
good points of the last play which they attended at their
sophomore society, and the "bum" held in connection
with it.   The general impression to be gained by an
outsider, from their conversation and otherwise, is that
the hall of the institution in question is a sort of club
room where Sophomores drop in on Friday nights to
play cards, smoke clay pipes and sip ale with one
another.   The junior class will often be represented
there, but never in force except on special occasions, as
when there is a play, or a regular supper, or a contested
election.   At such times Seniors also are wont to
appear.   A graduate rarely comes to the hall except
brought up there by a Senior, or under-class man.   Old
Sigma Phi men if members of Psi U are admitted to
Theta Psi, if members of DKE to Beta Xi, "and no
questions asked ;" though most of them in the two or
three classes preceding that of '67, which founded the
societies, were regularly elected and initiated as honorary members of one or the other organization, according
to the rule indicated.   Of course no old graduate ever
goes near one of the sophomore halls, unless invited
thither by some active or recent member.   But a Senior
would not hesitate to invite any old graduate to join
him in making a call at such a place, without any regard
to that old graduate's connection, or want of it, with
Sigma Phi, or any other sophomore or junior society.

Thirty is the number of elections generally given out

by each society, and as both combined make up less than half an average class, of course many desirable men are still left out, whom their luckier classmates wish to have "in" with themselves. They rarely give out any new elections, however, until the new year has opened and they themselves are Sophomores. Then, when they have succeeded in electing a classmate, he is either brought at once to the hall by a messenger and initiated forthwith, or the society—upper-class men and all—march in procession to his room, singing songs and offering congratulations, after the old manner, and 'escort him back to the society hall. As a class election usually comes upon a man unexpectedly, a treat is not expected of him, yet if several are elected at once they often combine to give a supper at the hall, shortly afterwards; or a single individual who happens to be free with his money may after his election bear the whole expense of a society "spread." When honorary members are elected from the two upper classes—and almost any Junior or Senior is glad to receive an election—a single classmate of the chosen one conducts him to the initiation. All names are voted upon separately by secret ballot, and a single negative vote is usually sufficient to reject a candidate. The ballot box is so arranged that each man can cast his vote without showing it or even seeing it himself; one compartment contains a number of white cubes (signifying Yes) and black balls (signifying No), and the voters selecting one of these thrusts it into the other compartment of the box undetected.

There is always considerably difficulty in reconciling the conflicting choices in the matter of elections. A man whose friend is blackballed, may vow to reject everyone else until his friend has been elected, and so on. An approved device for overcoming many difficulties is to "pair off" opposing candidates and elect them both on a joint ticket. In the case of class elections there is apt to be more than usual contention, for there is greater personal interest in the men, and the number allowed is much smaller, and the voters are bound by no pledge of any sort to say Yes. Pledged men, to be sure, are sometimes rejected, when formally offered for election; but it is accounted rather dishonorable for a society to do this in many cases without special reasons, and unless a man's reputation or social standing changes greatly for the worse after he obtains a pledge, he may feel pretty confident of receiving his election also. It is very seldom, too, that a single blackball keeps a man from a society. However stubborn the caster of it may be at first, the "pressure" brought to bear upon him by the whole society arrayed in opposition is so enormous, that he is at length glad to reverse his vote and submit to the will of the majority. As the mortality among sophomore-society men is usually large, the eight or ten class elections given at various times during the year rarely bring the active force above thirty in number. The last Sophomores are taken in just before the procession starts forth to give out elections to the Freshmen, and are not required to pay any initiation fees. The presidency and lesser offices of these societies are not accounted of much importance, and it is very rarely that there is the least excitement in regard to them. Even upper-class men seldom mention their incumbents, —though this is probably due more to the absence of any interest concerning them than to any settled objection against the betrayal of "secrets." The annual expenses of membership are perhaps ten or fifteen dollars greater than in the societies of freshman year.

The sophomore year is a sort of transition period, and the sophomore society fairly enough represents it.

Everything is unsettled; men's positions are every day changing both relatively and absolutely; and the fast, loud-mouthed element in the community is to all appearances the ruling one. For the first time the line between "society-men" and "neutrals" is plainly drawn, and the sheep are separated from the goats. There is a keener pleasure in sporting the sophomore badge, a sharper regret at the inability to do so, than is possible in after years. The lucky Soph, turning his back upon the "heavy literary" performances of his freshman year, thinks that the only true enjoyment of a select society must lie in going to the other extreme, and doing nothing whatever that smacks in any way of honest labor or improvement. The quiet, substantial men, who figure prominently afterwards, are in the class and society now, but they keep in the background, and are overshadowed by the light-headed, noisier crew who are suffered to have things all their own way. Next year, may be, the reverse will appear; for the societies of two different years, composed in succession of essentially the same individuals, may and in fact often do, differ widely in character and purpose. The faults of the sophomore society are usually exaggerated by friends and enemies alike. It does not as a matter of fact encourage drunkenness or immorality, — though it may sometimes affect to do so. Perhaps the worst thing that can be fairly charged against it is its frivolous and purposeless character. It inspires a sort of pride in its members, but no affection. They look back upon their connection with it as a joke, and are careless as to its subsequent fate. It would probably be more hopeless to solicit money from them in its behalf than to ask it for their freshman society. Yet, after all, few would willingly part with the host of conflicting memories reflected in the halo of very doubtful glory which encircles its name.

6*

CHAPTER III.

JUNIOR SOCIETIES.

Alpha Delta Phi — Psi Upsilon — Delta Kappa Epsilon — Badges, Vignettes and Mottoes—Catalogues, Chapters and Membership —The Death of Old Chapters and the Origin of New Ones— Names of Prominent Members—General Conventions—Intercourse between the Chapters—Giving out Elections—Initiation — Meetings and Exercises — Halls — Corporate Titles — The Course of Politics in '69 (the Freshman Societies; the Annual Jubilee Committee; the Gamma-Nu-Delta-Phi Embroglio; the Cochs and "Lit." Editors)—The Effect upon Delta Phi—Agreements concerning the Freshmen—Real Character of a Coalition —The Division of the Spoils—The Contested Elections of Members — Duration of Society Influences — Comparison of the Societies.

There are three junior societies, and they are the only ones ever established in that class,—a fact which no other year can boast of. The Skull and Bones of senior year is the only class society which has the advantage of two of them in point of age. And these two, it may be remarked, are the only Yale societies, aside from Phi Beta Kappa, which originated outside of the college. "Alpha Delta Phi," which was founded at Hamilton College in 1832, established four years later its "Yale" chapter, which was the eighth in order. The abbreviated title of Delta Phi should not be confounded with the society of that name which exists in several colleges. Outside of Yale, Delta Phi is always spoken of as Alpha Delt. "Psi Upsilon," which was founded at Union College in 1833, established its third ("Beta") chapter at Yale in 1838. The name is always shortened to Psi U.

" Delta Kappa Epsilon"—formerly called Delta Kappa Eps, but now invariably DKE—was founded in 1844 by the class of '46.

The badge of Delta Phi is an oblong slab, an inch in length, with rounded corners, displaying on a ground-work of black enamel a white crescent surmounted by a green star; below is the date "1832," and upon the crescent the letters "*A Δ Φ*," both in gold. The wearing of badges of this sort has within the last year been mostly abandoned, in favor of the "skeleton pins," which were formerly worn by none but Seniors and graduates. Of these pins there are many varieties. They are formed of the star and crescent simply, and according to the taste or wealth of the individual are made either of plain gold and enamel, or set off with pearls and precious stones—an emerald in the center of the star being perhaps the favorite one, though it some-times gives place to a ruby, amethyst, or diamond. Green and white ribbons are sometimes worn in the button hole as society colors. The wood-cut vignette was formerly an enlarged representation of the regular badge pin, and there have been several different pat-terns, but the one now commonly employed at Yale dis-plays a plain star and crescent upon a dark shield, crossed behind by a sword and spear, supporting below the motto, *Manus multæ, cor unum.* Above the shield is a ring of stars. The steel-plate poster is the same design more elaborated, with the letters indicated upon the crescent, the date below the shield, the words "Alpha Delta Phi, Fraternity," and the name of the chapter within the circle of stars. The Psi U badge is a simple diamond-shaped pin, a little more than an inch in length, displaying upon a groundwork of black enamel the sin-gle emblem of the clasped hands, with "*Ψ*" above and "*Υ*" below. The skeleton pin of this society is a monogram made up of the two letters which compose its name, sometimes ornamented with pearls and precious stones, though more commonly plain. A miniature copy of the regular diamond-shaped badge, ornamented with pearls, rubies, etc., is worn by some members of the western chapters, though not authorized by the society. The common vignette is an enlarged copy of the badge, surmounted by a peculiar kind of scroll-work which leave the date " 1833." Another one represents the pin surrounded by the chapter letters, enclosed in a wreath of oak and olive, with " 1833" in rays above and " Fraternity" upon a scroll below. The seal of the society represents an owl grasping a fasces bound together by the motto, *Fit via vi.* Νόμιζ' ἀδελφοὺς τοὺς ἀληθινοὺς φίλους, was the motto upon the title page of the catalogue of 1864. The DKE pin is of the same size and shape as that of the Psi U. Its device is a white scroll, bearing the letters "*Δ Κ Ε*"; below is the name of the college where the chapter is situated ; in each angle is a star ; the groundwork is the usual black enamel. The skeleton badge consists simply of the white scroll and letters, somewhat enlarged. At first, the vignette was simply a copy of the badge, but an entirely independent design was afterwards devised as a coat of arms, and this has since formed the chief part of the vignette : A white (argent) central shield—displaying a rampant lion, a pair of crossed keys and an ear—is surmounted by an outer shield, divided by various cross bars and chevrons, with the colors blue (azure), red (gules), and gold (or), indicated in the regular heraldic manner. An open eye looks forth from the upper part of the outer shield, and a pair of hearts, one on each side, are joined by a chain which sustains at the bottom the letter or letters denoting the chapter. In the usual vignette this double shield is surmounted by crossed swords, and a winged globe bearing the letters "*Δ K E*"; while the motto, *Κηρόθεν φίλοι ἀεί*, figures on a scroll beneath, and rays of light set off the whole design. There are several variations from this pattern, but all the vignettes agree in displaying the elaborate double-shield design. This is also the chief device in the steel-plate poster, which resembles a seal or medal —being circular in shape and three inches in diameter. The motto just given is expressed upon the upper part of the encircling band, and upon the lower, within a scroll, are the letters "*Δ K E*"; while ornamental wreath-work fills the space between the shield and the band. The Delta Phi poster is the only one often seen at Yale, as members of the other two societies prefer to display richly-framed photographic views of their respective society halls, in place thereof. The regular pins are essentially alike in all the chapters, though different manufacturers may slightly vary in the details of their workmanship. Phi U's badge is the neatest of the three, and Delta Phi's the ugliest. As for the skeleton pin of the latter, it would hardly be taken for a society badge at all, but rather for a bit of ornamental jewelry. Formerly, when the slab badge only was worn by the active members, Delta Phi men who were senior neutrals very generally wore the skeleton, and a few still keep up the practice. Very rarely, too, a skeleton Psi U badge may be noticed, but that of DKE is never seen at all. Chapter letters of gold, attached to the main badge by a minute chain, in the manner described for the freshman societies, are worn by some of the Psi U and DKE men, at a few of the colleges, though never at Yale. Upon the backs of the regular badges are engraved the owner's name and class and the peculiar Greek symbols allotted to him, together with the letter of the chapter; and in the case of Delta Phi a crossed sword and spear surmounting a sort of monument, are also added. Yale Seniors sometimes wear their junior year badges in such a position upon their vests as to be usually concealed from sight ; the Juniors occasionally wear their sophomore pins in a similar manner. Monograms of the society letters, carved in black walnut or other suitable wood, are sometimes to be seen ; and, aside from what has been mentioned, the number of engraved vignettes, ornaments, monograms, stamps and seals, in use by the societies, or their separate chapters, is quite large. Yale men, however, seldom display the insignia of their junior societies upon their note paper and envelopes.

It is through these third-year organizations solely that Yale shares in the general system of secret societies that is in vogue throughout most of the colleges. Though there are other important chaptered fraternities existing in American colleges, the three represented at Yale are undoubtedly the leading and most extensive ones, and a few statistical facts in regard to them may not be without value. The last catalogue of Delta Phi appeared in June, 1870 ; that of Psi U in December of the same year ; and that of DKE in May of the present year. The arrangement is similar in all of them : the chapters standing in the order of their establishment ; the members alphabetically by classes in the order of their graduation ; a list of chapters preceding, and an alphabetical list of members following, the main body of the catalogue. In this index are given the class and chapter of each man, so that his residence, symbols, and other facts concerning him can at once be found by turning to the main catalogue. The exact signification of these symbols is not generally known among the uninitiated ; yet it can do no harm to remark that, aside from being different in themselves, they are used by each society for an altogether different purpose.

The current catalogue of Delta Phi comprises 287 pages, and was printed by Curtiss & Childs of Utica, N. Y. Its title-page is surrounded by an ornamental border of green and red, and is faced by a wood-cut frontispiece representing the society emblems. Upon the outside of its green paper cover is a wood-cut monogram composed of the initials "*A Δ Φ*" and the date "1832." The last preceding catalogue was printed by J. H. Benham of New Haven, in 1860, and comprised 195 pages, of much less creditable typography. This society, unlike others, confers local rather than Greek-letter names upon its chapters. In the following list the name first given is that of the chapter, the date signifies the year or class in which it was founded, and the final numeral the number of its members up to the time in 1870 when the catalogue was issued:

1. Hamilton; Hamilton College, Clinton, N. Y.; 1832; 287.
2. Miami; Miami University, Oxford, O.; 1834; 185.
3. *Urban; NewYork University, N.Y. City; 1835 (*died1839); 24.
4. *Columbia; Columbia College, N.Y. City; 1836 (*died 1840); 32.
5. Amherst; Amherst College, Amherst, Mass.; 1837; 331.
6. Brunonian; Brown University, Providence, R. I.; 1837; 156.
7. *Harvard; Harvard Coll., Cambridge, Mass.; 1837 (*d.'65); 307.
8. *Yale; Yale College, New Haven, Conn.; 1837; 740.*
9. Geneva; Hobart College, Geneva, N. Y.; 1838; 162.
10. Bowdoin; Bowdoin College, Brunswick, Me.; 1839; 182.
11. Hudson; Western Reserve College, Hudson, O.; 1840; 138.
12. Peninsula; Michigan University, Ann Arbor, Mich.; 1845; 193.
13. Dartmouth; Dartmouth College, Hanover, N. H.; 1845; 273.
14. Rochester; Rochester University, Rochester, N. Y.; 1851; 117.
15. Alabama; Alabama Univ., Tuscaloosa, Ala.; 1851 (*d. '59); 51.
16. Williams; Williams College, Williamstown, Mass.; 1851; 132.
17. Manhattan; New York City-College, N. Y. City; 1854; 138.
18. Middletown; Wesleyan Univ., Middletown, Conn.; 1855; 152.
19. Kenyon; Kenyon College, Gambier, O.; 1858; 28.
20. Union; Union College, Schenectady, N. Y.; 1858; 84.
21. *Cumberland; Cumberl'd Un., Lebanon, Tenn.; 1858 (d.'61); 27.
22. Cornell; Cornell University, Ithaca, N. Y.; 1870; 16.

Deducting from the membership as here set forth about 25 names for repetitions and 35 for honorary members, and a total of 3650 is exhibited, against a total of 2300 shown by the catalogue of 1860. Delta Phi has also four alumni associations, or "graduate chapters": at Cincinnati, established 1846 ; Cleveland, 1866 ; Chicago, 1867 ; and New York, 1868.

The Psi U catalogue was published "under the supervision of the Beta chapter," and printed by Tuttle, Morehouse & Taylor, and comprises 233 pages. A tint-printed, wood-cut emblematical vignette, hinting at the significance of the chapter letter, serves as a frontispiece to each chapter, while the frontispiece to the main work itself consists of a finely-executed steel-plate engraving, —designed by Gavit & Co. of Albany,—representing a wall and archway, ornamented with the emblems and insignia of the society, while through the arch is seen the rising sun, lighting up the ocean waves as they dash upon a solitary rock. The work is by far the handsomest one of the sort ever issued by a college society. The last preceding Psi U catalogue was printed in March, 1864, by Baker & Godwin of New York, and comprised 207 pages. The arrangement of the following list of chapters corresponds to that in the case of Delta Phi :

1. Theta ; Union College, Schenectady, N. Y. ; 1833 ; 275.
2. Delta ; New York University, N. Y. City ; 1836 ; 200.
3. *Beta ; Yale College, New Haven, Conn. ;* 1838 ; 750.
4. Sigma ; Brown University, Providence, R. I. ; 1840 ; 180.
5. Gamma ; Amherst College, Amherst, Mass. ; 1841 ; 360.
6. Zeta ; Dartmouth College, Hanover, N. H. ; 1842 ; 340.
7. Lambda ; Columbia College, N. Y. City ; 1842 ; 220.
8. Kappa ; Bowdoin College, Brunswick, Me. ; 1842 ; 270.
9. Psi ; Hamilton College, Clinton: N. Y. ; 1843 ; 150.
10. Xi ; Wesleyan University, Middletown, Conn. ; 1843 ; 295.
11. Alpha ; Harvard College, Cambridge, Mass. ; 1850 ; 105.

12. Upsilon ; Rochester University, Rochester, N. Y. ; 1858 ; 100.
13. Iota ; Kenyon College, Gambier, O. ; 1860 ; 64.
14. Phi ; Michigan University, Ann Arbor, Mich.; 1865 ; 75.
15. Omega ; Chicago University, Chicago, Ill. ; 1869 ; 16.

The Theta chapter was suspended for a year or two preceding 1865, when it was revived, and the Delta chapter has also been once or twice near to death's door, while the Alpha chapter, killed by general edict of the Harvard faculty in 1857, was revived again in the class of '71. Psi U therefore possesses the distinction —which neither of its rivals, and probably no other similar extended fraternity whatever, can boast of—of being burdened with no dead chapters. Its total membership, as detailed above, foots up 3400 names, as against 2750 exhibited in the catalogue of 1864.

The DKE catalogue, " apud Phi editum, fraternitatis anno XXVII.," was printed by Tuttle, Morehouse & Taylor, and comprises a little less than 300 pages. Its only ornament is the circular, steel-plate poster before described, which serves as a frontispiece. Aside from a rather improved typography, it is the exact counterpart of the catalogue of 1867,—which was printed by Thomas, Howard & Johnson of Buffalo, N. Y., and comprised 259 pages,— except that the latter exhibited the society emblems printed in colors upon the title-page. The last preceding catalogue, printed in 1858, by J. H. Benham, had an " allegorical " steel-engraved frontispiece. The arrangement of the following list of chapters corresponds with that before employed:

1. *Phi ; Yale College, New Haven, Conn.* ; 1855 ; 746.
2. *Zeta ; Princeton College, Princeton, N. J.; 1845 (*d. 1857); 69.
3. Theta ; Bowdoin College, Brunswick, Me. ; 1845 ; 260.
4. Xi ; Colby University, Waterville, Me. ; 1845 ; 218.
5. Sigma ; Amherst College, Amherst, Mass. ; 1846 ; 344.
6. *Gamma ; Nashville Univ., Nashville, Tenn.; 1847 (*d. '61); 66.
7. *Psi ; Alabama Univ., Tuscaloosa, Ala. ; 1847 (*d. 1857); 82.

8. Upsilon ; Brown University, Providence, R. I. ; 1850 ; 144.
9. *Beta; Univ. No. Carol'a, Chapel Hill, N.C.; 1851 (*d.'62); 120.
10. Chi ; University of Mississippi, Oxford, Miss. ; 1851 ; 168.
11. *Delta ; Coll. of So. Carolina, Columbia, S. C.; 1852 (*d.'61);90.
12. Kappa ; Miami University, Oxford, O. ; 1852 ; 125.
13. Eta ; University of Virginia, Charlottesville, Va. ; 1852 ; 172.
14. Alpha ; Harvard College, Cambridge, Mass. ; 1852 ; 66.
15. *Omega ; Oakland College, Oakland, Miss.; 1852 (*d. 1861); 77.
16. Lambda ; Kenyon College, Gambier, O. ; 1852 ; 135.
17. Pi ; Dartmouth College, Hanover, N. H. ; 1853 ; 247.
18. *Iota ; Kentucky Mil. Inst., Frankfort, Ky.; 1854 (*d. 1860); 35.
19. Alpha (prime) ; Middlebury Coll., Middlebury,Vt.; 1855 ; 100.
20. Omicron ; Michigan University, Ann Arbor, Mich. ; 1855 ; 179.
21. Epsilon ; Williams College, Williamstown, Mass. ; 1855 ; 102.
22. Nu; New York City-College, N. Y. City ; 1856 ; 155.
23. Tau ; Hamilton College, Clinton, N. Y. ; 1856 ; 111.
24. Mu ; Madison University, Hamilton, N. Y. ; 1856; 133.
25. Rho ; Lafayette College, Easton, Penn. ; 1856 ; 100.
26. Beta-Phi ; Rochester University, Rochester, N. Y. ; 1856 ; 96.
27. *Theta-Chi ; Union Coll.,Schenectady, N.Y.; 1857 (*d.'69); 100.
28. Kappa-Psi ; Cumberland Univ., Lebanon, Tenn. ; 1857 ; 92.
29. *Zeta (prime); Centenary Coll., Jackson, La.; 1857 (*d. '62); 46.
30. *Alpha-Delta; Jefferson Coll.,Canonsb'g, Pa.; 1858 (*d.'65); 38.
31. *Tau-Delta; UnionUniv., Murfreesb'o,Tenn.; 1860 (*d.'61); 11.
32. *Kappa-Phi ; TroyUniversity, Troy, N.Y. ; 1861 (*d. 1862) ; 23.
33. Phi-Chi ; Rutgers College, New Brunswick, N. J.; 1861 ; 57.
34. Psi-Phi ; Asbury University, Greencastle, Ind. ; 1866 ; 40.
35. Gamma-Phi ; Wesleyan Univ., Middletown, Conn. ; 1867 ; 61.
36. Psi-Omega ; Rensselaer Polytech. Inst., Troy, N.Y. ; 1868 ; 25.
37. Beta-Chi ; Western Reserve College, Hudson, O. ; 1868 ; 23.
38. Eta-Alpha ; Washington-Lee Univ., Lexington, Va.; 1868 ; 55.
39. Delta-Chi ; Cornell University, Ithaca, N. Y. ; 1869; 16.
40. Delta (prime) ; Chicago University, Chicago, Ill.; 1870 ; 23.

The total membership of DKE thus appears to be about 4750, as against 3800 in 1867, and 2000 in 1858. At the latter date it possessed 29 chapters, as against its present 40, though it will be noticed that a dozen of these are dead. The war stopped most of the Southern chapters, and interrupted one or two which were revived at its close. The Alpha-Delta chapter had its charter withdrawn by order of the fraternity. The Zeta was killed by the general decree of the Princeton faculty in 1857. The same year, the similar decree of the Harvard faculty put the Alpha chapter under the ban, but it has nevertheless continued to exist in secret, as a sophomore club, and its delegates have always been recognized at the annual conventions, though its members do not, while at Cambridge, wear the society badge, nor have their names printed in the society catalogue.

Delta Phi also secretly kept up its existence at Harvard until 1865, when the organization now known as the "A. D. Club"—to which most of the DKE Sophomore are admitted in junior year—was established upon its ruins. Of course these "new Alpha Deltas," as Tom Hughes calls them in his sketch, are not recognized by the fraternity, and themselves make no pretence of being connected with it. The names of the Harvard men who belonged to Delta Phi after the suppression were not inserted in the catalogue of 1860, but appeared in the catalogue of 1870, as their classes had then all safely graduated,—the last one, as before remarked, being that of '65. The Psi U catalogue contains the names of no Harvard men later than the class of '57, because the society then gave up the ghost, in obedience to the faculty's edict, and the class in which it was recently reëstablished has not yet graduated. The names of graduated members will appear in future catalogues, however. The DKE catalogue contains the names of no Harvard men belonging to it after the suppression, because the club became too informal and disorganized to keep any records or lists of its members. Latterly the chapter has approached somewhat to a formal organization, and probably the names of recently graduated members will appear in the next catalogue. Indeed, it is not improbable that in the course of a few years the "Greek letter societies" may be allowed to exist as openly at Harvard as at most other colleges, since, under the more liberal administration recently introduced there, their existence is more than winked at already.

A comparison of the list shows the three societies existing as rivals in ten colleges outside of Yale, namely: Amherst, Bowdoin, Brown, Dartmouth, Hamilton, Kenyon, Michigan, Rochester, Union, and Wesleyan· Delta Phi and DKE in addition are rivals at Cornell, Miami, N. Y. City - College, Western Reserve, and Williams; and were formerly at Alabama and Cumberland; while Psi U and DKE in addition are rivals at Chicago, Harvard, and N. Y. University. The Yale chapter of each society is its largest, though not, except in the case of DKE, its most important or controlling one. The parent chapter of Psi U is its weakest, and that of Delta Phi is by no means its best, and no one chapter is allowed any preponderance of influence in either fraternity; but the original DKE is so much superior to any one of its many branches that it still exercises its parental control over them all, and while nominally deferring to their wishes, retains in itself the chief executive power. At Yale the real rivalry for the first place is between this society and Psi U, but at almost all the other colleges where the three exist DKE holds the lowest rank. There are of course many other local and chaptered societies in other colleges which dispute the ground with these three; and many which once existed have either wholly, or in the case of particular chapters, become absorbed in them. Thus, the Iota chapter of a western college society called "Beta Theta Pi" was changed into the Phi of Psi U at Michigan, and the Beta chapter of the same society at Western Reserve became the Beta-Chi of DKE. Not unlikely the society may have been the source of some Delta Phi chapter also, and perhaps some of its branches still exist as rivals of the two last mentioned societies. On the other hand, none of the chapters of these three societies have ever deserted from them, or attempted to reorganize under another standard.

An examination of the three catalogues brings to light a good many more or less notable names. There are college professors and tutors, doctors of divinity and of medicine, judges, lawyers and reverends, generals, congressmen and honorables, almost without number, who formerly sported the badges of these societies. Among Yale Delta Phi men may be mentioned: Rev. Dr. J. P. Thompson of '38, Prevost C. J. Stillé and Prof. J. D. Whitney of '39, D. G. Mitchell and B. G. Northrop of '41 [the names of Gen. W. T. S. Barry of Mississippi, Maunsell B. Field of New York, and several others, are included in the Delta Phi list of '41, though they revolted from that society and were among the founders of Psi U], W. L. Kingsley of '43, editor of the *New Englander*, Gen. Dick Taylor of '45, H. T. Blake of '48, founder of the Wooden Spoon, Prof. D. C. Gilman of '52, G. W. Smalley of '53, G. M. Towle of '61, and others. Alfred B. Street belonged to the Hamilton chapter; Gov. Dennison of Ohio and U. S. Senator Pugh to the Miami; Horace Maynard of Tennessee and Rev. R. S. Storrs, Jr., of Brooklyn to the Amherst; Senator Jenckes, the advocate of civil service reform, and Rev. Dr. Samson, president of Columbia College, to the Brunonian; James Russell Lowell, Rev. E. E Hale, Rev. O. B. Frothingham, and F. B. Sanborn of the Springfield *Republican*, to the Harvard; Rev. Dr. Hale, president of Hobart College, to the Geneva; Gov. Goodwin of New Hampshire to the Bowdoin; Manton M. Marble of the N. Y. *World* to the Rochester; Prof. A. W. Perry to the Williams ; Russell Sturgis, Jr., to the Manhattan ; Ngan Yoong Kiung of Shanghai, and Oronhyatehka of Canada, to the Kenyon. Chief Justice Chase, Rev. Henry Ward Beecher, Rev. Dr. Ray Palmer, Prof. Elias Loomis, and Cassius M. Clay, are among the honorary members of this society.

Taking up the Psi U catalogue, among the Yale members may be noticed : Rev. H. M. Dexter of '40, editor of the Boston *Congregationalist*, Henry Stevens of '43, F. S. A., Senator O. S. Ferry of '44, Col. E. G. Parker of '47, Dwight Foster of '48, attorney general of Massachusetts, C. G. Came of '49, editor of the Boston *Journal*, Champion Bissell of '50, publisher of the *American* (Whig) *Review*, Andrew D. White of '53, president of Cornell University, Chauncey M. Depew of '56, N. Y. secretary of state, A. Van Name of '58, college librarian, Engene Schuyler of '59, U. S. Consul at Moscow, and Wilbur R. Bacon of '65, Yale's most famous oarsman. At Union, are found Mayor Alexander A. H. Rice of Boston, Frederick W. Seward, assistant secretary of state, and A. C. Davis, Kansas attorney general; at N. Y. University, George W. Schuyler, State treasurer, and William Allen Butler ; at Brown, Lieut. Gov. Arnold of Rhode Island ; at Amherst, Galusha A. Grow of Pennsylvania, E. M. Wright, Mass. secretary of state (and, as honorary members, John G. Saxe, E. P. Whipple and Dr. J. G. Holland) ; at Dartmouth, Amos T. Akerman, U. S. attorney general, and W. H. Bartlett, judge of the supreme court of New Hampshire ; at Hamilton, Gov. J. R. Hawley of Connecticut and C. D. Warner of the Hartford *Courant;* at Harvard, Profs. Goodwin and Gurney ; and at Kenyon, James Kent Stone, " the youngest college president."

Among DKE men at Yale may be noticed : Charlton T. Lewis of '53, editor of the N. Y. *Evening Post*, Maj.

Gen. J. W. Swayne of '56, Brig. Gen. J. T. Croxton and Prof. Cyrus Northrop of '57, Dr. D. G. Brinton of '58, Joseph W. Shipley and Edward R. Sill, of '61, and Dorsey Gardner of '64; at Colby University, J. H. Drummond, attorney general of Maine; at Amherst, Gen. Francis A. Walker, of the statistical and census bureau at Washington; at Harvard, John Quincy Adams, Jr., Edward S. Rand, Jr., and Howard M. Ticknor. DKE's best-known men—Rear Admiral Foote, General Burnside, Vice President Colfax, Bayard Taylor, Nathaniel P. Banks, John R. Thompson—are all honorary members, elected as such on account of their notoriety. Though this society possesses the largest membership, the number of names in its catalogue that are even locally well-known is much smaller than is the case either with Delta Phi or Psi U.

Each society holds every year a general convention of all its chapters, which as a rule are each represented by two or three delegates. The exercises usually consist in the delivery of an oration and poem, by graduate—and, if possible, distinguished—members of the society, to which the public are admitted; and the transaction of business by the delegates, in private. The convention lasts for two days and winds up with a supper. It is held with each chapter in succession, except the very distant or the weakest ones. The presiding officer of the DKE convention is always a Yale man; in the case of the other societies, a member of the chapter with which the convention is held. It has been mentioned in the first chapter that at all other colleges except Dartmouth the societies draw their members from all the four classes. The exception at Harvard has been noticed, and at some of the other colleges also the freshman and sophomore members are not allowed to display their badges,—except when absent from the university town,

—nor to have their names printed with the others in the public lists. When a Freshman or Sophomore, who has become a member of one of the societies at some other college, enters Yale, he does not become an active member of the chapter until the time when the society is given into the hands of his own class. Previous to this his name is not published, in the list of members, neither is he expected to display his badge, nor to attend the society meetings unless specially invited by upper-class men. Most of the other chapters are more secret than those at Yale. At some colleges the songs are never sung outside the hall, neither are the places and times of meeting generally known, nor the societies in any way mentioned to the uninitiated. A fancy which Yale men sometimes have for displaying the splendors of their society halls to their lady friends is peculiarly horrifying to the other chapters. Not that the practice is much in vogue, but the few cases of it which occur are winked at by the societies, on the theory that the dear creatures comprehend too little of the mysteries which they behold to make any damaging revelations, even were they so inclined. Every chapter gladly entertains the representatives of every other chapter, whenever it chances upon them ; but though Yale members always accord welcome to the others, they are not always anxious to claim it in return, and sometimes when in the neighborhood of other colleges are inclined to fight shy of their brethren there resident. Yale DKE men in many cases do not wear their badges in the vicinity of certain of their chapters, of the extended numbers of which they are heartily ashamed. A report, which was perhaps meant for a joke, used to prevail about college to the effect that DKE raised some of the money to pay for its hall by selling charters to all applicants who would give fifty dollars apiece for them. However this may be, it is certain that the great number of its chapters is the chief source of its weakness as a fraternity. In the case of Psi U, also, were the first two and last two stricken from its list of fifteen chapters, its power and influence would be nearly doubled. A Yale Psi U man likewise, occasionally conceals his badge in localities where the wearing it does not confer much honor, and exposes him to the danger of being "brother-ed"—a word which in his view would hardly change in significance by the omission of its second letter. There is very little sentiment wasted upon one another by the Yale members of these societies, yet their friendship is probably not weakened by its omission.

The elections to the junior societies are given out to the Sophomores upon Tuesday evening, and the initiations are held two weeks and a half later, upon the evening of the Friday which precedes Presentation Day. The sophomore-society initiations always occur before this,—usually on the preceding Wednesday or Friday, —and in the interval all the Sophomores seem to be neutrals, for all alike are badgeless. The mode of giving out elections is the same as that of the sophomore societies, already described, but as there are only two classes, instead of three, to engage in the work, everything is more orderly and respectable. The elections are offered and congratulations exchanged, in a sober and gentlemanly way, before any movement is made toward the eatables. There are rarely any displays of greediness or rowdyism. There is less of noise and excessive drinking. But Sophomores are apt to get together after receiving their elections and "celebrate" the event, much after the manner of the year before. Election cards, too, are distributed ; the initiation fee of fifteen to twenty-five dollars is collected by

one of their own number ; and the members are individually summoned in writing to be present at a
particular college room at a certain hour on the evening
of initiation ;—all after the old custom. This time,
however, the members elect are conducted to the hall
in a body, and initiated without perceptible uproar.
It is generally understood in advance among them that
the ceremony is only a formal one, yet most men probably feel a trifle nervous about the matter, up to the
moment when the mystery is revealed to them. Then
come the oration and poem and display of theatricals,
and finally the supper. Like the old Sigma Phi initiation suppers, this used on some former occasions to be
served in a hotel dining-room, instead of in the society
hall as now. The Psi U initiation exercises generally
close the earliest, at about two o'clock ; the DKE the
latest, at about daybreak. The badges, engraved with
the new members' names, etc., are provided in advance
by the society,—the initiation fees covering the cost of
them,—and are "swung out" next day. The same is
true in the sophomore societies.

The regular meetings are held every Tuesday evening, beginning at nine or ten and ending at midnight
or later. In old times the hour of meeting was publicly
announced, by posting upon the trees in the college
yard large cards upon which were the society vignette
and a printed or written numeral which signified the
hour of meeting. This custom was also observed by
the sophomore and even the freshman societies. The
exercises are of a more varied character than those of
the societies of the two preceding years, and comprise
features from both of them. There is less formality
about the literary part of them than in freshman year,
and less prominence to their "social" features than in
the sophomore societies. There are music and dancing

as well as singing, and of course smoking, and card playing and occasional suppers. At the close of their meetings, each society marches in a body to the college yard, singing its songs on the way, and after giving forth some additional strains from a particular rendezvous therein, disbands. Psi U's station is in front of the Lyceum building, where, just before disbanding, it always ends up its final song, to the tune of "In a few days," with the chorus, "Hurrah! 'rah! 'rah! 'rah! Psi U! Psi U!—Hurrah! 'rah! 'rah! 'rah! Psi Up-si*lon!*" DKE always marches through Trumbull Gallery, and the south entry of North College, in front of which, after singing an additional song or two, it disbands with the cheer: "Hurrah! 'rah! 'rah! D! K! E!" One of its outdoor choruses to the tune of "All on a summer's day,"—very popular in the society during 1867–8,—was the best marching song known at the time in college. It closed with a "Slap! bang! here we are again, in jolly DKE." Delta Phi's most characteristic melody was to the tune of the "Old oaken bucket,"— but of late years this society has seldom sung any of its songs in public. DKE on its homeward march sometimes finds that the doors of North College have been barred against it by neutrals or under-class men, and is then obliged to pass around instead of through the building before giving its final cheer. The foregoing remarks, like the similar ones concerning the singing of sophomore societies, though expressed in the present, relate to the past, as the societies, obeying the edict of the faculty, sing no more, and disperse without ceremony of any sort.

The attendance upon the meetings is more regular than in the case of the sophomore societies. Some of the Seniors are almost always present, and on special occasions nearly all of them attend, and perhaps take part in the exercises. These occasions, aside from initiation night, are when the representatives of other chapters are present in force, in response to a regular invitation. At such times the society of course tries to appear at its best, and the festivities are often prolonged until nearly daybreak. Perhaps the entire assembly of seventy-five or more, march through the streets in procession, singing their society songs before the young ladies' boarding schools, by way of serenade, or shouting them forth beneath the college windows. Next morning, too, very likely the guests may be invited to attend chapel prayers, and be seated together in the galleries, where the best looking of them may act as "electioneering arguments" upon the unpledged under-class men who gaze up from below. Outside members who chance to visit town without formal invitation are likewise sure of good treatment at the hands of Yale men. Old graduates come more frequently to the hall than in the case of the under-class societies, though generally only by special invitation of the society or an active member of it. The night before Commencement is the time when many of them meet together there, to talk over the old experiences and perhaps partake of some refreshments provided for the occasion.

The hall of Delta Phi is in the upper story of the block at the south-west corner of Chapel and State streets, opposite the building wherein the Sigma Eps hall used to be. It was newly fitted up in 1867, and was said at that time to be the finest lodge room possessed by any chapter of the fraternity. As the Williams chapter has since then erected a $10,000 hall of its own, this can be no longer true, though the hall is undoubtedly a good one. It is protected without by a ponderous iron door, and current report adds a billiard table to its other inner attractions. The other two societies possess halls of their own. That of Psi U is on High street, a few steps from the north-west corner of the college yard. It was taken possession of on the first of May, 1870, having been about seven months in process of erection. It has a front of 26 feet, a depth of 66 feet, is about 40 feet high, and stands upon a lot whose dimensions are 40 by 70 feet. The material of the front is red pressed brick, inlaid with ornamental work in black,—one pattern running across just above the freestone foundation, another at the top of the entrance way, and a third just below the cornice of the roof. This is a Mansard, slated, and surmounted by an ornamental iron railing, which connects and partly conceals the two short chimneys which project at its extremities. Above the entrance is an arched window, the keystone of which bears the chapter letter, "*B*." The entrance and the arch above it make a slight projection from the front, and so a gable above the arch breaks the uniformity of the roof. The roof cornices and the massive doorway are of light Nova Scotia stone, and freestone is the material of the half-dozen steps which lead up to it. In relief, upon the inner slab which surmounts the doors, are the letters, "*Ψ. T.*" The doors themselves are of solid oak, though these will doubtless in time give place to iron ones. On the south side of the building, near its front, is a second arched window, covered like the ornamental one in front with a brown lattice-blind. There are two other square windows in the rear, protected by close black shutters. There is also a rear entrance to the basement, and two full-length basement windows, as well as half-a-dozen scuttle-windows upon either side, all of which are protected by iron bars. The other windows mentioned are all in the second story, and in the roof is a large skylight of thick, ground glass, which looks in upon the main

theater or exhibition hall. The usual assembly room is
on the lower floor, and there are various small apartments above and below. Ventilation is secured by
double walls and other special appliances, and the
building is heated by furnace, supplied with water, and
lighted by gas. David R. Brown was the architect ; the
masonry was superintended by Lyman Treat, and the
carpentry by William Judd. The whole property must
have cost some $15,000, and is probably not yet more
than two-thirds paid for. For a year or more before the
work was begun, the society owned the stucco house next
beside the Divinity College on College street, and intended to refit and occupy it for its own uses, but finally
decided to build the present hall instead. Previous to
this, Psi U had occupied for more than a quarter of a
century a hall in Townsend's Block, corner of Chapel
and College streets, where, since 1864, the hall of Beta
Xi had been, close beside it. This society, since Psi
U's departure, has added the vacated hall to its own,
and now controls the entire upper floor of the block.
Psi U's first lodge room was identical as to locality
with the present one of Delta Phi. At Middletown, the
society is said to be constructing a $10,000 freestone
hall of its own, upon a corner of the college grounds ;
and at Amherst it holds a long lease on the two upper
stories of the large block containing its hall, and rents
the rooms, which surround the hall, only as lodgings for
Psi U students. The DKE hall is on York street, near
the corner of Elm. It was built in 1861, chiefly through
the instrumentality of Henry Holt of '62, who advanced
the money for the work. This lot on which the building stands perhaps measures 30 by 60 feet, and the
hall itself has a front of 24 feet 6 inches, a depth of
45 feet, and is perhaps 35 feet in hight. Its material
is common brick, and the only ornamental work—aside

from the trimmings in front, made of wood in imitation of stone—is the slab of brown sandstone above the entrance whereon are carved the letters, "*Δ. K. E.*" The door at the entrance is of iron, and just above it is the chapter letter, "*Φ.*" There are no windows, save the skylights in the flat, tin roof, from the edges of which project several ventilators and short chimneys. Inside, the building is of course divided into two stories and several different apartments. Seen from without, the hall has an attractively mysterious look to an underclass man, though its appearance is much inferior to that of the Psi U structure. The present value of the property is probably about $8000, and the payment of $1500, instead of the annual ground rent hitherto claimed by the owner, is all that is now needed to vest the title wholly in the society.

The holding of real estate by these societies is rendered possible by the organization of "trust associations," composed of resident graduate members, who fulfil the duties of trustees, and receive no compensation for their services. Psi U was incorporated by the Connecticut Legislature, at its May session of 1862, when "James H. Trumbull [of '42, Conn. Sec. of State], Henry E. Pardee [of '56], and Simeon E. Baldwin [of '61], with all such other persons as might be from time to time associated with them, together with their successors," were "constituted a body politic and corporate, by the name of the 'Trumbull Trust Association,' for the sole purpose of the intellectual and moral improvement and culture of its members ; and by said name" were to "have perpetual succession and be capable in law to purchase, receive, hold and convey real and personal estate"—not exceeding a certain amount in value ; "to sue and be sued, implead and be impleaded, defend and be defended," and so forth. The "Winthrop Trust Association," incorporated three years later and consisting of Edward I. Sanford of '47, Cyrus Northrop of '57, Robert S. Ives of '64, Daniel C. Chapman and George C. Holt of '66, with their associates, and so on, is the legal style of DKE. It is named in honor of the most famous member of the society, Theodore Winthrop of '48. It is supposed that Delta Phi is as yet unincorporated.

Upon the junior societies at Yale, as at present organized, hinges the entire system of college politics. The election of the nine "Cochleaureati," or members of the Wooden Spoon Committee, and the five Editors of the Yale *Literary Magazine*, which election is held during this year, is the great thing about which they center, though they enter into and effect to some extent the previous minor elections. It was formerly the custom for each of the three societies, whose combined membership always formed a clear majority of the junior class, to nominate three of the candidates for the Spoon Committee and agree to support the nominees of the others. Each society thus obtained an equal share of the committee. But, as a majority of the nine choose the Spoon Man, a second coalition between two of the societies against the third was necessary to decide the matter, as well as to share the five editors between them by some regular agreement. The manner of pledging Freshmen to these societies has been already noted in the description of those of sophomore year. When the class of '69 entered college, the upper-class politicians had already prepared for them a "coalition," which was to decide their junior year elections. It was between Delta Phi and Psi U, against DKE. Each society was as usual to have three Cochs, but Psi U was to have the Spoon Man and three Editors, while Delta Phi was to have two Editors and the chairman of the editorial board. As soon as the nucleus of each society's pledged Freshmen was of respectable size, this coalition was ratified, and papers were signed in duplicate whereby each Freshman bound himself to faithfully observe these and other minor specifications, upon the arrival of his junior year. Each party to the coalition preserved one set of the papers, and every Freshman who thereafter pledged to either society was obliged to agree to support the coalition also. As many other Freshmen as possible were also "pledged to the coalition," being induced to take this step in the belief that it would better their chances of a pledge to one or the other of the societies composing it. This was not considered as preventing them from accepting a pledge to DKE if one were offered, but simply as binding them to vote against the DKE candidates until themselves regularly pledged to that society. Before the end of the first term of freshman year the political machine was in working order. The coalition held meetings and nominated candidates for the freshman-society offices; DKE did the same; and the two opposing factions then fought it out. The neutrals of each society, though outnumbering each of the parties, nominated no third candidate of their own, and made no effective opposition. They were without "leaders," or common interest to bind them together, and of course were unlikely to make an open fight against societies to which they hoped each day to be pledged. Neither did the neutrals know of the formality with which each party nominated its candidates in advance; they only observed that their presidents and other high officers were sure to be "pledged men," and the rival candidates the representatives of opposite political factions; and so they sided with one or the other of them, as caprice or interest dictated. In Delta Kap there was only one party, for after the first the coalition had things all its own way, and DKE gave up the fight. It was, however, allowed one place on the Initiation committee. Sigma Eps was more evenly divided, and each election was closely contested. The fight over the campaign offices was especially fierce, and the expedients then resorted to for effecting the result have been described in the chapter on Freshman Societies. DKE was finally victorious, but in turn gave the coalition one member of the Initiation committee. In Gamma Nu there was but little chance for politics.

Outside the freshman societies, the first opportunity for displaying their power was afforded by the election of the Annual Jubilee committee. The "ticket" was made up by a Delta Kap politician, who divided it equally between the pledged men of the three junior societies ; but after the election it was found on examination to represent the freshman societies in the proportion of Delta Kap 6, Sigma Eps 3, and Gamma Nu none. The latter society therefore resolved not to participate in the supper, but, one of the committee afterwards withdrawing from college, the class elected a Gamma Nu man in place of him, and all ended happily. No men in the class of '69 were pledged to the sophomore society Theta Psi, but its thirty elections in that class were conferred upon the coalition men pledged to Psi U and Delta Phi, in the proportion of two of the former to one of the latter. Among these Delta Phi men was the politician just mentioned, who, as campaign president of Delta Kap, had conceived such a hatred of Gamma Nu, that he vowed to debar its members from the upper-class societies which he himself might belong to. As Delta Phi was accustomed to depend upon Gamma Nu for its best men, it did not approve this decision of its representative, and threatened not to elect him if he persisted in his course. He, however, was obstinate, and Theta Psi was through him prevented from electing any Gamma Nu men in '70. In Delta Phi there was a long contest over the '69 elections, one faction favoring this man and his partisans, the other his opponents. By various compromises, about two thirds of the pledged men were finally elected, but the politician and his chief opponent, were not among them. On the Tuesday evening following the initiation, the meeting was adjourned early, on account of the Wooden Spoon Exhibition, and while their Gamma Nu opponents were absent the partisans of the politician reässembled, elected and initiated him. When the Gamma Nu members learned of the facts, five out of the seven sent in their resignations to the society, and took off their Delta Phi badges. In the course of the next term they became members of DKE. The originator of the trouble withdrew from college at the close of sophomore year. His chief opponent had in the meantime joined Psi U, and the few pledged men whom Psi U had rejected had been taken into Delta Phi. The opening of junior year found the two societies at swords' points. The paper coalition between them was seen to be but a rope of sand, and was soon formally repudiated. As the time of the great election drew near, an arrangement was proposed whereby Psi U and DKE were each to have four Cochs and two Editors, and Delta Phi one of each; but this being rejected by the latter, similar terms were offered to an association of neutrals, and accepted by them, and the "ticket" as thus made up was finally elected by the class,—Psi U according to agreement afterwards taking the Spoon Man and DKE the chairman of the editorial board. The Delta Phi men attended the class meeting, and voted for the three Cochs and two Editors whom they had—without hope of success—nominated in the usual way from among their own number.

For some years preceding the revolt, Delta Phi had been held in less repute than the other two societies, but had yet been treated by them as a political equal. Since then, it has altogether degenerated—having been obliged, in 1869, through fear of dissolution, to give elections to Freshmen as well as Sophomores, and transform itself into a mixed sophomore-and-junior society—and is no longer of any political or social importance. The rumor has been current of late that the fraternity is about to abolish its Yale chapter; and it would act wisely in doing so, for though it has other branches which, absolutely, are no better than this, yet there is probably no other college in which the relative position of Delta Phi is so low as at Yale. On the other hand, some ardent spirits profess to believe that its present decline is only temporary, and that in the future it will be able to regain its former importance in the college.

Agreements not to pledge or electioneer Freshmen have at times been entered into by these societies. The last was that made in the class of '70, whose members were not to be approached upon the subject of junior societies before a certain hour of the first day of February, 1868,—in the second term of their sophomore year. As a necessary tender to this agreement, the two sophomore societies were neither to pledge nor electioneer nor accost the Freshmen in any way until the evening which both should unite upon for the giving out of elections. At eight o'clock of the appointed evening they could address any Freshman in these words: "I offer you a pledge to Theta Psi [or Beta Xi]. Do you accept?" No argument or explanation of any kind was to be allowed. This programme was accordingly carried out, and two or three hours after the men were pledged the societies marched around and gave out elections in the usual way. Spite of the pledge, " the two crowds" were for all practical purposes "packed" in advance. Lacking but a day or two of the appointed first of February, the junior society agreement was openly broken,—DKE and Psi U each charging the other with its violation. Forthwith most of the Theta Psi men were pledged to Psi U, and the members of Beta Xi to DKE,—though the reverse was true in some cases,—and each society completed its number from among the neutrals. Neither society of course gained anything in the class of '70 by anticipating by a few hours the appointed time of pledging them. But the agreements as to the junior and sophomore societies were to be perpetual; and the object held in view by the society which broke the pledge was to prevent its going into effect in future classes. The '71 Freshmen were forthwith electioneered and pledged, and, spite of one or two attempts to do away with the practice, things have since gone on after the old fashion, though in the case of '74, Psi U and DKE agreed to offer no pledges before the third term; —Delta Phi's consent not being thought worth gaining. It is exceedingly difficult to keep such an agreement. Without any encouragement from upper-class men, cliques will be formed and crowds be packed in the interest of some particular society. When a society sees "the best men" plainly drifting away from it, it is apt to suspect treachery, raise a cry of foul-play, throw up the pledge, and fall to work to better its fortunes. The agreement, furthermore, does not offer equal advantages; relatively, the best society gains at the expense of the poorest. When a man has been a year and a half in college he comprehends the drift of things, sees the relative positions of the societies, and can make his choice wisely. But, as a Freshman, the chance of joining *any* upper-class society seems to him so desirable that he often takes up with the first one offered him. Thus, in an indiscriminate scramble among the Freshmen, an inferior society is likely to do better, than when a year later it seeks for recruits among the wily Sophomores. The cases are exceptional in which there is much electioneering for the upper-class societies. Occasionally a "big man" may hesitate between two societies, and be earnestly argued with by their representatives; but, as a rule, a man makes up his mind for himself which crowd he will go with if he can, and accepts an offered pledge to it with few words. When any arguments are offered for a society, they are of course similar to those used in behalf of the freshman societies, and relate to the honors, social position, and so on, gained by its members. Prize lists, however, are unknown after freshman year.

There is more harmoniousness and good feeling in the junior societies than in those of the two preceding years, yet bitter enmities not unfrequently arise within them. The bones of contention are not the society offices,—for the incumbents of them are chosen without dispute,—but, as may be judged by the sketch of junior politics in the class of '69, the positions upon the "ticket" for Cochleaureati and *Lit.* Editors. These are balloted for one at a time, and the order of nomination is known outside, so that the candidates are spoken of throughout the class as the first, second, or third Cochs or Editors, of this or that society. It is expected that the first Coch of one or the other society will be chosen Spoon Man, and the first Editor, chairman of the editorial board. What is known as a junior-society coalition is not really made between the societies as such, but between the individual members of them. The societies form a good medium through which to operate, but the agreement is a purely personal one, after all. For example, certain individuals, who belong to Psi U, and certain other individuals, who belong to DKE, promise to vote for one another's candidates in a certain class meeting. A formal writing is accordingly prepared in duplicate to which each individual party to the compact puts his signature. A majority, who order that their society accept a coalition, cannot force an opposing minority into it, nor bind their votes in class meeting. The compact " holds " just as many individuals as enter into it, and no more. If the thirtieth man in a society insists on voting in opposition to the twenty and nine who are his comrades, there is no one who can say to him, Nay. Of course, in practice, when a large majority urge the adoption of a coalition, the minority are prone to fall in with it, even though they may dislike to do so ; but their action is voluntary, and they have no one but themselves to blame if they lack the independence to assert their own convictions. Let it be understood, once for all, that the current talk of a man's society binding his vote or opinion upon outside matters, is nonsense, pure and simple.

Suppose a junior class of 115. Suppose two junior societies of 30 men each. Suppose these 60 men agree to elect a ticket made up from among their own number. Suppose the separate thirties nominate half of it. Then, 16 votes will ensure a man a majority of the 115 cast in class meeting. The disproportion is often greater than this. In the class of '69, with 120 members, a bare half-dozen nominating votes secured a man his election to a cochship. Of course a coalition is not arranged and ratified by the necessary number of individuals, without a vast deal of wire-pulling, and log-rolling, and pipe-laying, and the rest of it ; for all the separate and conflicting interests have to be consulted and reconciled, and the likely " men " held in view as well as the " measures." This work takes up the time of the professed politicians.

But, supposing that all the details have been at length satisfactorily arranged, and that the "nominations are now in order" in the societies, we can see how the strife has been narrowed down to very close quarters, and the fidelity of a man's time-serving "friends" is put to the crucial test. The general result is often to be guessed at in advance with tolerable accuracy, for the contest is not infrequently in regard to the order in which particular candidates shall be nominated, rather than to the fact itself of nominating them: though usually there are some unsuccessful candidates close upon the heels of the last ones chosen. In general, there is more uncertainty as to order in nominating the Cochs, more uncertainty as to the men themselves in nominating the Editors. However smoothly the elections may pass off, they usually occasion more or less hard feeling; and the "fence men" are certain to make enemies, whichever way, on the arrival of the decisive moment, they finally jump. Seniors announce the nominations from one society hall to another almost before the nominating meetings are adjourned, and they are discussed next morning at every club breakfast table. The only other elective honor of any account wherewith the society has to do, is the position of delegate to the annual convention, for which there may be several aspirants. The society also appoints a Senior as a member of the delegation, and pays his expenses with the others.

The nomination of the candidates for class honors, however, stirs up less of contention and bitterness than the election of new members to the society. There are fewer class elections given out than in sophomore year, because the interval between the time the members were pledged and the time they were elected was long enough for them to decide upon what other classmates they wished to have elected, and the society is not apt to refuse men thus recommended. In case there is such refusal, a class election probably results, soon after the new members are put in control. Perhaps a few may be given out for the purpose of gaining sufficient men to form an effective coalition. Perhaps a man, proposed before the class nominations are made, is at first rejected by those who fear his vote may work to their disadvantage, but elected when the danger is over. Perhaps a class election may be given a new man who enters college as a Junior. And, on the night of giving out elections to the Sophomores, a few Juniors who have been previously kept out may be allowed to slip in. Similarly, a few such honorary elections may be conferred on men in the senior class. Psi U, however, makes very few class and honorary elections, and never confers the latter upon members of the Scientific School, as do the other societies. The bad feeling which results from fighting over class elections, though worse in kind, is naturally less in extent than that arising when the new members are chosen from the class below. Among the pledged men who are to be balloted for there are generally factions, more or less clearly defined, each of which has its friends and enemies among the men who wield the ballot. Each wishes to be the controlling power in the society at the time of the class nominations, and so desires to keep out those likely to injure its chances, or interfere against a projected coalition. Aside from political considerations, too, there are many private and personal reasons which may make certain pledged men obnoxious to the rest, and cause the latter to work against them. When to these causes of confusion the private likes and dislikes of the Juniors are added, enough conflicting interests appear, to make the election meetings anything but harmonious ones. The pledged men really have the power

in their own hands, and occasionally some are found
fearless enough to assert it, by agreeing together not
to accept elections to their society, unless some enemy
be left out or friend taken in, as the case may be. But
as a rule, men feel too doubtful as to their own chance
of election to risk it by any such defiance ; and so the
societies are usually spared the disgrace of being
directly dictated to by under-class men. The strife over
elections of course varies in different societies and different years ; sometimes being very bitter, sometimes
hardly displaying itself at all ; but, what with compromises and the gradual wearing away of the weaker
party's opposition, the full crowd is at last made up, of
essentially the same men who were pledged, and the
society in due time given good naturedly into their
hands.

As a natural result of their political affiliations, the
active members of these societies mention them to one
another with less reserve than is wont to be maintained
by sophomore-society men, and do not resent as im-
pertinent any reasonable questions which may be asked
concerning them. They are usually careful to say little
about them in the presence of neutrals, however, lest
they be thought indirectly to boast of their own implied
superiority. DKE men are often called "Deaks" by
the others, but as this word is somewhat akin to an
epithet it is not employed in their presence, nor do
other society men often use it before outsiders, unless
intimate with them. Similarly, in sophomore year, Beta
Xi men are called "Dead Beats," or simply "Beats," by
those of Theta Psi, in the presence of their own number ; and neutrals, among themselves, though less commonly, designate them in the same manner. In freshman year, too, Gamma Nu men may be called Gamma
Nu-sters by the others, but the epithet is by no means a

common one. "Dickey E" and "Piecey U" are epithets sometimes applied to the third-year societies by the Seniors who belonged to them. Among Seniors, too, junior society transactions are talked of about as freely as the doings of the sophomore societies. A party of friends who belonged to rival organizations will "chaff" one another about them, and, in private of course, join together in singing their songs. Nevertheless, these societies are thought much more of than those of the two earlier years, and the affection for them is far more lasting. It induces undergraduates to give liberally of their money and labor for the erection of costly halls, and prompts former members to help them on, with generous subscriptions and friendly advice. A man's share in the ordinary expenses of a junior society is no larger than in that of the year before,—perhaps not as large; his share in the extraordinary expenses is unlimited. Suppose a new hall is to be built: a subscription of $50 is very fair; of $100, generous; of $200, munificent; while $500 makes a man a hero in society tradition ever after. Thus, these society "bonds of affection," et cetera, are shown to have a tangible cash value, and, even at Yale where they are wont to be made light of, are sometimes redeemed if not in gold at least in lawful money. At other colleges, where a man belongs to but one society, and perhaps may be a member of it during his whole academic course, his regard for it is naturally deeper and more enduring than it could be were his allegiance divided as at Yale. The graduates of the other chapters hence take a livelier interest in their welfare. If a new hall is to be built, or other extraordinary expenses are to be incurred, the brunt of the burden falls upon them. At Yale, it is the undergraduates who take the initiative; the aid of the old members, generous as it often is, comes in only as a supplement to their work.

The relative standing of the three societies has been incidentally alluded to ; a few direct remarks in regard to it may serve to close the chapter. Psi U, starting at Yale when Delta Phi was broken up by internal feuds, seems from the outset to have successfully disputed the ground with it as a recognized equal, despite its inferiority to it in age and reputation. These two were the important rivals until about the year 1862, when DKE, in the eighteenth year of its age, by the erection of a hall of its own, suddenly began to rise in college repute, and claim recognition as a rival of Psi U,— Delta Phi having been for some time on the wane,— and ever since the class of '69 entered college the real rivalry has been between those two societies. Since the graduation of that class, indeed, Delta Phi has practically sunk out of sight in college esteem, and is called a junior society only by courtesy. The material argument has all been on the side of DKE, and in view of this it seems remarkable that Psi U, with little else to back it save its traditional prestige, has maintained its old position so well. If the lift which its hall gave DKE be any index of the future, it seems likely that its rival, at length possessed of a more attractive one, will again take the lead in the race. Comparing the freshman societies with these, it is easy to see a general tendency in Sigma Eps men to choose DKE, Delta Kap men Psi U, and Gamma Nu men Delta Phi ; though since the catastrophe of 1868 the comparison in the latter case no longer holds. Thus, the campaign president of Sigma Eps is almost always a DKE pledged man, and of Delta Kap a candidate for Psi U ; while formerly the Gamma Nu president was quite as certain to be pledged to Delta Phi. Even before the latter's fall, it was not infrequently to be observed that a sneer would arise, when a man was mentioned who had " gone to Delta

Phi," which was only a little less pronounced than the old freshman derision of " Gamma Nu men." Now-a-days, hardly any one of any ability or social importance can be induced to join Delta Phi, and membership in it is thought to rather lower a man's dignity and self-respect. Indeed, the name " Delta Phi man " is fast becoming a synonym for " scrub," and " pill," and even the neutrals regard its members with a sort of pitying contempt. The sentiment concerning it is much like that which used to prevail in regard to Diggers of senior year : the average man " will go to one of the reputable societies or to none at all." But these two societies no one ever pretends to despise, however hostile he may be to them. For the last few years DKE has taken a good many more prizes and honors than its rival, and about all of the prominent boating and base-ball men have been among its members. Its men " work " more for their society than do their rivals, and take greater pains to display it. Psi U used to be called the " shawl society," in the old days when the wearing of that garment was deemed to smack somewhat of aristocracy and exclusiveness. Perhaps its place at Yale to-day cannot be better described than by saying that it still attracts most of the " shawl men " from every junior class. In place of twenty, political or pecuniary exigencies now require it to elect about thirty members, long time the established number of the less exacting DKE. As general college fraternities, their rank is : Psi U first, Delta Phi second, and DKE third ; or inversely as their membership and number of chapters. The lowest of them, however, as well as its two superiors, is probably of a good deal more importance than any of the other chaptered college fraternities in America,

CHAPTER IV

SENIOR SOCIETIES.

Peculiarities of these Societies—Skull and Bones—Its Badge Pin and Numeral—Hall and Corporate Title—Origin—Catalogue—Mode of Giving out Elections—Initiation—Mode of Summoning Members to the Annual Convention—Attendance upon the Regular and Special Meetings—Peculiar Customs and Traditions—Scroll and Key—Its Badge Pin and Vignette—Hall and Corporate Title—Origin and Growth—Customs and Traditions—Spade and Grave—Its Origin, Precarious Existence, Change of Name, and Final Catastrophe—The Societies and the Neutrals—Bull and Stones—The Coffin of '69—The Tea-Kettle of '53—Crown and Scepter—Star and Dart—Notable Members of the Existing Societies—Mode of Packing and Making up a Crowd—Comparison of the Societies—Their " Policies," Actual and Possible—Failure of their Imitators in Other Colleges—General Facts about all the Class Societies—Comparison of their Importance in Each Year—General Result of the System.

The societies of the first three years, though possessed of special characteristics, have yet such a general resemblance to one another and to those of other colleges, that their position in the system can be readily comprehended by any reader of these pages,—at least, if he be college-bred. But the senior societies are such peculiarly Yale institutions, that it will be difficult for an outsider fully to appreciate their significance. Nothing like them exists in other colleges ; and Harvard is the only college where, under similar conditions, they possibly could exist. In the first place, they are the only Yale societies whose transactions are really secret. Their members never even mention their names, nor refer to them in any way, in the presence of anyone not of their own number ;

and, as they are all Seniors, there are no "old members in the class above them" to tell tales out of school. There is no electioneering nor pledging for these societies, and no Junior is approached upon the subject in any way until an election is actually offered him. The number of elections given out to each class is small and never varies, and no class nor honorary elections are ever allowed. ˙ Both societies combined comprise but little more than one fourth the members of an average class, and the part played by them in politics is simply a negative one. A man's chances for office are never bettered because he belongs to a senior society, but are frequently, for that simple reason, injured or destroyed altogether. The societies do not take their names from the initials of a Greek motto, but from the peculiar emblems adopted as a badge. This badge is constantly worn by active members ; by day upon the shirt bosom or neck-tie, by night upon the night dress. A gymnast or boating man will be sure to have his senior badge attached to what little clothing he may be encumbered with while in practice ; and a swimmer, divested of all garments whatever, will often hold it in his mouth or hand, or attach it to his body in some way, while in the water. Only graduate members wear the badge upon the vest, where for the first few years they display it quite regularly. Old graduates seldom "swing out" except on special occasions, or while visiting New Haven ; and members of the faculty, except may be young freshman tutors, never display a society badge when engaged in their official duties. Members who have ceased to show the badge openly, nevertheless may wear it about them pretty constantly, perhaps by night as well as day, for quite a number of years. The senior societies, in theory, are composed exclusively of "big men" ; of those who, for whatever reason, have become preëminent above their fellows in college repute.   In this they differ from those of the two preceding years, which of necessity are half made up of comparatively second-rate men.   There are a certain number—say twenty—in each class, who, at the end of the third year, may be picked out as the confessed superiors of the others in popular esteem.   Were it possible to do this a year or more earlier, and were one junior society preëminently " the best," it is doubtful if the twenty could all be per-suaded to join it, or the society to elect them all ; for it is plain that their individual political influence would be greater in separate societies, partly made up of less important men.   The senior-society type, on the other hand, is an association with no weak members whatever ; and the history of the matter shows that unless this ideal is adhered to with reasonable closeness such a soci-ety cannot live long at Yale.

There are two of these societies, but as one takes its tone from the other it may be well to describe them sep-arately, and treat first of the oldest and most famous member of the modern system.   Its name is " Skull and Bones,"—formerly printed " Scull and Bone,"— and its badge, of solid gold, consists of the face of a skull, supported by the crossed thigh bones, with a band, bearing the number " 322", in place of the lower jaw. Its original badge was a rectangular gold plate, about the size and shape of the present Beta Xi pin, whereon the skull-and-bones design and the numeral were simply engraved.   Its wood-cut vignette merely represents the emblems, and is identical with that employed for general purposes in college papers elsewhere.   The number " 322" is always printed below it, though the size of the type is not invariable.   In the cut formally used, the design was smaller that now than in vogue ; but there never has been added to the simple emblems anything in the way of ornament or embellishment. Popularly the society is known as "Bones," and its members as " Bones men." The pin is sometimes called a "crab" from its supposed resemblance to that animal. The hall, erected in 1856, is situated on High street, near the corner of Chapel, about opposite the Yale Art Building. It is a grim-looking, windowless, tomb-like structure, of brown sandstone, rectangular in shape, showing a front of about 35 and a length of 44 feet, and is, at a guess, 35 feet in hight. The entrance in front is guarded by a pair of massive iron doors, a dozen feet high, finished off in panels, and of a dark green color ; while heavy clasps of brass close over the key-holes and are secured by padlocks, beneath one of which the bell-pull is concealed. Previous to 1864, when these doors were put in position, their places were occupied by commoner ones of iron, upon which the society emblems were displayed. The roof is nearly flat, and is covered with half-inch plates of iron, which in 1867 took the place of the tin before employed. There is a sky-light, similarly protected, and the chimneys and ventilators are ranged along the edges of the roof. Behind, are a pair of small windows barred with iron, and close to the ground are two or three scuttle holes, communicating with the cellar. The building is rapidly becoming covered with the " Virginia creeper," first planted there in 1864, and stands back a rod or more from the street, being separated from it by a post-and-chain fence. The dimensions of the lot upon which it stands are about 40 feet (front) by 70 (deep) ; and the total value of the premises must be upwards of $30,000. Before taking possession of its present quarters, the society for many years,—perhaps from its original organization,—occupied a low-studded back room in the third story of what is now the *Courant* building, opposite the college yard.

8

At the May, 1856, session of the State Legislature the society was incorporated as the "Russell Trust Association," with the same legal formulas as those quoted in the case of Psi U. The names mentioned in the act were William H. Russell of '33, John S. Beach of '39, Henry B. Harrison of '46, Henry T. Blake of '48, Henry D. White of '51, and Daniel C. Gilman of '52 ;—the first of whom has since acted as president, the one next the last as treasurer, of the association. All are residents of New Haven.

The society was originated in 1832 by fifteen mem·bers of the class which graduated the following year. General Russell, the valedictorian of that class, is its reputed founder, and the best known of his associates is Judge Alphonso Taft of Cincinnati. Some injustice in the conferring of Phi Beta Kappa elections seems to have led to its establishment, and apparently it was for some time regarded throughout college as a sort of bur-lesque convivial club. It is said that the faculty once broke in upon one of its meetings, and from what they saw determined upon its abolishment, but by the inter-cessions and explanations of its founder, then serving as tutor among them, were finally induced to spare it. The popular college tradition, that it was transplanted from a German university, is scouted by old neutral gradu-ates as absurd. But, whatever be the facts as to its origin, the mystery now attending its existence is genu-ine, and forms the one great enigma which college gos-sip never tires of discussing. Its catalogue is a unique affair, having a page six inches by four, printed upon one side only. Each right-hand page contains the members of a year—fifteen names indicated in full and alphabetically arranged—with the residences, printed in old-English text, and surrounded by a heavy border of black. A title page, bearing the society cut and the words " Period 2. Decade 3," precedes the list of the founders, and a similar one, " Period 2. Decade 4," stands before the class of '43, and so on for every successive ten years, the " Period" being always "2," but the " Decade" increasing each time by one. At the top of the first list of names—the class of '33—and separated from them by a broad line of black, are the characters, " P. 231.—D. 31.", which regularly increase by one with each succeeding class, and are therefore, for the class of '71, " P. 269.—D. 69." The first page of the book displays, in full-faced, old-English capitals, the letters, " Otirunbcditf," arranged in a semi-oval, between two black lines. The catalogue is black-edged, and is bound in black leather, with the owner's name and " D.", stamped in gilt upon the cover,—though of late the " D." is less often indicated. It will be observed that the " D." is always two less than the class ; thus, a catalogue labeled " John Smith, D. 62," would belong to a member of the class of '64, and so on. What these " Periods" and " Decades" and " P.'s" and " D.'s" may signify is known only to the initiated ; but, as the catalogue is never shown to outsiders, they were probably not put there for mystification solely. That the founders are put down as belonging to the " third decade of the second period" may seem to make in favor of the German university theory, in the minds of many ; and the blank space in place of the eleventh man's name in the list of the founders, may perhaps be thought a straw in the same direction. The last edition of the catalogue was prepared in December, 1870, and was as usual sent out in unbound sheets to each surviving member of the society. The total membership of the 39 classes represented was of course 585.

The elections to this society are always given out on the Thursday evening which precedes Presentation

Day.   Since no Junior is ever pledged or spoken to in advance, the excitement which prevails among the "likely men" is intense, though suppressed, as the hour of fate draws nigh.   All college, too, is on the alert, to find what the result may be.   It is said that formerly the fifteen Bones men, at midnight, silently moved from their hall to the rooms of the chosen ones, when the leader, in each case displaying a human skull and bone, said simply, "Do you accept?" and, whatever was the reply, the procession as silently departed.   As the neutrals got into the way of tagging about, insulting and annoying the society on its march, this plan was abandoned in favor of the less formal one now in vogue. According to this, at an early hour of the appointed evening, a Bones Senior quietly calls at the room of a Junior, and having been assured that "we are alone," says: "I offer you an election to the so-called Skull and Bones.   Do you accept?"   If the answer is affirmative the Senior—and perhaps the graduate member who sometimes accompanies him—shakes hands with the neophyte, and bidding him to keep to his room for the present, hurries back to the hall to report the result. If the election is refused, the result is likewise reported to headquarters, and influential members are sometimes sent back to argue the case; but, as a rule, the few men who refuse elections are not offered a chance to repent. Bones will not be dictated to, and when a man says, "I accept, in case So-and-So is elected with me," or "in case Such-a-One is kept out," he is never allowed to carry his point; Yes or No is the only answer recognized. Suppose the elections begin to be given out about seven, in case there are no refusals the whole number will be made up before nine o'clock; if there are refusals it may take an hour longer.   In anticipation of this possibility, a half-dozen extra men are chosen in Bones, in addition to the regular fifteen, and in case any of the latter fail to say Yes, elections are offered to a corresponding number of these "second choices," in the order in which they were elected. By going quickly and quietly about their business the Bones men manage to elude in great part the attentions of the rabble, which ranges about the college yard on the night in question, —barring up the entry doors, raising false alarms, and otherwise disporting itself. The names of the chosen men, however, are known about as quickly as the elections are conferred, and many in the crowd make out complete lists of them, for circulation at the breakfast table or in the division-room upon the following morning, when they form the sole topic of discussion throughout the college. Usually, the names are first printed in the *Courant* of the Wednesday following; though for a year or two past some of the city dailies have had the tact to secure them for their next morning's issue. The initiation begins, after the close of the Wooden Spoon Exhibition, at midnight of the following Tuesday, and lasts till about daybreak. The candidates for the ceremony are assembled in a room of the college Laboratory, which is guarded by Bones men, and are singly escorted thence, by two of the latter, to the hall. As the grim doors open for each new member, there are sounds as of a fish horn, as of many feet hurrying up an uncarpeted stairway, as of a muffled drum and tolling bell,— all mingling in a sort of confused uproar, like that from a freshman initiation a good many miles away. Perhaps, while being led to the hall, a candidate may pass between rows of neutral Juniors or other college men, some of whom may " bid him good bye," with expressions of congratulation and good will, if they think his election deserved, or insult and revile him, if their belief goes in the contrary direction. There is usually some one to flash a dark lantern upon each approaching candidate, and, if he makes no other personal comments, to at least shout forth his name, for the edification of the rest. To all this the Bones men of course pay no attention. It perhaps takes an hour or more thus to initiate the fifteen candidates; and when the self-constituted leader of the outside hangers on announces that "the last man's in," his followers agree that the fun is over, and sullenly disperse. If they stayed longer perhaps they might hear songs sung to strange old tunes, and the tones of the orator's voice, and the applause which follows it, and the prolonged cheers for "the Skull and the Bones." And of course there is a supper. Every resident graduate attends the initiation, as well as many from New York and elsewhere, some of whom come to town as early as election night; and the initiation itself, at least the outside part of it, is conducted by graduates alone. Long ago, it is said, the initiation took place on the evening of Presentation Day.

"The annual convention of the Order" is held on the evening of Commencement. Three weeks previous to this,—which, of late years, is therefore at the time of the first regular meeting, two nights after initiation,—a printed invitation is sent to every living member of "the Club" whose whereabouts are known. This invitation is upon the first page of a sheet of note paper. Below the society cut is the date—for example, "Thursday evening, July 22, 1869"—of Commencement night; followed by "☞ VI. S.B.T.;" a Latin quotation, playing upon the word "Bones;" the signature of the secretary, and the date. Upon the third page is the list of new members, printed alphabetically in old-English text, and surrounded by the black borders, exactly as in the catalogue, of which it in fact constitutes a new "P." and "D." Each one who receives it, by fitting the new leaf to his catalogue, thus keeps the same perfect from year to year. These pages are doubtless stereotyped, and preserved by the society, whose entire catalogue is thus always kept in readiness for the printer. With this invitation and catalogue-page, is also sent a printed slip specifying the exercises of Commencement week. A card-size photograph of the new members, grouped—in front of an antique clock whose hands point to the hour of eight—about a table on which lies a skull, is also sent to graduates, at this time or afterwards. In the picture, the thigh bones are held by certain members,—sometimes the table-cloth has the emblems embroidered upon it, and the whole arrangement of the group is apparently significant. Official notes to old members are written upon black bordered paper of the catalogue size, with or without the society cut at the head, and society communications sent through the mails are often enclosed in black-edged envelopes,—bearing at the end a printed request to the postmaster to return them to the society's post-office box if not delivered within a certain time,—sealed with a skull and bones and the letters " S.C.B.," impressed upon black wax. Bones men never display in their college rooms any posters or other reminders of their society,—though it is rumored that actual skulls were formerly used for this purpose,—but graduates often keep on the walls before them a richly-framed photographic group of the class-mates who made up their own special "D.,"— the picture being simply an enlargement of the card photograph before noted. As specimen jokes from the convention invitations the following may be quoted : " Nisi in bonis amicitia esse non potest " (Cic. de Am. 5. 1.) ; " Grandiaque effossis mirabitur ossa sepulchris " (Virg. Georgs. I. 497) ; " Quid dicam de ossibus? Nil nisi bonum " ; and, in 1856, at the time of erecting the hall,

"Quid dicam de ossibus? (Cic. de Nat. Deorum. II. 55.) O fortunati, quorum jam mœnia surgunt!" (Virg. Æn. I. 430,) At the head of the editorial columns of the city dailies, on Commencement morning, was usually displayed the " 322. VI. S.B.T." notice, between parallel black rules, but for the past few years the practice has been abandoned. Up to about the same time printed announcements of the place and time of the Commencement meeting, headed by the cut, were posted about college, and upon the notice-boards of the different churches, a few days in advance. Formerly, too, similar warnings were printed, in connection with the society cut, among the advertisements of the city papers. As their hall is called "the Temple " by Bones men, a current guess—and a wrong one—interprets "S.B.T." as "Skull and Bones Temple." A more likely reading makes "T." stand for "time," and so interprets the notice, "Six minutes before eight,"—the hour eight being "Bones time."

The meetings are held on Thursday evening, commencing exactly at eight o'clock, and every acting member is obliged to be in attendance from that time until the adjournment, at two or three in the morning. The society formerly had a way of marching from its hall in dead silence,—tramp, tramp, tramp,—to the north entry of North College, where it might leave a man or two, and so on, silently, in front of the row, growing smaller as it passed the different buildings, until at the south entry of South the few who were left disbanded. Formerly, too, it was customary, before breaking up, to sing a college song whose refrain was, " And I shall be his dad ;" but this practice, for lack of voices perhaps, was abandoned some years ago. A Bones Senior is never seen about New Haven after eight o'clock of a Thursday evening. Nothing but actual sickness ever keeps him from his society, except it be absence from town,—and those who have been absent are apt to appear for the first time at Friday morning chapel. A good share of the fresh graduates who are residents, and many of the older ones, are also ordinarily in attendance at the regular weekly meetings. Aside from the annual convention on Commencement night, there are two other "bums" held during the year,—one each at about the middle of the first and second terms,—which bring many graduates from out of town. These usually reach the city just before the meeting, and leave it on the midnight trains, so that their coming and going is not known to outsiders, except from the hotel registers or a chance contact upon the street.

Each Bones man has a nick-name by which he is known to his initiated classmates. One or two of these names, probably official titles, are retained from year to year, but most of them change with the classes, and are apparently conferred according to individual peculiarity or caprice. All members of the society are also spoken of among themselves by a certain general title ; another is conferred upon members of the other senior society, and a third is bestowed upon the neutrals. As these titles, especially the latter, might convey a wrong impression if generally known, they are not mentioned here. The society itself, among its members, is known as " Eulogia," or the " Eulogian Club." It is believed to have little or no regard to any formal, written constitution, but to be governed chiefly by tradition in its customs and usages. The hall is reputed to be a sort of repository for old college mementos ; like the " first college bell," the original " bully-club," the constitutions of defunct societies, etc., which are all said to be preserved there ; and when anything of the kind disappears, this is surmised to be its final destination. Though

Thursday night is the regular time of meeting, when attendance is compulsory, the hall is generally frequented on Saturday and other nights also, and is often visited in the day time besides.   An old member often goes there as soon as he reaches town, especially, if in quest of information in regard to classmates who were formerly associated there with him.   At convention time, the members who cannot in person attend, send to the society such facts as to their whereabouts and occupations for the year, as may interest old classmates and friends; and their letters are filed away for future reference. Every book or pamphlet written by a member is also preserved in the society archives; and its collection of printed and manuscript "Yalensia" is said to be very complete.

To discover the exact meaning of the inevitable numeral "322," has long been a problem for college mathematicians.   According to some, it signifies "1832," or the year the society was founded; others make it "3+2+2" or "7," which is said to be the number of "founders" in the class of '33, who persuaded the other eight to join them in making up the original fifteen; still another surmise sets it at "3×2×2," or "12," which might refer to the midnight hour of breaking up, or something equally mysterious; while a fourth guess interprets it to mean "the year 322 B. C.", and connects it with the names of Alexander or Demosthenes.   What these heroes may have in common with the Skull and Bones society, aside from departing this life on or just before the year in question, is not very plain; but it is pretty well established that Bones' "322" refers to that year B. C., whatever may be its additional significance. While the class of '69 were in college the hall, according to report, was twice broken into by neutrals, and strange stories were circulated of the wonderful mysteries there discovered by the interlopers. It is probably a fact that these men did really enter the hall, through the skylight in the roof; but there is no reason for trusting their own account of their exploits any further than this, since, if, as is not unlikely, the arrangement of things inside prevented their making any important discoveries, they would of course invent a sufficient number of supposititious mysteries, to clear themselves of the reproach of having ventured upon a fool's errand. None of their statements, therefore, have been thought worth repeating here. A surreptitious visit, real or pretended, was hardly necessary as a preliminary to assuring the college that "Bones keeps its most valuable documents locked up in an iron safe," since the same fact holds good for every society after sophomore year.

"Scroll and Key" is the name of the other senior society, which was founded nine years later than its more famous rival, that is to say, in 1841, by a dozen members of the class of '42. Popularly it is known as "Keys," though this abbreviation has only come into general use within the last half-dozen years. Its pin, of plain gold, represents a key lying across a scroll, and its wood-cut simply copies it. The design is such that it is difficult to tell the right side from the wrong, and the cut, when printed bottom upwards, as it often is, is rarely noticed as possessing other than its ordinary look. The original badge was a rectangular gold plate, of the same size and shape as the old Bones pin, whereon were engraved an eagle, poised above, suspending a scroll, and a right hand below, grasping a key. This is still worn, by a single member at a time, in place of the usual scroll and key, presumably as a mark of office, like society president or something of the sort. The letters "C.S.P.," "C.C.J.," are always printed with the society cut,—the former above, the latter below it,

—and with it usually serve as the only introduction to the lists of members printed in the *Banner* and elsewhere, though the name "Scroll and Key" is sometimes prefixed. The Bones lists, on the other hand, are always headed with the full name of the society. The posters which, until within a few years, were put up about the college yard and elsewhere at Commencement season, for the benefit of graduates, displayed an eagle poised above the ordinary emblems, with no print—in addition to the inevitable letters—except the day and hour of the meeting,—"9 P. M.," perhaps,—or the numeral "142." A small, seal-like wood-cut of the society, displays the clasped hands upon an open scroll, with "Adelphoi" in Greek capitals at the top, "1852" below, and at the bottom two hieroglyphic characters, the one like a Gothic "T," the other like an old style Greek "Γ;" while the only trace of the key is its head, which projects from the top of the scroll. Another, steel-engraved, seal, represents the eagle, looking down from above upon the central scroll and key, upon which the letters are indicated, while an open right hand reaches up from below. The framework of the device is made up of fifteen oblong links, and its shape cannot be better described than by saying that if there were sixteen links it would be an eight-pointed star; as it is, the ten lower links make up five points, but the upper five—in place of the six, which would make the remaining three—are simply rounded together. This, too, was the shape of the inner frame-work of the old gold-plate badge. The present pin has been said to be plain, because the eagle and hand, faintly outlined upon it, do not change this general appearance. Neither of the senior badges have their owners' names or anything of the sort engraved upon their backs. The invitations to the "Z. S."—or "bum" held at the middle of the first

and second terms—are printed within a scroll-like design
from which the key is absent ; or else with the ordinary
cut at the head of the note. The company of the
"brother" is simply requested upon the appointed evening, and he is directed to answer the secretary, which
officer is designated by the letter "G.," and is his "in
truth." Aside from these initial letters, there is no
mystery about the affair, which is either printed in gilt,
or, if in black, has mourning bands about the edges of
the page. All society communications are also forwarded in black-edged "return" envelopes, as in the
case of Bones, sealed in black wax with the society
emblems and letters. There have been several editions
of the society catalogue; and it is probable that a
printed list of the elections is forwarded each year to
every old member, in connection with the invitation to
the celebration of Commencement night. A card-size
photograph of each new group of fifteen is doubtless
similarly distributed, either then or afterwards. In this
picture, the central figure holds a large gilt model of
the society badge,—the six letters being indicated on
the scroll,—and each of the end men grasps a large key,
pointed towards the centre of the group. Eight are
seated, including the three mentioned, and the remainder are standing, but the position of each individual is
probably not significant. Enlarged photographs of the
same sort are handsomely framed and hung in the
rooms of graduates. The anniversary of Commencement night used to be announced among the ordinary
advertisements of the city papers, in connection with
the society cut. More recently, at the head of their
editorial columns of Commencement morning, " C.S.P.
—P.V.S.9.P.M.—C.C.J.," or something of the sort, appeared, between double rules of black. But this practice has now been abandoned.

The hall hitherto (since 1847, when the house where it stayed was destroyed by fire) occupied by the society is in the fourth story of the Leffingwell Building, corner of Church and Court streets, across from the Tontine Hotel. The headquarters of the Yale "law department" are upon a lower floor of the same building, and a Masonic lodge-room divides the upper story with Keys. Judged from the outside, this hall must at the most be limited to two not very large rooms, and the Keys men, when assembled in force, be cribbed, cabined and confined together in uncomfortably close proximity. This old order of things, however, has recently come to an end, and Keys is now in possession of a hall, far superior in costliness and architectural beauty, not only to Bones hall, but to any college-society hall in America. It stands on the north-west corner of College and Wall streets, and its erection had been planned and talked about for a dozen years or more. At midnight of Thursday, Nov. 25, 1869,—the date of the fall "Z.S.,"— the society, graduates and all, marched to the vacant lot, round which they formed a ring, while prayer was offered, and a society-song sung, after which, a graduate with a silver spade formally broke ground for the new edifice. Then came the singing of the "Troubadour" song, and the procession, dangling its keys, silently moved back to the old quarters on Church street. Only the foundation of the building was laid before the setting in of winter; but the work was resumed the following May, and rapidly pushed to completion; and it is presumed that the formal ceremonies of entering and taking possession will be celebrated at the next Commencement. The structure has a front of 36 feet on College street, with 6 feet of ground each side, and is 55 feet long, with an open space of about 20 feet before and behind, in other words, it stands in the center of a lot 48 by 92. Its hight is perhaps 35 feet. The light yellow Cleveland stone is the chief material of which it is composed. This is set off by thin layers of dark blue marble, while four pillars of Aberdeen granite, with marble cappings, sustain the three projecting arches in front. Each arch surrounds a narrow opening, provided with three bull's eyes for the admission of air. Below the central arch are a pair of paneled, massive iron doors, to which entrance a flight of half-a-dozen stone steps leads up from either side. Five similar arches, though without projections or supports, serve to adorn and ventilate each side, and a corresponding number of closely protected scuttle-windows communicate with the cellar below. Rows of short pillars—four at each end, six at each side—surround the top,—the central two at the rear end serving to hide the chimneys,—and a couple of stars are cut out in the stone between every pair of them. The architect was Richard M. Hunt of New York, and the builders were Perkins & Chatfield of New Haven. The value of the entire property cannot be much less than $50,000, and it is to be presumed that a good share of that amount has already been raised by the society. The "Kingsley Trust Association," which is the legal style thereof, was incorporated at the May, 1860, session of the State Legislature, in the names of John A. Porter of '42, William L. Kingsley of '43, Samuel C. Perkins of '48, Enos N. Taft of '51, Lebeus C. Chapin, George E. Jackson, and Homer B. Sprague of '52, Charlton T. Lewis of '53, Calvin G. Child and Josiah W. Harmar of '55, and Edward G. Mason and Mason Young of '60. These comprise its best known names, and were perhaps chosen on that account, since only the president, Mr. Kingsley, is a resident of the city.

In the Yale *Banger* of 1845, published by the Sigma

Theta Sophomores, is a burlesque of the Keys cut, representing the Scroll as a "Declaration of Independence from the Scull and Bone," signed by the "great seal," which consists of a view of the historical fox reaching after the equally celebrated sour grapes. This probably represents, with substantial accuracy, the motive which originated Keys. Its founders, not being lucky enough to secure elections to Bones, determined to start in business upon their own account, and hence the society. Its ceremonies, customs, hours of meeting, etc., have all been patterned after those of Bones, and the nearer it approaches to its model the more of a success it is judged to be, both by its own members and by the college at large. Its existence for the first dozen years was apparently a precarious óne. In only three classes before 1852 did it obtain the regular number of members (15), which Bones has never varied in electing, but ranged from nine—the lowest, in '51—to fourteen. Since that time exactly fifteen names for each class have always been printed in its public lists, and since 1860 exactly fifteen men and no more have joined the society from each class. Previous to the latter date, it was a common thing to give out one or two or more class or secret elections, so that in some classes there have been seventeen or eighteen members, and almost all the classes which at first fell below the regular number, now appear in the catalogue with their full complement of fifteen names apiece. The men who accepted these after-elections to the society usually displayed their badge like the others, though sometimes the fact of their membership was kept a secret and they were not allowed to wear them about the college, nor until after graduation. Hence in every class to the present day there are almost always one or two men, who are believed by many to be "secret members" of Keys, because, being friends of the "crowd," they naturally associate with it, as they would were there no such society in existence. It is also rumored, with less probability, that notable men are sometimes chosen as honorary members. George Vanderhoff, the reader, is one of them, according to the authority of the *Banger*, —which, however, may have meant the statement for a joke. Similar rumors are also sometimes started in regard to Bones, but are far less generally credited, and are probably altogether groundless. Certain it is that the fact of there being a secret or honorary member, of there being more or less than fifteen members from each and every class since 1833, has never been in a single case authenticated. Up to as recent a date as 1860, Keys had great difficulty in making up its crowd, rarely being able to secure the full fifteen upon the night of giving out elections, but, by dint of electioneering and "packing" in the interval between that time and initiation night, managed—after 1851—to swing out the orthodox number of new badges upon Presentation morning. Probably it would have given pledges in advance, like the lower-class societies, save that in those days any one standing the slightest chance for Bones preferred it to a "sure thing on" the other society. The true Cæsar-or-no-one sentiment seems to have had full sway, and the best men of the class who did not secure Bones elections apparently preferred to go through senior year as neutrals rather than as members of a confessedly inferior society. The proportion of "big men" among the neutral Seniors was consequently much greater then than in these latter days. Keys, in fact, up to the time when it attained its twenty-first birthday, occupied a position in college regard very much analagous to that more recently held by the Diggers' society, to be described hereafter. It is only within the last lustrum that it has come to be a rival of Bones, and that the half-loaf sentiment has grown common, which prompts a man when his chances for the latter are spoiled, to "lay" diligently for the former.

The Keys mode of giving out elections—as well as the rest of its customs—corresponds as nearly as possible to the practice of Bones. Formerly the fifteen members, each carrying a key some two feet in length, in a body silently marched to the rooms of the men who had been chosen ; and then the leader—possibly displaying the large gilt scroll-and-key model before mentioned—may have said simply, " Do you accept ?" Of late, however, the practice is for two members,—one a Senior, the other a graduate,—each carrying one of the exaggerated keys, to proceed together to the room of each chosen man. The Senior raps sharply with his key upon the door, and, both stepping in, says, " I offer you an election to the so-called Scroll and Key. Do you accept ?" If the answer is Yes, both Keys men shake the Junior by the hand, and tramp back to their hall, where the result of the first election is received before a party start out to confer the second, and so on for the others. On this account the elections progress much more slowly than in the case of Bones, and more opportunities are given to the rabble in the yard to yell " Keys ! Keys ! Keys ! " and surge about the bearers of those implements, whose approach is usually announced, by self-stationed outposts, in the neighborhood of the State House steps. In 1868, all the Bones elections had been given out for more than an hour, and the " packed Keys crowd " of '69 had begun to feel a trifle nervous, when the first key-bearers appeared in the yard. There seems to be no very great significance in the order in which the elections are conferred, except that the one first received is perhaps to be interpreted as especially honorable ; but on the other hand this is sometimes offered to a man, who is by no means the society's first choice, in order if possible to anticipate Bones in securing him.

The initiation takes place at the same time as the other one, and like it lasts till morning. The rendezvous for the candidates is probably some room in the neighborhood of the hall, at all events is outside the college yard, and as the hall is not so convenient to the colleges as that of Bones the neutrals pay less attention to what takes place there on initiation night. Visitors who may be stopping at the Tontine Hotel on the night of Wooden Spoon, however, seldom sleep very soundly, if their rooms chance to be situated upon the north side of the building. Resident and other graduates attend the initiations, and the regular meetings also,—though to a less extent than in Bones,—and the rule requiring the presence of active members on Thursday nights from eight o'clock till two, is also strictly enforced. An absent member of '68, suspected of make-believe sickness, was one time forcibly hurried off to the meeting by two classmates, who rushed up from the hall for that purpose, with a great display of crossed keys ; and the procedure may be gone through with in other instances which excite less attention than did that,—though the cases where it is necessary to enforce discipline are of course uncommon. At the close of its meetings, the society was in the habit of marching up through the green, past the State House, to the college yard, singing on the way, or just before disbanding, the well-known song, " Gaily the Troubadour touched his Guitar." Though this was always finely done, and very acceptable to all who heard it, the faculty—induced, it is said, by the discordant howlings of the " Stones men "—included Keys in the general edict promulgated last year against society singing, and ordered its discontinuance. The current traditions in regard to Keys are not very numerous, nor is the belief in its mysterious origin wide-spread, as in the case of Bones. Its letters are supposed to signify: "*Collegium Sanctum Pontificum; Collegium Conservat Jupiter.*" Bones having set up Demosthenes as its patron saint, Keys seemed determined to "go one better" and claim the recognition of great Zeus himself. "Zenome" is one the society words supposed to possess mysterious significance. According to rumor, a magnificent stuffed eagle forms one of the chief decorations of its hall; though as this report originated with a '66 neutral who professed to have "been there," not much reliance should be placed upon it. Keys, like Bones, also keeps the photographs of its members, a library, paintings, pictures, obsolete society badges, old college mementos, and general memorabilia.

A third senior society also existed during the time that the class of '69 was in college. Its name, taken from its badge, was "Spade and Grave." The spade, partly thrust into the grave, rested upon the footstone of the same, and upon the headstone was represented a crown,—gold of course being the material of the entire pin. The grave was perhaps a little more than an inch in length, and the badge had one or two variations in size and shape. The "Bed and Broom," it was at first called by outsiders; and, by the more respectful ones, the society was known as "Graves," and its members as "Graves men." None of these names were ever popular, however, and "Diggers" soon came to be the only title by which the society or its members were referred to. Bones men, among themselves, also adopted this name for them. "To give community and sweetness to the eating of sour grapes" was, even more notoriously than in the case of the original Keys men, the object for which the Diggers started their society.

The immediate cause which banded them together in the scheme was a quarrel in the class of '64. Of the five Yale *Lit.* editors in that class, three had been chosen to Bones and two were neutrals. One of these two published, as a leading article in the magazine for February of that year, a piece called " Collegial Ingenuity," reflecting on the mode by which men may worm their way into Bones, and, it was claimed, making personal insinuations against a particular member of that society ; and on this latter ground the Bones editors, who formed a majority of the five, voted to suppress the article, and requested its writer to produce another to take the place of it, — themselves meanwhile seizing upon all the printed copies. The neutral editor refused to obey, and called a class meeting which voted to sustain him, and commanded the Bones editors to surrender the magazines within a certain time, or be expelled from office. As they paid no attention to the order, the class elected three neutrals in their places, and these, with the two original neutral editors, duly brought out a new edition of the February number, " Collegial Ingenuity " and all, and edited the two following numbers, —with the latter of which their term of office expired by limitation. The Bones editors meanwhile issued the February number,—with an explanation of their action printed in place of the obnoxious "leader," but otherwise unchanged,—and duly published the two remaining numbers of their term, still keeping the five original names at the head of the title-page, as if nothing had happened. Thus, for three months, there were two issues of the *Lit.*, each of which claimed to be the " regular " one. The Bones editors were really in the right, as the class had no legal power to interfere in the matter, and the three magazines issued by the other editors have been known as the " second issue," The five members of that second editorial board of '64 have the credit of founding Diggers', and they with ten other classmates first swung out the Spade and Grave badge at the beginning of the summer term of that year. On the Thursday before Presentation Day, elections were given out to fifteen members of '65, who were the first Diggers to have their names in print (in the *Banner* of the following autumn). The grave scene in " Hamlet," wherein the digger tosses up the skull and bones with his spade, is said to have suggested the badge as a fit emblem to typify the hostility of the new society to the old one, and its power ultimately to work the overthrow of the haughty Skull and Bones itself. Its hall was in the Lyon Building, on Chapel street, on the same floor with that of Gamma Nu ; was supplied with common iron doors without and a billiard table within ; and was reputed to be elegantly furnished, and among other things to have one of its rooms entirely covered with black velvet. In February, 1870, as already stated, its premises were taken possession of and have since been occupied by the sophomore society of Theta Psi. Its wood cut was simply a copy of its badge ; and the same design, enlarged, carved in black-walnut and mounted in a frame of the same wood, was displayed in the rooms of members, as a sort of poster ; though the practice was not much in vogue after the first year or two.

The society started under a cloud, and never emerged from it, but rather seemed to fall deeper and deeper into its shade the older it grew. It was always despised and looked down upon. Even those who joined it, in many cases cursed and ridiculed it by turns, up to the very moment of accepting their elections. Spite of careful packing and electioneering in advance, it always had difficulty in making up its crowd on the same night with the other societies, and it always had elections refused.

No one standing the least chance for Bones or Keys could be got to go to it, and the best of those left out by these societies preferred to remain neutrals altogether. Psi U men used to boast that no member of their society ever became a Digger; and the four classes between the first and last were certainly composed exclusively of Delta Phi and DKE men. There was, however, one member of Psi U among the founders, and four in '69 accepted elections,—much to the chagrin of their comrades. Everyone sneered at the society, including many of course who would gladly have joined it had they been able ; but the scrubbiest neutral of them all would affect to take offense were such an idea hinted at, and stoutly assert that, " had the Diggers ventured to offer him an election, he would have indignantly hurled back the insult in their faces !" This show of independence after election time is past is quite a common thing ; but the men of '69, even as Juniors, used to shout a sort of chorus, " Todtengraber ist güt," to the tune of " Trunca-dillo" ; they equipped a burlesque " spade and grave" in the college yard one day ; and in other ways so defied the powers above them that it became a problem whether the Diggers of '68 could secure any successors. There was the usual amount of electioneering and packing, but on election night only three men could by the most urgent entreaties be secured, from the indefinite number to whom elections were offered ; so these three were released and no new Digger pins were swung forth upon the morning of Presentation Day. The next public appearance of the society was on the first Friday morning of the following October, when fifteen senioric shirt-bosoms were adorned by as many new badges, the design being a crown from within which projected the ends of a crossed sword and scepter. This was superseded the following term by a larger sized pin of the

same pattern.   By a pretty thorough canvassing of the
class, in the three months' interval, these new members
had been raked together, and induced to " run" the society for a year, in the hope that under a changed name
the same old story could not be told concerning them.
At least half of them were secretly pledged and initiated
before Commencement, and wore the old Grave badge
during vacation, in localities where they would be unlikely to meet with Yale undergraduates.   From the
headstone of this old badge, it will be observed, the
crown itself was taken.   Above the old cut, in the *Banner*, the name " Spade and Grave " was printed in full ;
while above the new crown design were simply the letters, " S. L. M. " (popularly translated " Slim " or
" Slimy"), which had not before been made public,
though reckoned among the original mysteries of Diggers'.   Freshmen spoke of the society as " Crown and
Scepter," or " Sword and Crown," but upper-class men
clung relentlessly to the old title, and the doom of Diggers' was sealed.   Its usual arts were wasted upon the
class of '70 ; not one of them would pledge, either
before, on, or after, election night ; and so, after a precarious existence of five years, it was forced to give up
the hopeless fight and the ghost.

Like Keys', its customs were all modeled as closely
as possible after those of Bones, which it was to spade
out of existence so quickly.   Three men always came
up from the hall to give out each election, two of the
trio walking abreast in front, and the third following
close upon their rear.   A dark lantern or a club was
often carried by one of them.   The yells and outcries
with which the rabble greeted the approach of Digger
election carriers were far more prolonged and uproarious
than in the case of the other societies.   The Juniors
upon whom they called would be invoked with such cries

as : " Kick 'em out, Jim!" "Oh, Tom! *don't* be a Dig-ger!" "Shut your door on 'em, Jack! Don't let 'em fool you!" and so on ; while the Diggers themselves would be treated to all manner of compliments and personal attentions, such as were never bestowed upon the other election carriers. "How can I leave Thee," was the song sometimes sung outside at the close of the meet-ings, either while marching, or on arriving at the col-lege yard ; otherwise the procession silently tramped up Chapel street to South College, and so on in front of the row, dropping its men at each entry until none were left. It was believed to have had a good many secret members, — even including some from the Scientific School, — and several '63 men are known to have be-longed to it. After the change of base in 1868, the graduate members ceased to wear the old Grave badge. The society was unincorporated, and had never printed any catalogue. Its letters were supposed to represent the motto, *Sceptrum Ligonibus Mors.*

Not only do senior-society men never mention their own society in the presence of others, but they never even refer to the existence of a rival society, and when an outsider mentions this in their presence, even to a third party, they appear to take offense, and perhaps withdraw. So, too, they are offended if a man sings, or even hums the air, of the songs which they sometimes sing in public ; though these are familiar melodies, and have long been procurable in the form of sheet music. This same fact holds true, to a lesser extent, in the case of the junior and sophomore societies. A certain air gets in a measure identified with a particular society song ; and as members of the society never use it except in singing together, they dislike to hear it whistled by an outsider. A Sophomore, for instance, a few years ago, by persistently whistling, "All on a summer's day," would probably have injured his chances of a DKE election; and, in the case of Psi U, perhaps the same would still be true of one who should be constantly humming, "In a few days." Senior-society men may also refuse to speak when passing in front of their hall, and in some cases to notice a neutral classmate whom they may chance to meet after eight o'clock of a Thursday evening. An instance is related in the class of '67 of two Bones men who brought from their meeting a sick classmate and put him to bed in his room, without paying any attention to his neutral chum who was there present, though he was also a classmate with whom they were on friendly terms. This exaggerated display of secrecy is quite a modern outgrowth, however, being altogether unknown to the old members of fifteen or twenty years ago, and it attained its highest pitch in the class just mentioned, — since when, senior-society men have conducted themselves much more sensibly. For many evident reasons, the costs of membership in a senior society are much greater than in any other, though most of their money is raised by voluntary contributions, and a man eligible in other respects is not kept out on account of his poverty. On the other hand, a man's wealth of course adds to his chances of election in senior year more than in any other. The annual running expenses of a society, in which graduates take so prominent a part, cannot and ought not to be borne by fifteen men alone, and there are doubtless permanent funds whose income is available for such purposes,—at least in Bones, whose property is fully paid for. To increase this fund, almost every old member sends in an annual contribution, according to his means, for five or ten years after graduation day.

It is in senior year alone that the neutrals largely outnumber the society men, that they have nothing to hope for in the way of class elections, and that they are not overawed by the presence of upper-class men. These three circumstances combine to foster in some of them a sort of reckless hostility towards these societies, such as is not felt towards those of the earlier years. This displays itself in a variety of ways. The conduct of the neutrals when the senior elections are given out has been already described, and the fact noticed, at least by implication, that they never in the least interfere with the similar ceremonies of the other societies. Nor yet do they ever attempt to break into the halls of the latter. It was in the class of '66 that this hostility first definitely displayed itself, in the institution of a sort of a mock "society" called "Bowl and Stones,"—the name being a take-off on that of Bones, and the duties of its members being simply to range about the colleges at a late hour on Thursday night, or early on Friday morning when the senior societies disbanded, singing songs in ridicule of the latter, blocking up the entries, and making a general uproar. The refrain of one song, to the tune of "Bonnie Blue Flag," was "Hurrah! Hurrah! for jolly Bowl and Stones"; of another, to the tune of "Babylon," "Haughty Bones is fallen, and we gwine down to occupy the Skull." Another function of the "Stones men" was to offer bogus elections to simple minded classmates, or even to under-class men,—whom they were sometimes able to "sell." In the class of '67 they were at their worst, and wantonly smashed bottles of ink upon the front of Bones hall, and tore the chains from its fence. On the Thursday morning which preceded the Presentation Day of 1868, the Stones men of that class posted up a comic handbill, purporting to show the "order of exercises" which would be observed by the senior societies in giving out their elections that evening. There was some little wit employed in the composition of this notice, and is was the only thing emanating from the "society" that was not at once weak and discreditable. The modified name, "Bull and Stones," then first appeared ; which form has since been retained.   Some members of the class of '70 even went so far as to procure a small gilt representation of "a bull" standing upon "stones," which was worn as a burlesque badge pin, even in public, and in some cases quite regularly, during the first term of their senior year. Of course there is nothing *to* this "society" except what has been told ; its "members" are few or many according to the state of the weather ; and any neutral senior who is ready to join a crowd for making an uproar on Thursday night is, from that fact only, a good and regular "Stones man." Indeed, the name has of late come to be accepted as a synonym for any senior-society neutral whatever ; and every one not elected to either of the two societies is said to "belong to Stones." At the time of the last initiation, the Stones men seized upon and confiscated for their own use the ice-cream and other good things which the confectioner was engaged in taking into Bones hall. Since then, one or two projected "raids" of the same sort have been frustrated by the presence of a policeman. Now-a-days, Thursday night is the favorite time for the more depraved Stones men to "go off on a bum" together, and afterwards wake the echoes of the college yard with their discordant howlings.

That this "society" showed no signs of existence in the class of '69 was perhaps due in great measure to the existence of another more creditable organization, some of whose members would probably, save for it, have been leading "Stones men." On the morning of Presentation Day, 1868, fourteen men, who had been neutrals since freshman year, were noticed to wear upon their shirt bosoms, gilt coffin lids, about an inch in length. Their names were printed in the annuals of the next term, under the "senior-society" heading, beneath a wood-cut of the badge, above which appeared the letters "E.T.L.," but no name. They were spoken of as "Coffin men," or "ETL's," when mentioned at all; and, so far as known, met quite regularly on Thursday nights, perhaps in some room rented for the purpose. They said nothing in regard to themselves or the regular senior societies, and they attempted to give no elections in the class of '70. The society passed in the class for a joke; but, for the negative benefit it effected in restraining some who would otherwise have been uproarious, as well as for the positive advantages it may have conferred upon all its members, it deserves to be held in grateful recollection. Perhaps somewhat similar to this was the "Tea-Kettle" society, established in the class of '53, which has left nothing behind it save the announcement of its birth in the *Lit.* Another short-lived association was the "Sword and Crown" which was existing in 1843 with fifteen members. Its badge was a rectangular gold plate, upon which, within an ornamental border, the appropriate emblems were engraved. These did not much resemble the last badge of the Diggers, as the crown was a much more elaborate and highly ornamented affair, and the sword and scepter were crossed behind rather than within it. An existing poster showing a wood-cut of the simple emblems bears the direction, " S.T.G. 8.30 A.M." Another poster, which perhaps had no connection with this or any other society, shows the three letters "Iota Kappa Sigma," printed in heavy black type, with "24 D" appended. Still another, represents a naked figure just trundling over a precipice a wheelbarrow in which are loaded a

skull and some bones and a scroll and a key and a star
and a dart. The "Star and Dart" society was established in 1843, and apparently occupied a position
somewhat analogous to the present one of Bull and
Stones, though it really had an organization of some
sort. The frame-work of its rectangular gold-plate
badge was an exact copy of that of the Bones pin, and
the emblems of the two societies now existing formed
the chief part of the engraved central design. The
eagle of Keys, that is to say, was represented as fiercely
picking to pieces the Skull and Bones at its feet, while
a Dart, appearing in the right upper corner, was about
to destroy the eagle, and a Star in the left upper corner
was supposed to denote "the prosperity and final success of the society over its rivals." A wood-cut copy
of this design surmounted the following notice printed
among the advertisements of a New Haven newspaper:
"*Nos in vita fratres sumus.* C. 2954 a. F. ∞ dd Z ∪ ⊣.
There will be a general meeting in New Haven on
Thursday evening, Aug. 15, 1844. Yale College, Aug.
10." Possibly there were other Commencement times
at which a similar notice was printed, and doubtless
posters to the same effect used also to be displayed
about the college buildings at such seasons. After a
period of suspended animation, the society was revived
in the class of '49, and the members belonging to it in
the classes of '50 and '51 (fifteen in one case, eleven in
the other) had their names published in the *Banner*, in
connection with the society cut and the numeral "2954."
From this publicity, as well as the character of many
of the members, it is to be inferred that there was
really a little something *to* the society, and that its
existence was not altogether contemptible. Whether it
had a hall of its own, and regular weekly meetings and
exercises; whether it made any pretensions to equality

with the two reputable societies; whether it was so hostile to them as its badge would imply; whether its crowd was made up before, at the same time, or after the other elections were given out; and whether it died by choice or by necessity,—all these things, on the other hand, must remain uncertainties, until some traitorous ex-member thereof shall reveal to an anxiously expectant world the real history and mystery of the late Star and Dart.

Among the many Bones men worthy of mention are: Henry C. Kingsley of '34, treasurer of the college; Prof. Thomas A. Thacher of '35; Col. Henry C. Deming of '36; Attorney General William M. Evarts, Profs. Chester S. Lyman and Benjamin Silliman, of '37; Rev. Dr. Joseph P. Thompson of '38; Prevost Charles J. Stillé of '39; Prof. James M. Hoppin of '40; Gen. William T. S. Barry and Donald G. Mitchell, of '41; Henry Stevens, F. R. S., of '43; Senator Orris S. Ferry of '44; Gen. Dick Taylor of '45; Henry B. Harrison of '46; Henry T. Blake and Dwight Foster, of '48; Charles G. Came, Profs. William B. Clark and Timothy Dwight, of '49; President Andrew D. White of '53; Dr. John W. Hooker of '54; Rev. Elisha Mulford of '55; William H. W. Campbell, editor of the Norwich *Bulletin*, Chauncey M. Depew, N. Y. secretary of State, and Prof. Lewis R. Packard, of '56; Gen. John T. Croxton and Prof. Cyrus Northrop, of '57; Addison Van Name of '58, librarian of the college; Eugene Schuyler of '59, U. S. consul at Moscow; Edward R. Sill of '61; and Prof. Edward B. Coe of '62. The most prominent Keys men have already been mentioned in naming its twelve incorporators, but additional names to be noticed are: Gen. Theodore Runyon of '42; Rev. Dr. Gordon Hall of '43; Robert P. Farris of '47, editor of the Missouri *Republican*; Rev. John E. Todd of '55, son of Rev. Dr. Todd, the opponent of college secret societies ; Sidney E. Morse of '56, publisher of the N. Y. *Observer ;* Gen. John W. Swayne of '56 ; Dr. Daniel G. Brinton of '58 ; Prof. Daniel C. Eaton of '60 ; and Joseph L. Shipley of '61, editor of the Scranton *Republican.* Five Keys men and one Digger made up the famous " Wilbur Bacon crew" of 1865.

Formerly, when Seniors took a more active part than now in the junior societies, men who did not belong to these were often chosen to the senior societies, but of late a membership in the former is a necessary stepping stone for admission to the latter ; not confessedly, of course, but by the rule which is sure to force a junior society into electing every man eligible for election a year later, and to compel every such man to accept such election. It has been noticed of late years that Psi U generally has a majority in Bones, and DKE in Keys, though in '71 Psi U had six men in Bones and nine in Keys, to DKE's nine and six. It should not be inferred from this that senior-society men allow their junior year or earlier society connections to prejudice them in elect-ing their successors. They apparently have regard for the interests of their senior society simply, and choose those whom they think will most benefit it, without much regard to outside considerations. Much of the excitement over the election of Cochs and *Lit.* Editors turns upon the question of senior societies. Each one of these officers is supposed to " stand a chance," and shortly after their election the two "crowds" begin defi-nitely to be made up. There are always some "sure men" to form a nucleus,—the Spoon Man for instance, is always certain of receiving a Bones election,—and about these the "likely" ones who are not quite so " sure" try to "pack" themselves. Thus a "crowd" is made up in the interest of each society. Its members

" run" together constantly, call one another by their first names, and make a great display of familiarity,—especially in the presence of "their" Seniors,—as much as to say, "We can't be separated. Take all of us or none." This sort of thing is practised chiefly by prospective Keys men, who can make up their crowd with a tolerable certainty that their evident wishes will be respected by the society. It is seldom that Keys ventures to keep out more than a single man from a well defined pack, and substitute one of their own choosing in his place. Such a pack really has the power in its own hands, and should the members of it agree to "stand by one another" they could of course carry their point ; but the refusal of a senior-society election, even conditionally, seems so terrible a thing, that they have rarely the courage to make a direct demand. Keys, however, has in some instances been obliged to submit to such dictation. The society undoubtedly winks at "packing," and indirectly gives it on occasions its official aid,— though not as frequently nor as extensively as is sometimes reported. There are so many conflicting elements in the Bones crowd that it is never organized into a regular pack, and there is always more doubt as to the way its elections will turn. The nearest approach to a pack is when two or three "sure men" take it upon themselves to persistently "run" another, and make such a display of their fondness for him as to secure his election also. However Bones may allow its action to be affected indirectly, it will not be dictated to when once its elections have been made up, and it is useless for a man to attempt to alter the result by conditionally refusing his election, in favor of or against some particular classmate. Though the Bones crowd may be pretty accurately guessed at for some days before the elections are issued, it is the chances of its individuals which are

9*

estimated, not of the crowd as such, as in the case of Keys. There is no such general collusion of all the members of the Bones crowd ; it is rather made up of separate cliques of twos and threes, and single individuals, who hope for Bones elections, but have not much else in common. The fact that elections to this latter society have been refused in favor of Keys is hence not very difficult of explanation. A man whose chances for Bones are rather doubtful may be willing to throw them away altogether for the sake of the comparatively "sure thing" which he gains by joining a pack for Keys. So, receiving an election to Bones, he is in honor bound to decline it, and cling to the men with whom he had joined his fortunes. It will be found that all the Bones refusals in '67 and '70, over which so much ado was made, came in every case from men previously packed for Keys. Thus, Bones' greater independence and ceremoniousness sometimes work to its own disadvantage. A man may go to Keys for the sake of taking a friend or two with him whose companionship he could not be sure of were he to become a Bones men ; and in general one has less uncertainty as to whom he will have to fraternize with when he packs for the former society.

In a direct comparison of the societies, it is seen that Bones in reputation, influence and prestige is altogether superior to its rival ; and it seems almost as certain that it must always retain this preëminence. It is, in its main features, essentially unique. No other college society can show so large a proportion of distinguished and successful members. It is probably not too much to add that of the Yale graduates of the past generation who have attained a fair degree of worldly eminence, nearly half will be found to have been included within the mystic fifteens of this organization. Its apparent aim is to secure at once the best of the good scholars, good literary men, and good fellows; the former to bring it dignity and "tone," the latter to preserve its social and convivial character; and its success in equalizing these three elements—one of which is apt to predominate in a society—has been remarkable. It develops in its members, too, a genuine pride and affection, such as they feel in or towards no other society. Men who are careless and frivolous and selfish as to everything else, manifest an earnestness and a generosity where Bones is concerned, that is really surprising. And this, too, in a way not calculated to attract attention, nor suggest an appearance of exaggeration or make-believe. Keys men, on the other hand, are rather given to displaying their society zeal as much as possible. Old members who come from abroad to attend the "bums" are apt to make their presence generally known, and take pains to exhibit the extent of their "interest." Their affection for the society is no doubt genuine enough, but their carefulness in displaying it suggests the idea that its inspiration comes quite as much from an oppressive self-consciousness of the need of "going one better" than Bones, as from the simple force of pleasant associations. Since the time, say about 1860, when Keys came to be recognized as a reputable society, settled upon an invariable membership of fifteen, and ceased to give out any class, secret, or honorary elections, its policy has seemed to be the making prominent of the social element, the choosing of good, jolly fellows,—men of ability if possible, but at all events congenial and in the college sense of the word gentlemanly. Ability in the absolute, that is to say, has been accounted of secondary importance as a qualification for membership. Upon a strict and more rigorous adherence to this policy in the future—if it be worth while to express a prevalent college opinion—

the success of the society will in great measure depend. In the latter's own chosen field, it can never hope to seriously rival Bones. To the "solid," thoughtful men of the class—the big scholars and writers—Bones will always be the more attractive, and if Keys enters into competition for them it will as inevitably have to take up with second-rate representatives of the "heavy," "respectable" element, at the same time that, by this very action, it renders itself less alluring to the "popular men," who are and should be its "best hold." If, on the other hand, it has the tact to depart for once from its Bones model, and set up an independent standard of qualifications of its own, it may in time gain in its own particular field a recognized preëminence. Keys' real "mission," as it seems to an outsider, is to draw together a genial, gentlemanly crowd, rather than an "able" one. If a pleasant, agreeable fellow chances to be possessed of something more substantial than popularity,—if besides being a gentleman, he be also a scholar, a writer, an energetic worker,— he should of course be all the more desirable ; yet the first mentioned, more trivial, qualities should be regarded as the essential ones, after all, which recommend him for election. Ability, real or reputed, should never of itself elect a man to Keys. The prestige the society may gain by taking a man simply for his reputation cannot make up for what it thereby loses in attractiveness for "popular men." Keys' great opportunity is, by excluding all others, to make itself the most desirable society for the agreeable, jolly fellows in every senior class. If it resolutely adopts this "lay," it may, with the help of its hall, ere many years, leave Bones in the lurch, so far as "popular" men are concerned; and, by occupying an independent field, prevent the possibility of direct comparisons which must always be to its own disadvantage.

This seems so manifest that nothing but a foolish over-confidence in its own strength can induce it to engage in a " straight fight " on Bones' own chosen field, where, with all the odds against it, it must ever suffer defeat. Bones, on the other hand, would do well to consider whether it will be worth its while much longer to take in men for their popularity and agreeableness simply. It is just here that it has met with its most humiliating rebuffs hitherto, and that it is likely to meet with worse ones hereafter, unless it changes its policy. Four of the five '70 men who rejected Bones in favor of Keys, were simply " good fellows," who would have been somewhat out of their element in the crowd of the former society ; and the case in the class of '67 was very similar. If Bones should insist more strongly than now upon ability as a prime essential in all its members, and upon this basis, modified by a reasonable regard for social qualities and harmoniousness, elect them, it would secure itself almost absolutely from having an election rejected, as well as add to its own lasting reputation,—even at the sacrifice of one of its cherished traditions, which it has managed to perpetuate thus far on the whole with a fair share of success. Whether Bones makes this concession with good grace at the outset, or waits to be forced into it by the success of Keys, when the latter shall turn all its energies upon this one point, remains to be seen. But appearances certainly point to the coming, at no distant day, of what may be termed a senior society millennium, when Bones and Keys shall each occupy an undisputed field of its own, and each be recognized as in its own sphere preëminent ; and when the only question in a man's mind shall be, " In which field, on the whole, is supremacy the more desirable ? " Then shall the Death's head be, even more certainly than now, the badge of intellectual superiority in college repute, and the unfolded Scroll be, even more invariably, the emblem of gentlemanly good fellowship and social popularity.

It was remarked at the beginning of the chapter that societies like Bones and Keys would be possible only at one other college than Yale, and that as a matter of fact they are peculiar to the latter institution. They are not, however, without imitators. At Columbia College is an "Axe and Coffin"; at Michigan University an "Owl and Padlock"; and at Wesleyan University are a "Skull and Serpent" and an "Owl and Wand." None of them are of any importance, and with the possible exception of the second, are in every way inferior to the Greek-letter societies connected with their respective institutions. There is no special difficulty in imitating the peculiar names and mummeries of the Yale senior societies, but the gaining of a similar prestige and influence is quite another matter. It is the high character of their members, not their names and forms and ceremonies, which give the Yale societies their fame. It was a belief in the power of these latter non-essentials that induced the Diggers to persist so long in a worse than hopeless fight. At Yale, the strictly class societies of the first three years supply the machinery by which every class is carefully sifted and its best men are "brought out" in readiness for the senior societies. Yet even here, with from one hundred to one hundred and twenty men to pick from, and the three years' sifting process reduced almost to an exact science, it has been absolutely demonstrated that no more than two societies, of fifteen men each, can exist. Indeed, it was for a long time a problem whether more than one could live, and even now the two, to be at their best, must occupy somewhat different fields. But at other colleges, where no such class system prevails, where the numbers to select from are much smaller, where the competing societies are more numerous, the attempt to ape Bones and Keys can succeed in nothing save in making the would-be societies ridiculous. In view of their real worth, people may be willing to overlook the silly practices of the Yale senior societies; but when mock mystery and cheap ceremonials are the only things which a society has to boast of, it cannot well help falling into contempt. The statement is therefore again repeated that Bones and Keys are peculiarly Yale institutions, genuine outgrowths of a system that flourishes nowhere else, the only organizations of the kind existing in the country.

In concluding this account of the class societies, it may be well to add a few additional facts that are true alike of many or all of them, and to compare directly their general character in the different years. Each society, save Gamma Nu, has a "grip" of its own, but society men, in either of the four years, do not generally employ it in greeting one another. It is not a popular device with them, and comparitively few would be able, a year or two after graduation, to give the four different grips correctly, were they to try. Many of the active members, even, of these societies cannot remember their grips without an effort, and in junior year, when visitors from other chapters are expected, there is need of some preliminary practice before the guests can be welcomed in true mysterious fashion. At other colleges the society grips are constantly made use of, and when a Yale man who has forgotten his grip meets an outside brother he extends his hand with all the fingers separated, and returns the grip that he receives, in full faith that he has given "the right one" and concealed his ignorance. It is easy enough for an outsider to find out from someone or other the reputed grips of the dozen or less societies, and it is more than likely that these are really the true ones in many cases. But the whole matter is made so little of by Yale men that none of these peculiar hand shakings are worth describing. In the published report of a recent DKE convention, that society announced that it had adopted a new grip and motto,—presumably on account of the discovery of its old ones, and probably at the instance of the outside chapters. Whether the changes were really made, or the announcement offered simply as a "blind," the result was of course the same. The only two Yale society mottoes that seem to be unknown to outsiders are, oddly enough, those of Delta Kap and Theta Psi. That of the former used to be, *Δεσμός Κρύφιος*, and was as well known as Sigma Eps's is at present, but the one which superseded it and is now in vogue has been by some miracle prevented from leaking out. Every junior society man can find out without much difficulty the mottoes and " secrets" of the other societies in his class, but he feels in duty bound not to make public his knowledge, and the neutrals are generally in ignorance of these matters. At Yale, one society never thinks of breaking into the hall of another, and making public all its mysteries, as is the practice at some of the smaller colleges. It is through these that some of the Yale junior-society secrets are divulged. Chapters which think it a fine thing to steal the constitution and documents of as many rival societies as possible, when they chance to gain those of societies which are also rivals at Yale, may forward to their brothers at the latter place their ill-gotten knowledge : knowledge which the latter are usually honorable enough to keep to themselves. It is only in the songs of the first two years that the societies mention the names of their rivals,—to ridicule them, of course, but in a good natured way. A secret ballot, upon each candidate separately, in which a single blackball rejects, is the mode of election in all these societies. Every society has a janitor whom it allows to wear its badge. While '69 was in college the same individual was at once janitor of Delta Kap, Theta Psi and Psi U, and wore either one of the badges indifferently, though never displaying two at a time. A senior-society janitor is not allowed to serve for under-class organizations. The present Bones janitor is a negro named Robert, who assists the professors in the experiments at the philosophical lectures, and is a sort of college supernumerary. His predecessor, also a black man, died in the service, and was followed to his grave by the whole Bones society, resident graduates, solemn professors, and all. The societies of the two upper years have boxes at the post office wherein is placed all mail matter directed either to their popular or official, trust-association, titles. A letter directed to either of the lower-class societies is exposed to view beside the general-delivery window, until discovered and called for by one of the members. Society men as a rule preserve all their badges,—sometimes, in senior year, mounting their previously gained insignia in a velvet-lined, ornamental frame or case. Quite a number of freshman pins are disposed of, however, when the time for wearing them is past, and some sophomore and a very few junior badges go the same way, but a senior-society pin is kept by its owner until death doth them part. By other college men their junior-society badge, usually the only one they ever possess, is as a rule always preserved, and is in many cases steadily worn for some years after graduation. Yale men, who were senior neutrals, sometimes display their junior badge, on special occasions, after graduation, but never the pin of a lower society. When a Freshman leaves college he usually takes off his society pin, but a Sophomore, if a society man, is likely to wear his badge for some time after his withdrawal.

In taking a general look at the societies of the four years, the first seems a working ground where Freshmen may display their abilities, and induce the Juniors to pledge them ; the second, a place where these pledged men as Sophomores may be kept quiet until they are further inspected, and the poor ones got rid off ; the third, another working ground of narrower limits, where the select Juniors who have passed safely through two sifting processes may, by making the most of their talents before the Seniors, prevail upon the latter to spare them in the last grand turn of the sieve, and elect them into the fourth, beyond which there is nothing higher. It is a fault of the system that each society save the last is only a stepping stone to the next, and when the last is reached the time left to enjoy it in is short indeed. The size of the classes, and the class feeling thereby engendered, makes any other system impossible, while the system in turn tends to strengthen and perpetrate the class feeling. From his freshman society, a man usually gains considerable solid advantage, and a fair amount of pleasure. The direct benefit of a sophomore-society experience is not very great, and a man loses less by being a neutral this year than any other,— sophomore neutrals being often elected to senior societies,—but still, he does lose something, both in a peculiar sort of " fun," and in general social position. In a third-year society the advantages are many, and are of a general as well as local character. The occasions thus afforded for members of different colleges to fraternize together, the opportunities given for making pleasant acquaintances at unexpected places, are evidently of considerable value. A man's interest in his junior society is not as intense or as lasting at Yale as at other colleges, yet it is altogether greater than that which he feels toward any lower-class society. One

Yale graduate would not be apt to claim introduction to another on the score of belonging to the same junior society, yet, once acquainted for some other reason, this fact would form a sort of bond between them. The attempt to make an outsider realize the overwhelming fascination, which a senior society exerts upon the mind of the average Yale undergraduate, would probably be useless. An election thereto is valued more highly than any other college prize or honor ; and in fact these honors derive a good part of their attractiveness from their supposed efficacy in helping to procure the coveted election. There is nothing in the wide world that seems to him half so desirable. It is the one thing needful for his perfect happiness. And if he fails in gaining it, the chances are that he becomes a temporary misanthropist, that is to say, an ardent " Stones man." Though the advantages of membership are no doubt exaggerated in anticipation, the real benefit gained in belonging to a senior society is certainly considerable,—far more valuable, in fact, than that which accrues from membership in any other. Quite aside from the enjoyment of the senior year itself, the facts that in after life a man is thus introduced to the best graduates of the college, wherever he may meet them, and that, whenever he visits New Haven, he is sure of being entertained by the best of the oldest undergraduates, and instructed as to the doings and whereabouts of the best of his former classmates,—these facts, other things being equal, of themselves make membership in a senior society especially desirable.

College friendships do not at Yale run very closely in society lines. A pair of friends may be brought together or separated by almost numberless society combinations. They may belong to the same society in each of the four years, or in the first and last, or in the second and third, or in none at all, or one may be a society man and another a neutral for all the course, and so on through all the possible permutations. Still, it is pleasant for friends to keep in the same societies, and a general tendency of certain crowds to go together, year after year, has been already remarked upon. No neutral as such is looked down upon or avoided by society men. If the latter usually "run" together, it is because of similar tastes and proclivities, which would induce them to do so, were no societies in existence. In senior year there is hardly a society man without one or two special friends who are neutrals, and with whom he has quite as much to do as with his own regular associates. Such pairs oftener chum together than do two from rival societies; though this sometimes happens, and previous to senior year is not at all uncommon. Aside from a man's real or reputed ability, good nature, and popularity, a thing which often helps to elect him is his relationship to a former or active member of the society. If a father or an uncle or a brother has preceeded him, the fact helps him to follow in their footsteps, especially if they were in any way famous. An older brother in the class above, or even one or two classes removed, is almost certain to secure the election of a younger one, unless the latter is peculiarly unqualified or obnoxious. This species of favoritism attracts the most attention in the case of the senior societies, into which nearly every year, by his relationship with an older and worthier member, is dragged one man at least who is without other qualifications sufficient to recommend him. The cases of poor men taken in are, by the bye, a good deal more common and noticeable than those of desirable men left out. Every year almost there is a great show of indignation over the injustice in the senior-society elections which bring several big men to grief, yet it rarely happens that the good policy of the society in leaving them out is not vindicated within a twelve month. When fifteen men are to be shut up together for six successive hours, every week, and be thrown in with each other constantly, it is essential that they should be reasonably harmonious if not congenial ; and an organization whose members should be chosen for their reputation and ability simply, could not be in the right sense of the word a society.

Without now discussing whether college opinion always awards men the positions they deserve, it may be said, in conclusion, that the society system, viewed as a means for separating those who, for whatever reason, are high in college esteem, from those who, for whatever reason, are not, must be admitted to be in the main a fair and successful one. No one can reasonably deny that it has this effect, and that the society men of every year are as a class superior in college repute to the neutrals. It would of course be foolish to judge an individual solely by his society connections, but it would be far less foolish than to judge him solely by the number of prizes, or scholorships, or honors he could lay claim to, as is not infrequently the practice. To set up any one arbitrary standard whereby to judge character is manifestly unfair, yet, if it is to be done, there is no single test which embraces so many, in making an estimate of a Yale man's importance, as his share in the society system. Blockheads and simpletons certainly find their way into the senior societies, yet there are few generalities of the sort deserving of more confidence than these, that in a Bones man you will find ability and force of character, in a Keys man politeness and geniality, and in both the most favorable samples of the Yale graduate of the period.

CHAPTER V.

SOCIETY INSTITUTIONS.

Linonia, and Brothers in Unity—Their Origin and Early History—
Rivalry in Gaining Members—The Statement of Facts—The
Campaign, a Dozen Years Ago—The Rush—Latest Modes of
Distributing the Freshmen—Initiation—Meetings and Exercises
—Exhibitions—Officers, Politics, and the Campaign Election—
Attendance—Management of the Finances—The Society Halls
—Catalogues—Libraries—Reading Room—The College Book-
store—The Prize Debates—Annual and Centennial Celebrations
—Analysis of the Society Tax—Calliope and Phœnix—Phi Beta
Kappa — Its Origin and Peculiar Organization — Names of the
Chapters—Meetings and Exercises—Orations and Poems—Qual-
ifications for Membership — An Invasion of Barbarians — The
Society Badge Key—Initiation —The Annual Business Meeting
—Catalogues—Significance of the Fraternity—Chi Delta Theta
—Its Literary Character—The Present Wearers of its Badge.

Some of the societies which were the precursors of
the modern system still have a sort of semi-animate
existence in the college, in the form of mere "institutions," and they, and the customs springing from them,
are therefore all described here under that general title.
The first, both in age, reputation and importance are
the societies of "Linonia" and "Brothers in Unity."
Except where great formality is required, the latter title
is always abbreviated to "Brothers"; and each member of the society was called a "Brother." Each member of the "Linonian Society," as the favorite cere-
monious name for it used to be, was termed a "Linonian." These titles are rarely used of late, and a man
is simply said to "belong to" Linonia or Brothers, as
the case may be. Both are spoken of indifferently as

the literary, the large, the open, the general, or the college societies,—the comparative frequency of the names perhaps being in the order given. Linonia was founded September 12, 1753. Of the class which graduated that year, numbering 17 in all, one only belonged to the society. He was the seventeenth on the list—the names at that time being arranged according to the " gentility " of the families they represented, instead of alphabetically—and his name was William Wickham. Besides this, little more is known concerning him, save that he afterwards took his Master's degree, lived on Long Island, and died in 1813. According to repute, he was the founder of the society, and its first chancellor,—that being the name applied to the president up to the year 1789. In the first 15 classes (1753–67), Linonia had 150 of the 400 men who graduated, or an average of 10 to a class,—the highest number being 16, and the lowest, after the first class, 4. Of the 250 not included in its catalogue, it is likely that a large portion were members of " Crotonia," a rival society which had been for some time in existence when Linonia was founded, but which must have died out within 15 years thereafter.

Brothers was founded in 1768, by 21 individuals in the four classes '68, '69, '70, and '71,—seven being upper-class men who seceded from Linonia, and the remaining 14 being Freshmen, who were of course neutrals, as in those days of servitude no Freshmen were ever admitted to any society whatever. Oliver Stanley of '68, the first president of Brothers, was said by tradition to have been the founder of the society, and was so mentioned in the eulogy pronounced at the time of his death in 1813. But the popular hero of the affair was David Humphreys of '71, " who stood up for the dignity of his class ; and having found two

Seniors, three Juniors and two Sophomores, who were willing that Freshmen might be admitted to a literary society, he, with thirteen of his classmates fought for and established their own respectability." He was afterwards a colonel in the Revolution, served as aid-de-camp and secretary to Washington, fought bravely at Yorktown, presented to Congress the British colors surrendered by Cornwallis, and was awarded " an elegant sword " by direct vote of that body. He was dubbed LL.D. by both Brown and Dartmouth, was Fellow of the Royal Society, and ambassador to Spain. He died in 1818. Of the 19 who graduated in his class, 15 were Brothers and 4 were Linonians. In the class of '75 the corresponding figures were 3 and 33. And so it changed about, one society being specially successful in some years, the other in others ; but the disparity was not usually as great as in the cases indicated, and in most years the classes were about equally divided. Hence, in the 33 classes, 1768 to 1800, Linonia claimed 560 and Brothers 569 men, all of whom were said to be graduates ; but as only 1110 men graduated from college in the interval, and some few of these in the earlier classes remained neutrals, several of the non-graduates must have remained upon the lists. It may be noted that the class ('68) which founded Brothers was the first whose names in the college catalogue were arranged alphabetically.

The exclusion of Freshmen from Linonia seems to have been the only attempt ever made at selectness in membership, — all who applied for admission in sophomore year or afterwards having been, apparently, welcomed to the fold. As soon as Brothers had established the precedent, of course Linonia was obliged to elect Freshmen also, and the two societies soon settled down into an annual strife to decide which should gain the largest number of each incoming class. As the average number obtained by each was about equal, in 1801 it was agreed that all new comers should be allotted in alphabetical order to the two societies,— the first man on the list going to Linonia, the second to Brothers, the third to Linonia, the fourth to Brothers, and so on to "Z," or the end of the class. It happened that John C. Calhoun of '04 was allotted to Linonia, but refused to join that society, as most of the Southerners went to Brothers ; and hence both societies have claimed him as a member until this day. Doubtless an arrangement was effected whereby two men allotted to different societies could exchange places, if they cared to, but the system of alphabetical distribution remained in vogue until the year 1830. Then, open war was once more declared, and each society again began to plead its cause before each freshman class. The custom known as "Statement of Facts" was now introduced. In theory, and perhaps originally in reality, the plan was as follows : On the first or second Wednesday of the college year, the entire freshman class was invited to a public hall, and there addressed by the president, senior orator, and junior orator of each society, on the relative merits and advantages of the two organizations ; and at the close of the speeches, each freshman was called upon to indicate the society of his choice. Such was the theory, which, if ever practised in all its simplicity, was not long in becoming a mere farce, owing to the campaign meetings, and electioneerings, and pledgings, which preceded the Statement of Facts. The mode in which the freshman societies now gain their members is the same as that formerly used for recruiting Linonia and Brothers. The lesser campaign has simply superseded the greater, and the description already given of it will in most points apply well enough to the latter ; but it may be well to quote from an account written in 1859 of the way in which the large societies were accustomed to manage affairs :

" The campaign of warfare commences with the fourth week of the summer term, when the campaign presidents are chosen for the new senior class, and the new sophomore class—which is to bear the brunt of the battle—is marshalled for the fight.   The officers, on whom falls the personal responsibility of victory or defeat, remind them, with serious earnestness, of the great responsibility which has fallen on their shoulders ; they tell them that they are carrying into the contest the banner that has long waved in victory over their old fraternity ; that thousands are waiting anxiously to see if its folds, as of yore, are still to wave in honor and glory, or whether they are to droop in ignominy and shame before the foe who have so often cowered before them !   But they by no means trust merely to nicely worded speeches.   The class is thoroughly organized for the battle.   The labor is divided and sub-divided as far as the interests of the campaign demands.   General committees, and special committees of correspondence, are appointed to find out by every means in their power who are coming into the next freshman class and whence.   To the larger academies, and usual tributaries of the college, special electioneerers are sent, and skirmishes are fought long before the main battle begins in New Haven.   Meantime, the weekly meetings are the occasions of enthusiastic speeches, the subjects of which are the history and glory of one society, and the faults imaginary or real of the other.   As the battle thickens, the cohorts increase in activity and enthusiasm.   The committees for the Tontine Hotel and the New Haven House scan closely the journal of names, and follow to his room every suspicious-looking youth.   The steamboat committee are on duty at five in the morning and at eight at night. The depot committee grow hardened to their work, lay aside all gentlemanly feeling, and pounce upon the unwary. The railroad committees ride from New Haven to Springfield, to Guilford, to Bridgeport, and New York. They endeavor to make themselves agreeable to any fellow travelers, provided they be young, and look haggard, in view of some specter like an approaching examination. The room committee report the items of knowledge that they have culled in a careful survey of every tree and dilapidated building around the college, to headquarters, to be put in immediate requisition, should any Freshman desire a night's abode. With such an array of preparation on both sides, the harmless Freshman runs a poor chance of escaping the fiery ordeal. Many come pledged to join one or the other society, and over them there is of course no struggle. Others fall into the hands of one party only, and any access to them is denied the other until they shall have decided. But to those whose destiny throws them into a crowd of contending Sophomores, in the dark and smoky cavern, called the New Haven depot, especially if the least sign of indecision or perplexity is perceptible, there is no longer hope of rest or quiet or comfort ; not even liberty and the pursuit of happiness being allowed them until they decide the momentous question.

"During the days of examination for admission to college, and a few days previous, the societies put forth their utmost energies, and instead of meetings once a week they are held two and three times a day. For every Freshman that enters the hall, speeches must be made, to recount the incomparable history, the superior prize-lists, the immense advantages of this society over its rival. The work of the officers and of the various committees is at this time exceedingly laborious, and would never be undertaken were it not for the personal honor attending it ; and would never be completed were it not for the enthusiasm which the contest always inspires.   The enthusiasm is undoubtedly real, and although the fight is renewed from year to year, the same notes rung, the same old story told, from meeting to meeting, there is music in these notes and a strength in that story which, especially to a class for the first time engaging in those scenes, is stirring and effective. The vociferous applause which is given to the speeches, the hearty greeting with which every new-comer is met, shows the presence of unbounded enthusiasm.

"There are comparatively few who come to college without a knowledge of the system of electioneering. Most are prepared for it.   But even then, if they have not decided, they cannot remain free from interruption, unless at all hours they lock their doors and demand freedom.   Some, however, arrive at New Haven before they know even of the existence of such societies. Their ignorance affords opportunities for successful mis-representations and cunning duplicity, of which many take advantage.   The temptation, coming together with the excitement of the campaign is greatly increased. The contest is generally decided before the second week of the fall term.   At the close of the first week, when there is scarcely one who has not already joined one or the other society, is repeated the annual farce of what was once a Statement of Facts in behalf of each society, by appointed orators.   It is now rather a field for the display of empty eloquence and skill at repartee. Any distortion of facts which seems to confound their opponents, or to turn the laugh upon them is considered as the most acceptable part of the proceeding.   The Freshmen, for whose enlightenment the exercises are specially intended, attend in mass. A general struggle with the Sophomores—whose duty, now that electioneering is no longer necessary, tradition says, is to prevent the Freshmen getting into the hall without first taking off their hats—is the first thing on the programme. They then take the seats that are reserved for them, with fragments of their hats in their hands, and of their coats on their backs, amid a yelling, screeching and cheering which is perfectly indescribable. After their indignation against the Sophomores has cooled down, they begin to applaud almost continually their own and hiss the orators of the rival society. At the close of the meeting, the students adjourn to the halls of their respective societies, where the result of the campaign is officially proclaimed. One society celebrates a jubilee : the other waits for a 'better time coming.'"

Brewster's Hall was the usual place of holding the "Statement," but Union Hall served instead on at least one occasion, and in 1861, the last time any such meeting was held, the faculty granted the use of Alumni Hall. The "rush" attendant upon this celebration seems to have been regarded as in some sense a substitute for the old Foot-Ball Game, and both seem to have degenerated into the common street rushes of to-day. The meeting of 1860 was thus described: "It began of course with the usual abominable 'rush.' Defiant Sophomores dared hopeful Freshmen to 'come on.' They did so. They sopped each other in the gutter, crunched each other's toes, and, when they got tired, adjourned up stairs ; the Freshmen to look attentive and listen to the arguments offered by the societies, the Sophomores to look depraved and throw beans at nearly everybody except the speakers. Seven o'clock, post meridian, was the hour for reassembling. The Sophomores looked as wicked as ever, and the Freshmen as hopeful as ever. Again the initiatory plunge, again the wallow in the gutter, again the tugging, straining, button-bursting operations, and then they all crowd into seats and listen to the remainder of the story each society is anxious to tell."

In 1859 an unsuccessful attempt was made to bring both societies to an agreement, whereby all private electioneering should be done away with and no Freshman should be pledged to either society, until the close of the Statement of Facts, when each should signify the one of his choice. The campaign meetings of each society were to be held on alternate evenings, and the society which had the last meeting, was to give up to the other the first chance for speaking at the Statement. This plan was adopted on the following year, and perhaps in 1861 also; but for the next four years thereafter there was open war again; and the only thing at all resembling a Statement of Facts, was a gathering in one of the society halls, where the two presidents simply announced the official figures of the campaign,— the result being of course received with tremendous cheering and enthusiasm by the partisans of the victorious society. The Sophs, as of old, waited outside to rush the Fresh who might try to attend; but the faculty probably interfered with the sport, for when '69 —which was the last class electioneered—entered college in 1865, there was no attempt at a rush, nor was it generally known among the Freshmen when the final results of that last campaign were proclaimed.

For the next two years, the new-comers were distributed alphabetically between the two societies, and allowed to "pair off" in cases when they had any preference. In 1868, this plan was somewhat modified by the introduction of a sort of travesty on the old Statement of Facts. Eight orators, two from each of the two upper classes in each society, were appointed to make as ludicrous speeches as possible in regard to the "merits of the societies." In the old times, statements utterly without foundation in fact were common enough, but they were earnestly made, with the intention of misleading and deceiving the Freshmen, and the speakers did not ridicule their own societies. Now, the speeches all take their point from their simple absurdity, and want of purpose. Everything that is said, whether of praise or censure, is spoken ironically, and accepted as a joke by the upper-class men who know how dead the societies are. The Freshmen also laugh with the rest, without exactly knowing the reason why. At the close of the addresses, they are called upon to join one society or the other, and those who are not present—that is, a large majority of the class—are distributed alphabetically, as before. Though there is no regular "rush," the Sophs annoy the Fresh in coming up the stairway— the meeting being held in one of the society halls—and interrupt proceedings generally, by snapping beans about the hall, and making other diversions of a similar character. The two upper classes, especially the Juniors, respond to the president's calls for "order" by attempting to eject from the hall some disorderly Sophomore ; whereupon the classmates of the latter rally to his defence, and a wild tumult ensues,—the result of which is that most of the Sophomores are forcibly thrust out and the door locked behind them. In revenge for this indignity, they smash the windows of the hall, and raise discordant outcries, while their comrades who were left inside loudly clamor for their readmittance. At last they are allowed to enter again, and the "exercises" proceed as before.

The form of initiation in vogue when '69 entered college was for each new-comer to assent to the pledge of fidelity to the society—thereby promising to be "true to its interests and faithful to its secrets"—and sign his name in a book supposed to contain its constitution. The pledge was read off by the president, and three cheers were proposed by him or some other member for each one as he signed his name. A good part of each freshman class joined during the progress of the campaign meetings, and as some of them were unable to pass their entrance examinations, the lists of each society very often contained names of men never actually belonging to the college. The same fact is still true of the freshman societies,—one or two men who never "make up their conditions" being initiated into them almost every year. Now-a-days, a large share of college never formally join either Linonia or Brothers, although in the *Banner* and *Pot Pourri* the letter "L." or "B." is still prefixed to every name, to indicate membership in one or the other of them. Formerly the *Banner* gave each society separately, though arranged as now in classes. Nobody now cares which society he is assigned to ; and few, when asked, can readily tell which, without reference to a catalogue. No one ever pretends to remember the open-society connections of any one save himself ; and often in the making up of a joint committee, a man is appointed to represent one society when he really belongs to another, and perhaps he may even fulfil his duties without discovering the mistake.

It was perhaps during the first third of the present century that the societies saw their best days. The time when they came together was thought the gala night of all the week, and all classes met then on a footing of perfect equality,—though the Seniors naturally took the lead in affairs, and the Freshmen were for the most part interested spectators rather than actors. The literary efforts of the latter were mostly confined to their own class society or debating club, which held fortnightly meetings in one of the recitation rooms, had little organization and no name, and was disbanded at the close of the year,—the freshman clubs of no two successive classes having any connection with each other. Fifty years ago, when the general societies were absolutely secret, it was thought a great—as it was an infrequent —triumph for a man to find out the name of the president or other officers in a rival society. About a third of the members regularly attended the meetings; as many more went to the halls half of the time, and the remainder frequented them only occasionally. Attendance was not compulsory, except to fulfil appointments, and an "excusing committee" passed judgment on all excuses, at the close of each meeting. They reported to the librarians the names of those who refused to pay their fines, and the librarians in turn forbid such delinquent the privileges of the library until the claims of the society were satisfied. Brothers was nicknamed "the Cider Mill" by the men of Linonia, because it was said to conduct its debates strictly according to the catalogue,—obliging each man to speak in his "turn" as the alphabet had arranged it, and allowing no voluntary efforts outside this regular order.

Originally the societies were strictly secret, as already stated, and as late as 1840 none but members were expected to attend their meetings, save by formal invitations on special occasions, but for fifteen or twenty years past all college has been at liberty to frequent either hall, as much or as little as has seemed good to it. The ordinary meetings are held every Wednesday evening of the term, beginning at eight o'clock,—the hour of assembling being indicated by a ringing of the college bell. The chief feature of these exercises is a debate between four appointed disputants, two of them speaking on each side, on some question chosen by them or the president, three or four weeks previously. This debate is also "sustained" by as many impromptu speakers as can be induced to volunteer. Besides this, there are occasional essays, orations and poems. On "election nights," when the debate is suspended, an unusually good oration or poem is looked for, and "the other society" is often formally invited to hear it,—which invitation it as ceremoniously accepts or declines. The present tense is here employed, for the sake of convenience, to describe the state of things existing when '69 entered college, and still kept up in theory. As a matter of fact, no such meetings are now held. Sometimes a crowd of a dozen or fifteen chance together in one of the halls of a Wednesday evening, and hold any kind of ex-tempore exercises they may happen to think of. Often no one goes to the halls at all. Even the posters are not often seen now, and are never read or regarded. Formerly, almost every tree in the college yard had its red (Linonia) and blue (Brothers) posters tacked to it each Tuesday morning. On these were indicated the question for debate for the next meeting, with the names of the speakers, the names of the orator, essayist, etc., and the names of those appointed to speak at future meetings. A special notice of the time and nature of his appointment used also to be sent to each individual.

A custom which doubtless saw its best days within the fifteen or twenty years following 1825, was the giving of occasional "exhibitions," in which each society endeavored to surpass the other. The chief features of each of these "exhibitions" consisted of a dramatic poem, a tragedy, and a comedy, all written for the occasion by members of the society. These were never printed, but the "fragments of unpublished dramas," occasionally to be met with in the earlier volumes of the

Lit., give some notion of their quality. Except for the smaller type, the programmes resembled ordinary play-bills, being printed on one side of narrow strips of paper, sometimes two feet in length. The names of the two "managers" appeared at the foot of them. Some-times the true names of the actors were printed, and sometimes their fancy titles only. Each society accumulated quite a wardrobe of costumes, which it displayed to the Freshmen as an electioneering argument ; though the dresses were really common property, as each borrowed from the other. It is said that the faculty finally put an end to these "exhibitions," on the ground of their engrossing too much attention from the students.

The society offices—of president and vice-president in the senior class, secretary in the junior class, and vice-secretary in the sophomore class—used to be considered high honors, and were sharply contested for. Originally the officers served for a year, afterwards for a term, while for the past thirty years or more they have been chosen five times annually. A wide field was thus spread open for the practise of junior-society politics, and the wranglings over the elections were protracted and bitter. The office of campaign president or one first chosen from each senior class—the Juniors being recognized as Seniors within the meaning of the regulation, and the other two classes proportionate advanced, on the evening of the campaign election—was the special object of ambition, being considered the highest general elective honor of the college. All of the minor "campaign offices" were more eagerly sought for than the same positions at subsequent elections. Hence the amount of political intrigue, and wire-pulling, and log-rolling, expended in deciding the first election in these two societies was almost fabulous. The three lower classes were vitally interested in the matter, for each had a share in the spoils, and a vice-secretaryship might be as valuable in taking one man to Sigma Phi as a presidency in taking another man to Bones or Keys. The bargains and coalitions and combinations and cross-combinations made between the six junior and freshman societies were therefore all but innumerable, and far surpassed in intricacy anything now possible, when each class has its own independent politics. The class-society connections of the candidates seem always to have been considered, though it was only for the campaign election that formal coalitions were made. The mode of voting on that occasion was as follows : First, "the Seniors" were called for, and each member of the junior class, as his name was read, in alphabetical order, stepped forward and cast his ballot ; then " the Juniors" were called, and the Sophomores voted ; then, instead of calling "the Sophomores," "the Freshmen" were called for. Upon this, the Fresh would shriek, yell and hiss, until the secretary, correcting his " mistake" would address them as "Sophomores," when, with tremendous cheering and enthusiasm, the Freshmen would in turn march to the ballot-box. Should the first Fresh on the list be unaware of the trick, and start forward to vote at the first calling of his name as " a Freshman," he would be dragged back by his more watchful comrades, and the storm of hisses would grow terrific until the coveted name of " Sophomore" was announced. Printed blanks for voting were provided by the society ; but regular ballots, with the names of their candidates indicated in full, were usually supplied by the rival factions.

The vice-president was expected to sit in a chair at the side of the president, and was usually elected his successor. The secretary seems to have been a sort of ornamental officer, for all his work was performed by the vice-secretary, who sat at a table in front of the president's desk. The "censor" was an officer peculiar to Brothers, and perhaps used to read an occasional critique on the proceedings of the society. From this seems to have originated the comic "censor's report" of the Thanksgiving Jubilee. Now-a-days, the offices are filled by default, and any one who chooses to take a half-dozen friends with him to the hall on election night can have whatever one of them he may want. Who the officers may be, college in general neither knows nor cares; and they are all regarded with a mild sort of derision in the rare cases when they are thought of at all. Each society, with a nominal membership of 250, used to consider an ordinary meeting well attended when a tenth of that number were present. This was in the first of '69's four years: in the last, for a twentieth of the members to frequent the hall was considered extraordinary. The quorum needed to adopt the constitutional changes establishing a reading-room was only got together after repeated attempts, although the project was favored by every one. No quorum has assembled since then, and it is hardly probable that another will ever be drawn together. Up to 1860, a treasurer was included among the society officers, and the funds were managed by direct vote of its members. At that time the faculty were induced to have the college treasurer made tax-collector, and since then a society tax of $6—increased in 1867 to $8—a year has been assessed, in three equal instalments, upon the official term-bills. In the old times, about a third of the society dues were never collected, but now no undergraduate can shirk paying his "society tax" without defying "the president and fellows of Yale College," in whose name it is collected. Save for this arrangement, the societies, even as " institutions," would have ceased to exist, by the refusal of new-comers to join them or pay any money in their behalf. The $400 now annually collected in their names is expended under the direction of the assistant treasurer of the college.

The two society halls are in the upper story of the Alumni Hall building, and are of exactly the same size and shape,—measuring 50 by 25 feet, and 25 feet in hight. Both are handsomely furnished, though perhaps that of Brothers presents the most elegant appearance,—the upholstery and hangings being of blue, the society's color. The walls are also frescoed, and a large painting in which Col. Humphreys forms the chief figure hangs above the president's desk. In Linonia the seats are arranged in the form of a semi-circle, rising one above the other. Two life-size marble statues—the one of Demosthenes, the other of Sophocles—stand in the corners. They are copies of the antique, and were executed at Rome in 1858, by E. S. Bartholomew, especially for the society. It has long been a standing joke in college that no one is able to tell " which is which." As a set-off to the statues, Brothers appropriated a large sum of money in behalf of the " Pilgrims' Monument " at Plymouth, and a small bronze copy of the same stands upon its president's desk. Before taking possession of its present quarters in 1852, Linonia had rented a hall on Chapel street, in the third story of the building opposite the college yard, for nearly fifty years. In this hall, which is now the *Courant* composing room, this book was put in type. Brothers hall used to be further down Chapel, in Glebe Building, corner of Church street. During the last century, the societies had no halls of their own, but met in the various recitation rooms and other general resorts.

Catalogues of their members were first published in

1841. The names were arranged alphabetically by classes, and repeated in an index like that of the college triennial catalogue. Residences and the various honorary titles and achievements of members were indicated, and the society presidents were also noted. The Brothers catalogue contained in addition a special list of these, in the order of their succession. Each catalogue made a pamphlet of about ninety pages and was printed by Hitchcock & Stafford. The second one of Brothers (1854) also came from the same press. It contained a steel-engraved view of Alumni Hall, and was bound in a blue paper cover. The second of Linonia was printed by Baker, Godwin & Co. of New York, in 1853, to celebrate its one hundredth anniversary. Each society professed to publish the names of none save its graduate members, and—though the rule was somewhat infringed upon—its total membership was by this means reduced at least one fourth. Neither were lists printed of the "honorary members," elected from the world at large, and estimated to comprise in each case from five hundred to a thousand individuals. The necessary errors were many, but besides these each society charged the other with the commission of many intentional ones. The motto of Linonia was, *Quiescit in perfecto;* of Brothers, *E parvis oriuntur magna.* The former society once boasted of a watch-key badge, consisting of a thin gold plate, heart shaped, on one side of which was engraved "Linonia, Sept. 12, 1753," and on the other, in five separate designs, a dove, a swan, a dog, a phœnix, and a library of books. This design—in connection with the motto, *Amicitia, concordia, soli noscimus*—also formed a part of the illuminated book-label, for many years employed.

The accumulation of books seems to have been begun at a very early period. In the last catalogue of the Linonia library—printed in 1860 by J. H. Benham, and comprising 300 octavo pages—the number of volumes named was 11,300, and subsequent additions make the present number 13,300. "In 1770 there were stated to be nearly 100 volumes ; in 1780, 152 ; in 1790, 330 ; in 1800, 475 ; in 1811, 724 ; in 1822, 1187 ; in 1831, 3505 ; in 1837, 5581 ; in 1841, 7500 ; and in 1846, 10,103." Brothers' last catalogue, of the same size as Linonia's, was printed in July, 1851, by T. J. Stafford, and contained a steel-engraved view of the Library building. It mentioned 11,652 volumes, while its present number is 13,400. "The old catalogues show the number of books at successive periods to have been as follows : in 1781, 163 ; in 1808, 723 ; in 1818, 937 ; in 1825, 1730 ; in 1832, 3562 ; in 1835, 4565 ; in 1838, 6078 ; and in 1846, 9140." Brothers occupies the north wing of the Library building, and Linonia the south, and originally there were no inner passage ways between the wings and the main building. In 1860, by vote of the societies and consent of the faculty, the partitions were cut through and connecting doors inserted. This seems to have been considered as an essential part of the plan of having the college librarian's assistants act as librarians for the societies, though these inner passage-ways are never made use of now. Up to the time referred to, the librarians had been active members of the societies, and received no return for their services save the "honor," and possibly the fines they were able to collect. Since then, resident graduates, usually Theologues, have been employed on a salary, at first quite small, but now increased to $225 per annum. Each of these librarians has two Seniors as assistants, who are also paid $75 a year for their services. The libraries are open for the drawing of books for the half-hour succeeding dinner every afternoon, and during this time, according to the old plan, no one save the officers was allowed "behind the railing." Each man attached his name to a slip of paper on which he had marked the numbers of the desired books, and these slips were attended to by the assistants, in the order in which they were handed to the librarian. More recently the plan has been adopted of allowing those who wish to themselves select their books from the shelves. By an arrangement adopted in 1848, every member of either society can draw four volumes at a time from each of the libraries. Resident graduates are allowed the same privileges; and honorary members can also draw their eight volumes daily, on payment of a fee of one dollar a term. For an hour succeeding the time of taking out books—and of course, under the recent plan, during that half-hour also—the libraries are kept open "for consultation," and the alcoves and inner seats are made accessible to every one. This opportunity for consultation was first given in 1860, and until within a few years the consultation hour was in the forenoon. Before the present edifice was built, the society libraries were stored in the Athenæum. Formerly, it was customary for every member as he graduated to give at least one book to his society library, as in duty bound, but now the additions are all made by purchase.

The college reading-room is another thing, carried on by the faculty, in the name of the dead societies. The attempt to organize something of the sort had been often made without result. About the time that '69 entered college, a joint committee from the two societies reported in favor of combining the two libraries, and using the vacated building as a reading-room, but nothing was done to carry out the plan. Another proposal was to use the Calliope hall for the purpose; while newspaper writers called for the surrender of one of the vacant rooms in the Art Building. Finally, a petition, calling upon the faculty "to take immediate steps for the establishment of a reading-room," was circulated and very generally signed, which resulted in the arrangement whereby the faculty promised to provide a reading room, and the societies to supply the money to carry it on. The four middle rooms on the ground floor of South Middle were accordingly made into one by the tearing away of the partitions, and an enclosure for the College Bookstore was built in the middle of it. The doors on the west were fastened but the other two were left open, and with new floor, plaster, paper, and paint, the old quarters were transformed into a very respectable reading-room, which was first opened with the summer term of 1867. Upon a fixed desk or rack, extending about the sides of the room, are kept the files of about 25 daily newspapers, and a dozen weekly journals like the *Saturday Review* and *Nation*, as well as *Punch* and the *Illustrated News*. High stools are provided for those who do not wish to stand while consulting the files. Some 30 reviews and magazines, and as many more religious periodicals, may be obtained on application at what was formerly the Bookstore window, and must be returned there by the applicant before leaving the room. On Sundays, all the newspaper and other "secular" literature is locked up, and the "religious" papers and magazines are spread out upon the tables. All in all, there are about 120 different periodicals. The newspapers are kept on the files for about a week, and are then piled in the Treasurer's office, and are ultimately sold for waste-paper. The magazines and more important periodicals are bound and placed in the society libraries. These magazines had been taken by the societies before the reading-room was established, but were never accessible to the students except in the form of bound volumes, that is, until they were six months or a year old. An indigent Senior is employed to take charge of the reading-room, open and close it at the specified hours, —eight in the morning and ten at night,—give out the magazines from the office-window, and attend to the keeping of the files. This work was formerly performed by the proprietor of the College Bookstore, in consideration of paying no rent. A committee of three from the faculty decide what periodicals to purchase, and have the annual spending of $1000,—the "society tax" being, by constitutional amendment, increased from $6 to $8 per member on account of the reading-room. It should be remarked that all the "religious" literature is supplied by the Yale Missionary Society. The reading-room is a very popular resort both for readers and for loungers, and is a much frequented rendezvous during the half-hour preceeding recitation time. The largest crowds of actual readers assemble there immediately after dinner and supper, though there are few hours in the twelve when it is entirely deserted. Few but undergraduates make use of it, and those few rarely pay anything for the privilege, though an admission fee is nominally required of them. The room is lighted with gas, well heated, supplied with tables, chairs, settees, etc., but has no carpet or other covering upon its floor. Its forerunner was a rack, beside the bowling alleys in the basement of the Gymnasium, upon which were filed a half-dozen daily newspapers, which the faculty paid for.

The College Bookstore, though combined with the reading-room, did not spring into existence at the same time with it, but had led an independent life for quite a number of years. Doubtless some of the poorer students had attempted to turn an honest penny by selling text books before that time, but the first mention made of college booksellers was in the fall of 1851, when a

Senior, in North, and a Theologue, in Divinity, opened their rooms to "the trade." On the following summer, the latter sold out to Pliny F. Warner of '55, who seems to have been the real founder of the Bookstore, for though he disposed of its "good will" three or four times in the interval, he was called back to the rescue when the concern was in trouble, and so may be said to have " run" it for five years, or until 1857, when he finally sold out to a Sophomore of '60. The latter remained proprietor until graduation, when a '61 man bought it and held it for two years, after which time all the owners were Theologues until 1868, when it was bought by a '70 man, who, when he graduated, sold out to Charles C. Chatfield & Co., and so put an end to it as a college institution. The " store," migrating first to 17 South, and then to 155 Divinity, finally reached 34 South Middle in 1861, and remained in that locality— after 1867 as the central feature of the reading-room— until its final absorption, in the fall of 1870. Various city booksellers had often tried to crush the enterprise, by underselling, and by calling their own establishments "college bookstores," "student's bookstores," "Yale bookstores," and the like, but the students generally looked upon their own institution as a protection against monopolists, and rallied to its support. Previous to 1867, the proprietor of the Bookstore performed all the work himself, and kept his shop open only at certain stated intervals each day ; but, after that, a clerk was employed, whose office hours corresponded with those of the reading-room, and the business of the concern was enlarged so as to include not only the selling of text books and stationery, and the delivery of the college prints and periodicals, but the selling of miscellaneous books and publications, and the delivery of newspapers, photographs, etc., of every sort. In short, it had become transformed into a general bookstore and news agency, and was monopolizing a good share of the reading-room's space, and was making itself a public nuisance, when it was ordered out of the college limits, and passed into the hands of its present proprietors, whose establishment is on Chapel street, opposite the college yard. It is still advertised as the " College Bookstore." For a year after the establishment of the reading-room, a branch post-office was connected with the Bookstore, the "boxes" whereof were rented for a dollar each, or one half the price of those in the general office. Among other advantages, the branch office was kept open two hours later in the evening than the other; but all who wished to make use of the branch were obliged to secure boxes, as there was no "general delivery" in connection with it. The office grew in popularity, and at the beginning of the second year the number of boxes was doubled; but just then word came from the department at Washington that the establishment was contrary to the official regulations, and so it was abandoned forthwith—and an after attempt to resuscitate it was in vain. Though New Haven has a "free delivery," the carriers will not deliver letters to the colleges, even when directed to particular rooms, and hence the students who room in college are obliged to rent boxes, as a large portion of them do, or frequent the lobby of the " general delivery."

The Prize Debates, now held under the auspices of the two societies, are about the only reminders of their former "literary" character. The introduction of these superseded the idea of a "Test Debate," which it had been attempted to establish at about that time, as a means of deciding the question of literary superiority among the rival societies. The present system was inaugurated by William D. Bishop of '49, who, a year after graduation, presented Linonia with \$1000 in 7 per cent railroad bonds, the interest of which was to be divided into two first prizes of \$25, a second prize of \$15, and a third prize of \$5, for the encouragement of debate in the two lower classes. One of the first prizes was always to be given to a Freshman, and the other three could be competed for by Freshmen and Sophomores on equal terms. Other regulations in regard to the matter were these: "Five graduates of Linonia shall be chosen by the society by ballot, and their names put by the secretary into a box from which the president shall draw out indiscriminately three who shall constitute a committee to hear the discussion and award the prizes, their decision being based upon the 'argument,' the 'style,' and the 'delivery.' Each disputant shall have the privilege of speaking but once and of occupying but twenty minutes. Those who are desirous of competing for the prizes shall hand in their names to the president at least one week previous to the discussion. The chairman of the committee shall call upon the disputants by lot, and each disputant shall immediately respond to his name or be debarred the privilege of taking part in the debate. The discussion shall take place during the last half of the second term of the college year." Twenty men entered the first debate, March 2, 1851, and with slight changes and modifications the plan mentioned remained in vogue until 1860, when the joint debate was abandoned, and each class has since had an independent trial of its own, for three prizes of \$20, \$10, and \$5. Under the old rule, it rarely happened that the Freshmen were able to win more than the single prize necessarily allotted to them. In 1854 there was a senior debate in which one prize was awarded, but it was not until four years afterwards that the regular senior prize debate was instituted by the society.   Two prizes only were awarded during each of the first three years of the senior debate, but since '62 three have each year been given.   The junior debate was introduced in the class of '65, and with that class, therefore, was perfected the system, since in vogue, of competing in debate, for three prizes, in each one of the four academic years.   The value of the prizes in each of the two upper classes is $20, $15, and $10.

Brothers, meanwhile, had of course felt in duty bound to be equal with its rival in the encouragement of eloquence.   So, in 1853, each class had a prize debate, —the Sophomores on February 16, the Juniors on February 19, the Freshmen on March 2, and the Seniors on March 9.   One prize in each upper class, and three prizes in the freshman class were competed for.   Next year, the Juniors competed for one prize, and the Freshmen for three prizes.   For the five years following, only the two lower classes debated,—the Sophomores for two prizes, the Freshmen for three as before.   In the former class the number of prizes was first increased to three in the class of '62.   In '59 came the first regular senior debate, for two prizes, to which a third was first added in '61.   The class of '65 omitted their sophomore debate, and held one, for three prizes, in junior year, instead of it.   With '66, therefore, or a year later than in Linonia, was perfected the present system of four prize debates a year—each for three prizes, of $20, $15, and $10.   Hence, both societies together now award twenty-four debate prizes a year, amounting in the aggregate to $340 in value, but as a large proportion of them are "split" the number of individuals "honored" in this way is from 30 to 40 annually.   Of the prize money all but the $70 (or less, in years when the bonds are depreciated) derived from the Bishop fund, comes from the taxes assessed on the term-bills of the students.

By order of the faculty the debates must now be held within ten days from the opening of the term. Those of the Seniors and Sophomores introduce the second term; those of the Juniors and Freshmen, the third; though the junior debate came at the former time until within a year or two. The question for discussion is chosen a month or two in advance, by those intending to discuss it, and the order in which they are to speak is also determined in advance, by lot. The three persons who act as judges are usually graduates of the college and society, though little attempt is made to adhere to the original rule in regard to this matter, and any gentleman of requisite age and "weight," who can be persuaded to serve, is quickly accepted as judge, without much regard to his college or society antecedents. Members of the faculty are usually the first ones applied to, and some of them serve as judges on nearly every debate. Wednesdays and Saturdays are the times preferred, though the other days of the week are selected almost as often, for holding the contests. Frequently, though not always, the debates of the two societies are in progress at the same time. When only eight or nine speakers take part, the debate is finished in a single session, which is held in the evening; but, with twice that number of disputants, a preliminary afternoon session is required. The freshman and junior debates are generally the most closely contested of any; for in the one case is offered the first opportunity a man has for displaying his "literary abilities" to the college public; and in the other the last one for gaining laurels that may take him to a senior society. The junior debates of the present year, however, attracted barely as many competitors as there were prizes offered, and it was at one time rumored that they would be abandoned for lack of participants. In senior year there is little to fight for save the keeping up of previously made reputations, unless it be that the chances for class oratorship are sometimes affected by the result of this last debate. As for the Sophomores, perhaps some of the successful ones of the year before do not care to run the risk of a second trial, and some of the unsuccessful ones are too much discouraged to do so; for at all events their debate perhaps creates the least excitement of any. But all these prize trials attract great attention, and are, during their progress, the common talk of class and college. Large crowds go up to hear the speeches, and though different men "draw" different sized audiences, the attendance upon all is considerable, and it is rarely that the hall is entirely deserted, even for the poorest speaker. Programmes bearing the names of the judges, the question for debate, and the names of the disputants in their order, are freely circulated, and as fifteen minutes are allowed every speaker, it is possible to guess very nearly the time when each one of them will "come on." Between every speech the doors are left open for a minute or two, to allow the entrance and egress of spectators, but are kept locked in the meanwhile, so that no speaker need be interrupted. The president sits at his desk to announce the speakers, and the judges are ranged below him. At the conclusion of the debate, which often lasts till nearly midnight, they withdraw for a few moments to compare opinions, and then announce their decisions. The result is usually received with loud applause and cheerings, both within and without the hall, the prize takers are congratulated by their friends, and the excitement is ended. Partisans of the different class societies add up the "honors" each one of them has taken in the persons of its past, present, and prospective members, and discuss the result of their comparisons at the breakfast table next morning. The

Courant has also sometimes published the society connections of the prize men, in announcing their names.
It should be understood that these prize debates have
nothing to do with the ordinary exercises of the society,
and the men who participate in them rarely venture at
other times within the society halls.

Annual reunions of their graduates used to be held
in the halls on the day before Commencement, when
speeches were made, old stories re-told, songs sung, and
an enthusiasm for the society re-awakened. These exercises were among the most prominent and attractive
ones of the week, and were largely attended by the
undergraduate members; but with the decay of the
societies they have lessened in interest and for a few
years past have been neglected altogether. The cen-
tenial celebration of Linonia in 1853, the day before
Commencement, was quite a grand affair. The literary
exercises consisted of an oration by William M. Evarts
of '37 and a poem by Francis M. Finch of '49, delivered
in the North Church, and attended in a body by all the
assembled alumni. Afterwards came a banquet in
Alumni Hall, then for the first time dedicated. "It had
been finely decorated for the occasion by ladies of New
Haven. Festoons of pink, blue, and yellow—the badges
of the societies—adorned the walls, with four shields
enveloped in green, pink, blue and yellow, as representing Yale, Linonia, Brothers and Calliope." Names and
portraits of famous ex-members, mottoes and inscriptions, etc., were also displayed. Daniel Lord of '14
acted as president, and other big men helped to make
the after-dinner speeches. "Much good feeling and
cordiality prevailed, and Brothers and Linonians made
common cause in having a good time." A pamphlet
containing the oration and poem, and a full account of
the proceedings, was afterwards issued, as well as the

centennial catalogue already referred to, in commemoration of the event. The Brothers centennial was celebrated the day before the Commencement of 1868. A reunion was held at the hall in the forenoon; in the afternoon at the North Church an oration was delivered by Thomas M. Clark of '31 and a poem by Theodore Bacon of '53 ; and in the evening came a "social reception" at the Art Building, to which the sisters as well as the Brothers were invited,—a "collation" ending up the solemn festivities of the day. The affair was in every way inferior to the celebration of Linonia, for the fifteen years which had elapsed since then had been years of decay and dissolution, and the show of enthusiasum in all but the older members was too evidently feigned to be effective. The undergraduates took no interest in the exhibition, and what little trouble a few of them incurred for it was in deference to the faculty's request.

Various reasons have been offered from time to time to account for the dying out of all regard for these once proud institutions, and as many remedies have been stoutly urged. The commonest cry of the past seems to have been, "The class societies are causing the ruin of the others ; therefore, let the class societies be abolished." Another and more reasonable theory has called the class societies a consequence rather than a cause of the decay of the general ones. Whatever may be its true explanation, of the fact itself, that the general societies are dead past all hope of resurrection, there is no longer any reasonable doubt. The college children of this generation may not be wiser than their predecessors, and their society system may not be a better one ; but their modes of life and their society ideals are not like the old, and nothing can now make them take an interest in a system which in their view has outlived its usefulness. The fraudulent farce of keeping it up, however, is a wastefully expensive one, and appeals are all the while being made to the college authorities to step in and put an end to it. Were they to combine the two society libraries with the general library of the college, and from the lighter literature of the three sections form a special undergraduate department; turn the society halls into recitation or lecture rooms; and dispose of the duplicate volumes and other useless society property, they would effect a saving of at least $1500 a year, and could either reduce the "society tax" to $5, or, by keeping it as at present, could accomplish much more for the undergraduate library and reading-room,—the use of which is the only benefit which nine tenths of the students receive from their "societies." As very few undergraduates now sign their names to the constitutions of the societies to which they are allotted, the college treasurer would in most cases be unable to enforce payment of the tax, were it refused; and perhaps a general refusal to pay this illegal tax will finally be the means of forcing the authorities into assuming direct control of the property which is now so sadly mismanaged. From a recent article in a college paper is extracted the following summary, which, allowing for few unimportant variations, will fairly enough represent the society expenses for each and every year: "It appears, from the annual reports of the financial agent of Linonia and Brothers, that for the twelve months ending May 31, 1870, the college treasurer collected from the students, under the name of 'society tax,' the sum of $3718.12. As the number of undergraduates during this period averaged more than 500, and as the tax is $8, it would seem that some fifty or more made no payments; and no doubt these were the same individuals whose entire dues to the college treasurer were by authority remitted. Of this large sum of money, $2061.09 was expended upon the libraries. The salary of each of the two librarians is $225, and of each of the four assistants $75 ; but a part of the same was still unpaid when the report was made out, so that the salary item amounted to but $735. Of the remaining $1326.09, a great proportion was undoubtedly spent for books, though exactly how much is not stated. Next in cost to the libraries, was the reading-room, upon which (no items given) $967.80 was expended. Third may be noted the direct expense of 'running the societies,' $680.64 ; which was made up as follows: debate prizes, $284.75 ; coal, $106.06 ; janitors' salary, $65 ; fire-making and sweeping, $62.85 ; repairs, $43.18 ; gas, $42.56 ; printing, $41.25 ; incidentals, $28.24 ; and bell-ringing, $4.75. It is possible that the expenses for coal and gas should be charged in part to the libraries and reading-room ; though the report itself encourages no such inference. Fourth and last are the salary of the financial agent, $100 ; the charge of the college treasurer for collecting the tax, $80 ; the interest on the $400 debt of Linonia, $27.50 ; and the insurance of Brothers, $11.25 ;—a total of $218.75. In prize money Linonia annually distributes $160, and Brothers 180 ; but the total has been put at $284.75, because $55.25 of Linonia's money is derived from the ' Bishop fund,' and so does not enter into the account. The four divisions of the report as above given foot up a total of $3928.28 ; and the excess of $210.16 over the amount received for taxes, is made up of the $55.20 collected by the librarians for fines, etc., and the $154.96 by which the cash brought over from the old year exceeded the cash carried over for the new one."

A third society, after the same pattern, which lived out the time allotted to a generation of men, was "Calliope," or "the Calliopean Society" as its members preferred to call it. On July 8, 1819—because of a political fight which had resulted in the election of a northern man to the presidency of Linonia—32 members of the three lower classes withdrew from Linonia and Brothers, and set up this society of their own, to which they soon attracted 37 others, making Calliope's membership in that first year, 69, or larger than at any subsequent period. All the founders were, with two exceptions, Southerners, and to "the South" the society ever afterwards looked for its chief support. It never electioneered the Freshmen, or sought to increase its membership by any adventitious aids. All who came from the South went to the society as a matter of course. Some from the Middle and Western States also joined it, but the members from New England hardly averaged one a year. Its hall was in Townsend's Block, on Chapel street, oppose the college yard. When Alumni Hall was built, though the society was evidently moribund, it persisted in having a room made for it in the new building, and the apartment now known as Calliope Hall was the result. It lies between the other two society halls, and has seldom been put to any service since the disruption of the society, which happened before the new quarters were taken possession of. The society library, at the start in 1819, numbered about 400 volumes; in 1828, 2300; in 1831, 2900; in 1837, 4100; in 1840, 5000; and at the end in 1852, about 10,000. The books were kept in the apartment between the Library proper and the south or Linonia wing, and when Calliope was dissolved were given to the college, which by the sale of them to the Bridgeport city library realized $2100, from which fund two of its "general scholarships," yielding $66 a year are supported. Its first and perhaps only catalogue of members was an octavo of 32 pages, printed in 1839 by B. L. Hamlen. The names were arranged by years rather than by classes, and the States were brought into prominence by being separated from the residences. During its first twenty years the society seems to have had in all about 300 regular members, and half that number of honorary ones. All of the latter were obliged to come at least once to the hall and "pass through the regular form of initiation,"—a thing not required by the other societies, many of whose "honorary members" never set foot in New Haven, or even in America. The catalogue was embellished with a steel-engraved frontispiece, representing the society's patron goddess—"the queen of the sacred nine"—in her usual posture, accompanied by another female figure bearing a scroll labeled "Calliope, 1819." Upon the cover was displayed a six-pointed star, with a "C" supported within its open hexagon. The letters "*Φ E M*," initials of the motto, appeared upon the "C," and in the lower angle of the star was the date, "1819." This design was doubtless a copy of the society badge, worn as a pendant to the watch chain. In the *Lit.* for February, 1853, it was announced that the society had been dissolved, and that the committee appointed to pay its debts and wind up its affairs would publish a report of their work in the next number of the magazine, together with a statement of the causes which led to the dissolution. But the promised report and explanation were never printed. Still another "literary society" was the "Phœnix," founded in 1806, chiefly by Thomas S. Grimké, who graduated the following year. The society does not seem to have long survived his departure, and its members were quickly absorbed by Linonia and Brothers—the name of Grimké himself afterwards appearing on the former's catalogue.

Another sociey institution, almost as aged as Linonia and Brothers but of quite a different character, is the "Phi

the penalty for tardiness ; of $10, for absence ; of $20, for flunking an appointment.   There were never any eatables provided except on the night of December 6, when the society's anniversary was celebrated by a supper.   The oration on that occasion was delivered by a graduate, and the annual officers were chosen.   The president was always a graduate, and was often reëlected, —Prof. Kingsley, for example, holding the office for six successive years.   Afterwards, the annual supper was abolished and the only "bum" was that of initiation night, when with singing, and story-telling, and eating and drinking, "a general jollification was kept up till a late hour."   The occasion constantly increased in importance and expense, until in 1835 the initiation supper cost $150, which was judged to be so utterly extravagant, that the corporation passed a vote forbidding any future celebration of the sort, as being a waste of money. The day after Commencement, it was customary to hold an "exhibition," when two orations were delivered, by tutors or other graduates, and a debate was engaged in by four undergraduates.   As these exhibitions gradually grew in interest and importance, it was decided to make them public, and in September, 1787, the great uninitiated, "assembled in the brick meeting house," were for the first time allowed to listen to one of Phi Beta's representative orators.   The next public oration was pronounced five years later, and in the 42 years, 1793–1834, there were only 12 Commencements when the society failed to display itself; while from 1835 onward there has been no break in its annual exhibitions.   Before that time, there had been but seven poems delivered, of which only one had been printed.   Of the orations, ten had been printed.   There were but 28 of them, for on two occasions the poet had been the only speaker before the society.   Since 1835, the oration has been three times and the poem eight times omitted ; and, of those delivered, two orations and two poems have not been printed.

At the annual September meeting of 1793, it was voted, that an oration should each year be delivered in public on the day after Commencement ; that on the morning of that day the society—assembled at the State House at 8 o'clock—should always choose two orators, the first to speak upon the following year, and the other to be ready as his substitute ; that the substitute for one year should be in turn chosen the orator for the next ; and that the orator should notify the president, two months before Commencement, of his intention or not to fulfil his appointment. These rules are in effect still adhered to, though for many years the society's anniversary has been the day before instead of the day after Commencement ; the morning business meeting has been held in one of the Lyceum lecture rooms ; and the oration and poem have been delivered in the evening at one of the churches on the green. But the orator and poet and their substitutes are still chosen for one year in advance, and the substitutes are duly promoted to the first places, so that in effect each man appointed has two years to prepare himself. Perhaps three-fourths of the persons selected to speak before the society, have been regular members of it at Yale,—the others being regular or honorary members of other branches or honorary members of the Yale branch. Doolittle's Hall— in the old building on College street, near the corner of Elm, which was torn down to give place to the new Divinity College—used to be, in the old times, the only public hall which the city possessed, and Phi Beta Kappa, as well as Linonia and Brothers, used to hold its ordinary meetings there. Originally, the hall was said to have belonged to the Freemasons ; and of course the different college societies which met there rented it on different evenings. In 1825, or shortly afterwards, a clamor against Masonry and secret societies generally, which swept over the country, seems to have resulted in the removal of its secret character from Phi Beta Kappa, both at Yale and in other colleges. With its mystery departed its activity also ; and for forty years past it has been simply a " society institution" possessed of but little more life than it claims to-day, though membership in it was thought an honor worth striving for until quite a recent period. High scholarship was always as now the prime qualification which recommended a man for election, and, also as now, about a third of each senior class were annually elected. The bulk of the elections were given out to the Juniors during the third term, and the regular initiation was held then, but there seems to have been occasional class elections subsequently given out in senior year. Personal prejudice sometimes kept a few high-stand men out, and personal favoritism sometimes brought a few low-stand men in, but, in general, scholarship alone decided the matter,—the society confining its elections pretty closely to the list recommended it by the faculty, in response to its own application therefor. Elections were nominally unanimous, but each one who cast a black-ball was obliged to avow the reasons which influenced him in doing so, and the single " No" was always expected to be withdrawn, as a matter of course. For fifty years and more, admission to the society was considered one of the greatest honors of the college, and was the object in view of which the hardest exertions of the first three years were put forth. Its key, in fact, seems to have been thought about as desirable as a senior-society pin is now-a-days, and to have been as generally recognized in the college world as a badge of exceptional honor and distinction.

"This society," say its oldest archives, "continued to increase and become more and more respectable in the view of the students of college. The younger classes were sensibly ambitious of recommending themselves to the society by regular behavior and uncommon exertions of scholarship. At the same time, the candidate in the successive senior classes who finally failed of the honor of an election, were mortified and irritated by disappointment. Under the united influence of envy, resentment and curiosity, Hugo Burghardt, Nathan Stiles and Richard McCurdy, three Seniors, combined together, and on the evening of December 19, 1786, broke open the secretary's door, in his absence, entered his study, and feloniously took, stole, and carried away the society's trunk, with all its contents. They, however, by no means satisfied their expectations of learning the mysteries of the society and of the institution, as there was no written explanation of them in the archives; and fortunately they were detected before they had an opportunity of divulging their discovery. Upon their detection, they restored the papers as they found them, paid for the damage done the trunk, appeared in the presence of the society assembled in a general meeting, voluntarily made a written confession, which is still lodged in the trunk, and bound themselves by a solemn oath to confine within their own breasts all the knowledge of the secrets of the society which they had so criminally obtained by violating the sacred security of locks and keys. In compassion to them and their friends, the society generously pardoned them and engaged to conceal their names from the world. An attested copy of their confession and oath was entered on record and also transmitted to Cambridge. Thus tranquillity was restored, and the affairs of the society proceeded without interruption until on or about July 20, 1787, when the trunk was unlocked in a clandestine manner, and the secretary's and register's books were again stolen; though the latter was soon found. No discovery was made of the perpetrators of this second burglary, nor has there since appeared any publication of the contents of the book of records."

The badge of the society is a flat rectangular watch-key of gold, across the central portion of which are engraved the letters "*Φ B K*"; and upon the right lower corner, a right hand, with the index finger pointing diagonally .across to several stars in the left upper corner. The number of these stars seems for some time to have been made to correspond to the whole number of chapters, for there were five of them upon the key of thirty years ago. As the number of chapters became too extensive for representation, only as many stars were expressed as there were chapters in the State; and hence there are now three of them upon the Yale key. Another explanation is that they are intended to correspond with the number of Alphas. The flat portion of the key, which is almost a square, measures an inch upon its longest side. In all the colleges the badge has never varied, save in the number of stars, from that instituted at William and Mary in 1776. According to Allyn's "Ritual," it was "a medal of gold or silver, sometimes worn on the bosom, suspended by blue or pink ribbon, but more commonly as a watch key. Upon its back was engraved, "S. P. Dec. 6, 1776,"—the initials signifying, '*Societas Philosophiæ*." "The sign is given by placing the two forefingers of the right hand so as to cover the left corner of the mouth; draw them across the chin." "The grip is like the common shaking of hands, only not interlocking the thumbs, and at the same time gently pressing the wrist." At Yale and other colleges, the lists of members which are occasionally published are sometimes headed by a wood-cut seal, an inch and a half in diameter, consisting simply of the name of the chapter—"Alpha of Connecticut," for example — in a double circle within which appear the emblems of the key. The constitution of the society required every member to wear the badge, but only about a third of them did so, fifty years ago, when their society was a living, wide-awake affair ; and, now, as for a dozen years or more past, the sight of a Phi Beta key would raise a cry of derision. The last Yale Senior who once or twice ventured to expose such a thing to the gaze of the populace belonged to the class of '67.

This was also the last class for whose initiation a special meeting was held. Since 1850 or before, elections to the society have been entirely a matter of form. The faculty's record of scholarship alone decides the matter, and in accordance with this about a third of the junior class, comprising all the appointment-men save the lowest, were each year requested, by printed notice, to present themselves at one of the Lyceum lecture rooms, on the Wednesday evening preceeding Presentation Day, for the purpose of being initiated into Phi Beta Kappa. Here they were met by one or more of the graduate officers of the affair, and the significance of the society, and of their election to it, was formally explained to them. While awaiting the arrival of these officers the society was wont to take up a collection and institute an impromptu "peanut bum." The two or three of their number who were entrusted with the money, having purchased a bushel or so of peanuts at the nearest fruit store, would on their return be pursued by a ravenous crowd of their non-elected classmates, even to the very door of the lecture room, and sometimes be obliged to surrender a part of their booty. After the meeting, with its "bum," was over, the newly initiated were very liberal in the distribution of peanuts among the non-elect, or were beset by the latter and compelled by force to disgorge the remnants of their feast. Sometimes, also, the new members marched in procession about the college buildings,—having fastened to their watch-chains, as burlesques on the authorized badges, the large pasteboard rectangles used in recitation for the demonstration of mathematical propositions, —shouting " Phi, ai, ai ! Phi Beta Kappa !" which was a sort of cheer or rallying cry in the palmy days of the society. The bell which called their meetings together used also to be rung in a peculiar, jerky fashion, to imitate as nearly as possible this society shout. In the class of '58, for some unknown reason, only three men accepted elections to Phi Beta.

Besides this meeting, there were the Deccember aniversary for the election of officers, and the meeting at Commencement time for the choice of orator and poet. The latter is the only one now held. For a dozen years past, the general officers have been chosen at that time, and begining with '68, the " active members " have been " elected " then. Printed notifications of the time and place of meeting are posted upon the trees in the college yard. At the appointed hour, a sprinkling of graduates and two or three undergraduates assemble. A president for the next year is chosen in the person of some graduate, usually a non-resident of New Haven, who may or may not be present ; then the vice president (Prof. A. C. Twining of '20) secretary (Prof. D. C. Gilman of '52), and treasurer (Prof. H. A. Newton of '50), are reëlected ; and the remaining two officers— recording secretary and assistant treasurer — are appointed from among the " active members." The names of the first 30 or 40 persons upon the faculty's appointment list are read off and they are " unanimously elected " ed" to the society. They form the "active members" for the following year, without further ceremony, and their most active duty resulting is to laugh when they see their names in the society's printed list. The substitute orator and poet having been chosen orator and poet, and new substitutes having been chosen in their places, perhaps a few honorary members are elected. Then the official reports are read and accepted, financial and other resolutions are adopted, and the "society" disbands, to be resurrected and go through the same galvanic formalities at the close of another year. In its early days, an initiation fee of $10 was demanded; but this was abolished long ago, and the society expenses have to be met by subscription, and most of them doubtless fall upon the college professors who are its officers. At all events, it is supposed that they alternate with one another in making up the annual deficit caused by the printing of the oration and poem. At last year's Commencement meeting a committee of five old members was appointed to enquire into the expediency of rejuvenating the society or abandoning it altogether. No substitute orator and poet were elected for the Commencement of 1872, and it is therefore possible that this year's will be the last appearance of Phi Beta at Yale.

A sixteen-page catalogue, printed by Oliver Steele & Co. in April, 1808, was perhaps the first one published. It contained about 400 names, all arranged in one alphabetical list, with their " places of abode," "college titles" [" Senr.," "Junr.," or "A. B."], and "times of admission" annexed. The last catalogue — of 50 octavo pages, printed by B. L. Hamlen—was issued in 1852. In this the names of the members were given by classes, together with both "original and present residences," honorary titles, etc. Special lists of the "honorary members, not graduates of Yale College," comprising but forty names; of the presidents; and of the orators and poets, were also included. An index to the 1700 individuals mentioned succeeded the whole. Each separate chapter of the fraternity has doubtless published similar lists, but no general catalogue of the members of all the chapters has ever been issued. With each branch showing signs of life but one day out of the three hundred and sixty-five, there can of course be no tangible tie between them, and any general work in the name of the whole fraternity is clearly out of the question.

The history of the chapters elsewhere has been essentially the same as at Yale, save that the younger ones have never known any active life, but have been form the outset simply society institutions. Characteristics common to all the chapters are: the delivery of an oration and poem in public, at Commencement time, and the holding of a business meeting in private, when the officers and members for the ensuing year are chosen of whom the former are graduates and the latter the best scholars of the incoming senior class. In short, "Phi Beta Kappa" is, always and everywhere, a mere official compliment paid by the faculty to high scholarship. Its key, or the right to wear it, is simply a medal, or "reward of merit," certifying that the owner ranks with the first third of his class. This fiction, myth, abstraction, pious fraud, or what not, is naturally the object of much merriment at Yale. References are often made to its profound secrecy, to the wire pulling and electioneering resorted to in choosing its officers, to favoriteism and unworthy personal prejudices shown in conferring its elections, to the hilarious joviality and boisterous uproar attendant upon its weekly gatherings, to the low and disreputable character of its members, who are "in constant danger of being dropped from the class through excessive attention to their society duties,"—and so on. Such are the sarcastic and derisive utterances now heard in regard to that venerable fraternity which, almost a century ago, started out upon its mission of inculcating the doctrine that "Philosophy is the guide of life."

Youngest of the society institutions is "Chi Delta Theta," established in 1821. Prof. James L. Kingsley was its founder and perpetual president. Its object was to compliment and encourage literary as distinguished from scholastic ability. About a fourth of the senior class, including all the "good writers," were annually elected to it, and met fortnightly, in one of the Lyceum lecture rooms,—Tuesday evening at eight o'clock being the time of assembling. Sometimes the meeting was held at the house of the president. The exercises consisted of the reading of essays—one, two, three or more in number—and the subsequent discussion of them. Classical literature was at one time especially affected, and a select classical library was formed, which numbered about 100 volumes when the society dissolved and was then given to the college. All the books were from choice or rare editions. In Phi Beta, there were no written essays presented, but all the literary performances were in the form of debates, orations, etc., orally delivered; while in Linonia and Brothers, the two methods characteristic of both the societies were in vogue. Chi Delta and Phi Beta were neither rivals of each other nor of the general societies. Seniors might belong to all three of them, and it was of course thought an especial honor to be able to swing both the senior-society badges. At the time of Junior Exhibition, that of Chi Delta was very prominently displayed by the appointment-men who had just gained it,—for the elections seem to have been given out at that early period in the year.

The badge was in the form of a gold "Δ," or triangle, with sides an inch in length, upon the lower one of which was engraved "$X \Delta \Theta$ 1821 ;" and was usually hung as a pendent to the watch chain, though sometimes attached to the vest as a pin. The officers were chosen annually, and the founder of the society was always reëlected president. Chi Delta died out in the clan of '43 or '44, having had only a nominal, or honorary existence—like that of Phi Beta at the present time—in several preceding classes. No catalogue of the members seems ever to have been published. It naturally happened that the editors of the *Lit.* were always elected to it, and in 1868, at the suggestion of one of them, it was decided to revive the old society, by making it an institution connected with the magazine. The '68 editors were accordingly initiated as members of Chi Delta Theta, and pledged to turn over "the society" to the five elected to succeed them in the management of the *Lit.* A similar transfer has been made by subsequent editors, and the society in its present form seems as certain of long life as "the oldest college periodical" itself. Since the editors are supposed to be the "five best literary men" of every senior class, the name and mantle of the old society may be appropriately left in their keeping. The triangle is now worn, in the place of a watch chain, simply as a badge of the editorial office. Upon the reverse are graved, "*Yale Lit.* 1836," and the name and class of the owner.

PART SECOND.

THE STUDENT LIFE.

CHAPTER I.

FRESHMAN YEAR.

Board and Lodging—Eating Clubs—Their Formation and Characteristics—Names, Mottoes and Devices—The College Club or Commons—The Old Commons Hall System—The Old Buttery—Smoking Out—Stealing—Hazing—Put Out That Light!—Rushing—The Foot-Ball Game—The Painting Disgrace—Gate Lifting—Lamp Smashing—Thanksgiving Jubilee—As it was Known to '69—Its Previous Origin and Growth—Interference of the Faculty—The Last Jubilee—Its Character in the Future—Pow-wow—The Annual Dinner, and its Predecessor, the Biennial Jubilee—The Freshman Laws of the Last Century—The Old Manner of Lecturing.

On the same printed form which certifies that the candidate has been "admitted on probation a member of the freshman class" is a notification of the tutor to whom he is to apply if he desires a room in the college buildings. As none but indigent Freshmen ever occupy these rooms, which are poor in quality and few in number, the newly-admitted probably leaves this official alone, and starts off in quest of a room in some private house of the city, since college law forbids him either to lodge or board at a public hotel. According to the locality, size, equipment of the room or rooms, and the fact of his occupying it or them alone or with a chum, the Freshman agrees to pay a rent of from $1.50 to $5 a week, though the ordinary price of course lies between these two extremes.   "Fire" and "light" and "washing" are always "extra," and a stove is never included with the other furniture.   Towels, too, the lodger is expected to supply for himself.   If a house is supplied with furnace heat and gas, the "roomer" is charged a dollar for the former and a half dollar for the latter, per week.   It will usually cost him about as much if he has a stove of his own,—aside from the trouble of attending to it, which he must do himself,—but he can furnish his own "light" at half the indicated expense.   His "washing" costs from sixty to seventy-five cents per dozen pieces, and is either done at the house, or by private washer-women who call for and deliver his clothing, or by the public laundries.   If the entrance door of the house where he rooms is usually closed, the lodger is supplied with a latch-key, which will admit him at all times, and he commonly leaves the door of his own room unlocked in his absence ; but if the entrance door is always open, as is apt to be the case in a house where there are many lodgers, he is careful to lock up his own room when he departs therefrom.   He does not, save in exceptional cases, "board," that is, take his meals, in the same house where he "rooms."   "Eating clubs," especially in freshman year, are the approved mediums through which he obtains his food.

A "club" is in theory a coöperative affair, whose members " pay only for what they have," and " have just what they want," and whose steward obeys their orders in supplying the provender, and receives simply his own board in consideration of his trouble.   Such a thing may sometime have existed, but for some years past it has been an abstraction merely.   The real club is more a thing of this sort : The steward, usually a poor man, engages some woman, accustomed to the business, to supply a dining room, dishes, table furniture and waiters, and do the cooking for his proposed club. For this, he agrees to pay her a certain price per plate,—not including his own, which is free,—and engages that the club shall be above a certain minimum number as to size. He has probably secured beforehand the requisite number of classmates as members, or, if not, he soon gets them together, and the club is formed. A steward has little difficulty in making up a crowd among Freshmen, who are unacquainted with one another, and so without likes or dislikes. Those who have been acquaintances at a large preparatory school, however, sometimes join together in a club, or form a nucleus for one, when first they come to college. The steward generally attracts his men by suggesting a basis of "about" so many dollars per week; giving them to understand that this may vary according to their orders; and that his own board is the only compensation which he himself is to receive for his trouble. Meanwhile he agrees, in consideration of a certain percentage paid to himself by the latter, to order from a single market-man everything which the club requires, and the trader looks to him alone for payment of the supplies which he furnishes. The steward occupies the "head of the table," does the carving whenever necessary, and gives his orders to the market-man each day for the provisions needed the day following,—consulting in doing this the expressed wishes of a majority of the club, and warning them when their demands are bringing up the price of board above the estimated amount. At the close of the term he divides the amount of the provision bill by the number of members, and adding to this quotient the sum due from each one for table service and cookery, announces the result as the price of board for the term, which price is pretty certain to be in excess of the estimate on which the club was based. After collecting his board bills and paying his cook and market-man—from whom he receives back the percentage agreed upon— his work for the term is over. Very likely the club breaks up ; or perhaps it may go on for another term under the same auspices. It will be seen that in this arrangement everything depends upon the integrity and shrewdness of the steward and the woman whom he employes. The latter has the chance to appropriate as many of the club's stores as she may need, either to board her own family or to use for other purposes, and the former can put the figures of the provision bill almost as high as he chooses,—without there being in either case any sensible chance of discovery. For these reasons the plan is not a popular one, after men have found out its defects ; and they are apt to demand that a steward shall leave out the "about" in his proposals, and agree to board them at a certain fixed rate per week. If he does this, the peculations of the cook of course tell against himself simply instead of the club as a whole, and his only way to make himself good is to supply cheaper food, which of course raises an outcry from his comrades. Still another way in which a poor man may earn his own support is this : he offers some woman, in want of boarders at a certain price per week, to supply enough men for a table, a dozen being commonly the minimum number, to serve at the head of the table as carver, and perhaps to collect the board bills when due, as well as to act as a general go-between, in communicating the wishes of the boarders to their hostess, and the reverse. For these services he receives his own board without payment. In the fourth and last variety of eating club, there is no steward or head-man of any sort. The members of it simply agree to pay a certain price for board, and are as individuals directly responsible to their hostess.

The essential thing in a club, which, in all its forms, plainly distinguishes it from a boarding house, is this, that its members " make up their own crowd," and alone decide who shall be admitted to their number. A club once formed, neither the hostess nor the steward can secure the admission of a new member without the consent of the others. A club, too, adopts its own rules of table etiquette, and pays only such regard to the conventionalities as seems to it good,—no woman or other person of authority ever having a place at its table. Men in clubs, as everywhere else, are certain to be dissatisfied either with the quality of their food or the price at which it is afforded, and changes are continually going on. New clubs are started and old ones reorganized at the beginning of each year, and in fact nearly every term. Before the close of freshman year the " popular men" of the class are pretty certain to drift into a club together, which is nearly as certain to go to pieces before the close of the year which follows. In junior year, may be, each society is represented by its eating club, which perhaps had its beginning among its pledged representatives in the year before, when a neutral Sophomore who could get elected to the Psi U or DKE club would think his chances good for an election to the societies themselves : generally, with reason. Senior-society clubs are not very feasible, since to make up a table would require the presence of about every member, a thing which pecuniary and others differences would render all but impossible. The Coffin society of '69, however, took their meals together. Of late years, too, Seniors are getting much into the way of boarding at hotels, in defiance of the absurd rule which forbids any undergraduate so to do.

Some clubs are exceptionally long-lived. The " Pie Club" of '68, for example, which began with the third term of the first year, lasted through the course, and one in the class before it was nearly as aged ; but such instances are not numerous. It was in 1854 that a club —the " Hyenas"—first set a precedent, by publishing in the *Banner* a list of its members, beneath a wood-cut device. This practice has greatly varied in popularity. Ten years ago, nearly all the clubs of college engaged in it. Four years ago it seemed likely to be abandoned by all but the Freshmen. More recently, it has regained some recognition among the upper classes, though the Seniors are content simply to print their names, without device of any sort. The freshman clubs are naturally its best supporters, and they apparently labor to confer upon themselves as absurd titles as possible, in which they are more successful than in their attempts at witty mottoes, which are usually far-fetched and silly. Among the earlier clubs which figured in the *Banner* were the " Vultures," " Tigers," " Harpies," " Ostriches," " Anacondas," and " Crocodiles"; the steward of the first being called " Oecumenical," of the second, " Tigridum Curator," of the third, " Obsonator Harpyiis," and of the fourth, " Struthamelactor" and " Superintendent of the Des(s)ert." There were the " Dyspeptics," four of whom were represented as dragging some meat from a hungry dog ; the " Skel-e(a)t-ons," who were " Membra" and whose steward was the " Dissector"; the " Knicker-bockers" [both these clubs attained considerable age] ; the " Ruskins" ; the " Gastronomers"; the " Cœna-tors"; the " Frolicksome Oysters"; the " Beavers " ; the " Munch(ch)aw-sens"; the " Euphagonians" ; the " Musk-Eaters," whose steward was the " Gallinipper," and whose device represented a dozen musquitoes seated at table. Of course there have been the inevitable " Eta Pi" clubs in all their variations ; likewise the " Ace" and the " King" of clubs ; likewise all manner of "Greek" titles, like *Οἱ Βῆτ-ἡτερς, Οἱ Γόββλερς, Οἱ Στυφάγοι, Οἱ Γαστριμάργοι, Οἱ Παντοφάγοι, Οἱ Ὀλιγουφάγοι, Οἱ Ἱπποφάγοι, Οἱ Ὁμοτράπεζοι, Οἱ Ὀρτραφάγοι,* and *Οἱ Ἀμνίσκοι,* where a man named Lamb was steward. Another motto of the latter club was " Agno vivimus." The " Pinesthians," the " Epicureans," the " Choke A-e(ters), whose steward was the " Choker," the " Kukluxes," the " Fowl Fiends," the " Gobble-ins," the " Cherubs," the " Merry Eaters," the " Hard Cases," Case being the steward's name," the " Peacemakers," the " Lickapillies," the " Tasters," les " Miserables," les " Bon Vivants," die " Junggesellen," are among the more recent " eaters." The " Pick Quick," " Sans Souci," " Help (M)eat," " Hung(a)ry," and " Farewell" clubs were also recently existing. Other club names, past or present, are : " The Rect-ory," " Chou Chou," " Merchants' Union," " Water Club," " Ours," " House of Lords," as distinguished from the " Commons" or college club, and " Knights of the Knife and Fork." The " 'Cher' Club" of '63 was perhaps the most happily named of any.

The college club—usually called the " Commons," though it bears no resemblance to the obsolete institution of that name—was started in the summer term of 1866, under the auspices of the college authorities, for the purpose of furnishing a cheap but respectable board at its cost price. The old wooden structure next the Art Building was fitted up for its use, one large dining room being formed of its upper, another of its lower floor. The Seniors and Sophomores occupy one, the Juniors and Freshmen the other, though the classes are seated at separate tables. A few members of the professional schools are also admitted when there happens

now the case in the English colleges, the students had supper in their own rooms, which led to extravagance and disorder."

"Cellar room was rented for the storage of their apples and other provisions, and this cellerage cost more than the rent of a college room. The waiters at Commons, about 16 in number, were appointed by the faculty from the poorer students of the junior class, and were generally supposed to look out for number one. The beverage for dinner was cider, which was contained in large pewter pitchers at each end of the table. Up to 1815, tumblers were an unknown luxury. Each man drank in turn from the pewter, the galvanic effect of which gave a perceptible addition to the flavor of the contents. The breakfasts consisted of an olla podrida, hashed up from the remnants of yesterday's dinner, and fried into a consistency which baffled digestion, This compound was known as 'slum,' and was served both dry and wet. The morning drink was coffee. Any one who could get a doctor's certificate to the blessings of a chronic dyspepsia, or an incipient cholera-morbus, was sent to the Invalids' table, where he enjoyed better fare. To these accommodations a Senior or a tutor prefixed and affixed a grace, during the delivery of which two forks were sometimes observed sticking into each potato on the table. The tutors themselves sat at elevated tables, and getting but little chance to eat, from time to time rapped with their knife-handles to call to order some indecorous malcontent who compared the bread to bricks or started up the 'second perfect indicative' of βαίνω, to denote a disinclination to ill-cooked lamb. Connected with these times, was the custom of 'podding,' as it was called. Whenever peas were to be boiled for dinner, all undergraduates were summoned to
, assist in shelling them, and if any man was absent, the

rest collected the pods and threw them, without cere-mony into the delinquent's room. It is related that as many as 600 tumblers and 30 coffee pots were destroyed or carried off in a single term. Just before the old hall was abandoned, in 1819, there was a three days' rebel-lion of the Freshmen and Sophomores, and nine years later came the 'great rebellion' when about forty stu-dents were expelled from the college." "In the Revolu-tionary war the steward was quite unable once or twice to provide food for the college, and this led to the dis-persion of the students in 1776, and 1777, and once again in 1779 delayed the beginning of the winter term several weeks." In the days when the Cabinet served as the dining hall, the Sophomores entered at the north, the Freshmen at the south, and the Juniors and Seniors at the middle door. The waiters, like the monitors, lost nothing in social standing on account of their po-sitions. From this description it is not very difficult to imagine the kind of etiquette and order which prevailed in the old Commons Hall. Under the best conditions students, and other men also, are seldom contented with their food, and when arbitrarily restricted in obtaining it their dissatisfaction must have been extreme. Hence the "bread-and-butter rebellions," the destruction of unpalatable food, the smashing of dishes and furniture, the wastefulness and rioting and uproar;—vague ac-counts of which, like traditions of another age, have come down to the present generation of undergraduates.

Another old college institution of similar nature, which flourished for a century, but has left no sign be-hind, was the Buttery, abolished in 1817. It was kept in South Middle, south entry, lower front corner room (at present No. 33). "The butler was a graduate of re-cent standing, and being invested with rather delicate functions was required to be one in whom confidence

might be reposed. His chief prerogative was to have
the monopoly of certain eatables, drinkables and other articles desired by students, which went under the general
name of 'sizings.' The Latin laws of 1748 give him
leave to sell in the Buttery cider, metheglin, strong beer
to the amount of not more than 12 barrels annually,—
which amount as the college grew was increased to 20,
—together with loaf sugar ('saccharum rigidum'), pipes,
tobacco and such necessaries of scholars as were not
furnished in the commons hall. Some of these necessaries were books and stationery, but certain fresh fruits
also figured largely in the butler's supply. No student
might buy cider or beer elsewhere. The butler, too,
had the care of the bell, kept the book of fines, distributed the bread and beer provided by the steward into
equal portions, and had the lost commons, for which
privilege he paid a small annual sum. He was bound
·in consideration of the profits of his monopoly to provide candles at college prayers and for a time to pay
also 50 s. stg. into the college treasury. The more
menial part of these duties he performed by his waiter.
The original motives for setting up a buttery in college
seem to have been to put the trade in articles which appealed to the appetite into safe hands, to ascertain how
far students were expensive in their habits, and prevent
them from running into debt ; and finally by providing
a place where drinkables of not very stimulating qualities were sold to remove the temptation of going abroad
after spirituous liquors. Accordingly laws were passed
limiting the sum for which the butler might give credit
to a student, authorizing the President to inspect his
books, and forbidding him to sell anything except permitted articles for ready money. But the whole system,
as viewed from our position as critics of the past must
be pronounced a bad one. It rather tempted the stu-

dent to self-indulgence by setting up a place for the sale of things to eat and drink within the college walls, than restrained him by bringing his habits under inspection. There was nothing to prevent his going abroad in quest of stronger drinks than could be bought at the buttery, when once those which were there sold ceased to allay. his thirst. And a monopoly, such as the butler enjoyed of certain articles, did not tend to lower their price, nor to remove suspicion that they were sold at a higher rate than free competition would assign to them."

There are certain lodging houses in the vicinity of the colleges which, being occupied year after year almost exclusively by Freshmen, come to have a reputation as "freshman headquarters." An occupant of one of these, or of any room near the college square, is more likely to be troubled by sophomoric visitations, than one who rooms by himself in some comparatively distant locality. Most of the ill-treatment of Freshmen is inflicted upon them simply as such, not as individuals who are personally obnoxious ; hence a crowd of Sophomores on the look out for "fun" attempt to get it from the Freshmen who chance to be the most accessible. Perhaps it is eight or nine o'clock of a Freshman's first or second evening at Yale, when he may be studying his next morning's lesson, that a rap comes upon his door, which he may or may not suspect to proceed from Sophomores, and in reply to which he may or may not say, " Come in !" or himself open the way. If he does not so do, however, all doubts as to the personality of the knockers are quickly removed, by cries of " Open that door, Fresh !" " Let us in, Freshie, if you don't want to die !" and similar cheerful imperatives and imprecations. Perhaps the Freshman then opens the door; perhaps if he doesn't, the Sophs burst it open, lock and all ; perhaps they came in, or attempted to come in, at first without knocking at all; but the result of any of the numerous possibilities that have been suggested is, that the Freshman, before he has time to think up any rational plan of action, finds his room full of swaggering, loud-mouthed Sophomores, and himself at their mercy. Perhaps if he said " Come in !" to the first rap, one of the visitors advances and shakes hands with him with a great show of mock deference, and presents him to the others as a worthy member of the class of such-a-year. They order him to mount the table, and place him there if he does not of his own accord obey, perhaps supplying a chair for him to sit in. After darkening the room somewhat, they shut down the windows, call for cigars and tobacco, and if the Freshman has none they themselves produce the latter and proceed to load their pipes, and light them, taking pains to puff as much smoke as possible in the Freshman's face. Meanwhile he is requested to "scan"—that is, recite metrically— a proposition in Euclid, or a rule of the Greek grammar, or a passage in any other prose work that may be convenient ; to make a speech ; to sing a song ; to dance ; to recite the alphabet backwards ; to tell his name and age ; to do every unpleasant and absurd thing that the evil ingenuity of a Sophomore can conjure up. Unless he makes some show of obedience to these requests, his visitors "stir him up" with their bangers, or if he is obstinate and refuses to do anything, or even attempts to defend himself, they cover his head with a blanket and blow tobacco smoke up under it until he is stifled or sick. This is a complete "smoking out," and unless some such plan is resorted to the Freshman, even though not a smoker, can usually endure the process without much more inconvenience than his entertainers themselves, and is seldom sickened by it. The Sophomores of course improve their time in saying would-be smart and witty things at their victim's expense,—a style of wit that is pointless save when indecent or obscene,—and on their departure may take with them any little articles of property that fall in their way.

The regular time for pillaging the Freshmen, however, is when they are absent at recitation, especially on the first and second Saturday noons of the term, when the Sophomores are at leisure. They proceed to the Freshmen's rooms, in parties of three or four, and carry off anything they find there likely to please themselves or, by its loss, to inconvenience the owner. Pipes, tobacco and cigars are the first things confiscated, and are seldom returned. Combs, hair brushes, shaving brushes, clothes brushes, blacking brushes, looking glasses, pens, ink, and paper, pencils, knives, and paper cutters, collars, shirts, and neck ties, towels, soap, hones, razors, scissors, picture frames and ornaments, text-books and lexicons, anything and everything, all are seized upon. In a week or two, or after a longer interval, the Freshman may have the most valuable of his missing article mysteriously returned to him. Or even within a few days a Sophomore may openly bring them back, and perhaps go so far as to apologize, by saying that he thoughtlessly lugged them off in a drunken frolic. This practice of stealing is apt to surprise and enrage a Freshman more than the "smoking out." The latter he was in a measure prepared for by the rumors current in the newspapers, but of the other "custom" he had probably had no previous intimation. By the time the college catalogues are issued, during the second week of November, he has probably grown wary enough to be more on his guard, though he may not yet have learned that a specific aim of the Sophomores is to seize upon these pamphlets, so soon as the Freshmen shall have purchased them. On the day of publication, the catalogues are distributed among the latter by their division officers, at the close of the noon recitation, and charged against them on their term-bills, at the rate of ten cents per copy. They are given to the upper classes in the same way, but the Fresh are of course the chief purchasers, many an individual taking a dozen or more copies. If the Sophs should meet such a one alone upon the street they would not hesitate to wrest his catalogues from him forthwith, but their usual procedure is to visit the Freshmen's rooms while they are at dinner, and then rob them of their pamphlets. A Freshman's tobacco, catalogues, and umbrellas are looked upon as lawful prey by many who scorn the indiscriminate pilfering of his possessions. Cap snatching is also quite a common practice. Though a Soph would not steal a cap from a Freshman's room, he would think it a great exploit to "gobble up" the head coverings of an entire club from the hall or entry of the house where they were taking supper. A solitary Fresh passing near a crowd of Sophs also stands in danger of losing his hat, particularly if it be evening. To such an extent was this practice carried by the Sophs of '71, that the Fresh of '72 were for a time in the habit of wearing caps made of paper, when they went upon the street after dark, so that if they chanced to be "scalped" their loss would be trifling.

It was said that "smoking out" is generally practised upon Freshmen before they become known as individuals. "Hazing,"—which according to the dictionary would include this, and all other outrages, annoyances, and impositions to which Freshmen are exposed—signifies among Yale men the punishment of those who have become personally obnoxious to the Sophomores. It is a more deliberate and cold-blooded thing than "smoking out," in which the participants do not—certainly at the outset—entertain any feelings of revenge or malice toward their victim. The one thing naturally leads to the other, however, and a "subject" for "smoking out" who "shows fight," and perhaps gets the better of his entertainers, may be marked for more elaborate and formal attentions. A Fresh who is notably "loud" and defiant in his bearing; who takes pains to hurl contempt upon his "natural rulers"; who returns an "Oh, Soph!" for every "Oh, Fresh!" more than all, who tells tales to the faculty, is thought a proper subject for "bringing down." The self-appointed committee who are to carry out this process manage to entrap their man in a close carriage—and this, by means of disguises and other deceptions, is not usually a very difficult matter—where he is gagged, blindfolded, and rendered powerless. They then drive off to the appointed rendezvous, some desolate locality like East or West Rock, where others are perhaps awaiting them. The indignities here inflicted depend upon the ingenuity of the torturers and the extent of their dislike for the victim. The cutting off of his hair is the commonest device. Perhaps they mark upon his cheek the numeral of his class, employing for the purpose some chemical that will remain for several days indelible, or strip him and smear his naked body with paint; or pour cold water upon him; or practice certain things which cannot be named: finally leaving him, half-clothed, with a gag in his mouth perhaps, and his hands bound behind him, to find his way back to the city; or possibly dropping him, in this plight, within the walls of the cemetery, where he would probably have to stay until the opening of the gates in the morning. This is what "hazing" means at Yale, and it has been thought proper to be thus explicit in describing it. It should be understood that while all the things mentioned have, on the authority of accredited rumor, really been practised, they have not all, or many of them, been practised at any one time. And it may be further stated that, of late years and probably always, the cases of hazing have averaged less than one for every class. It is a sort of freshman bugbear, whose occasional appearance induces a belief in its continual presence. There can of course be no word of defence said in favor of the barbarity, yet it is nearly as certain that the victims of it always bring it upon themselves. For this reason, however great may be the indignation against the hazers, there is very little sympathy felt for the hazed, even by his own classmates. The justice of the " taking down " has to be recognized, even though its high-handedness be deprecated. On the other hand, no one is surprised when a hazed Freshman afterwards turns out to be a "big man" in his class, and stands high in college repute. As for one's conduct toward "smokers out," this may be said : once in his room there is no chance for a boy of ordinary physique to make an effective defence against them. If he be of the heroic mould, and wishes to "die game," he may be enabled, by singling out an individual interloper, to "smash" him, with the certainty of being himself "smashed" in return. A more logical proceeding for a boy of self-respect, is to remain passive but obey no orders at any price. Abuse of a lay figure is not exhilarating—even for Sophomores. A more natural and alas! common one is to obey just so far as may seem necessary to escape personal violence. With sufficient warning on both sides, a pistol-shot through the door is the surest way to scatter a crowd of Sophs pressing against it, and though they vow dire vengeance against him in consequence, a Freshman who thus defends himself will not be likely afterwards to suffer at their hands, save for some additional reason. The attempt to drive Sophomores out of a room by a threatening display of a pistol is, on the other hand, sheer folly.

Another amusement of this gentry, is, of an evening, when passing a Freshman's room which fronts upon the street, to shout, "Put out that light, Freshie!" and, if the obedient Freshman douses his glim, to cry, "Light her up again, Fresh!" and so to keep him at work until the Sophs grow tired of the sport. If he pays no attention to their clamors, or even shouts back a defiance, they will probably let him alone, though, if the locality be a safe one for the practice, they may hurl a stone through his window in return. "Oh Fresh! Freshie! Freshman!" are the cries which constantly greet him upon the street, especially when he passes near a crowd of Sophs, seated upon the college fence, or hanging about their club headquarters after dinner, in which cases delicate personal compliments are added, as: "What a pretty Freshman!" "See his new necktie!" "How his boots shine!" "Keep step there, Freshie! Left! right! left! Left! right! left!" and so on. Another diversion for a crowd of scoffing Sophomores is to attend the gymnasium, and make comments on the Freshmen there performing,—thereby of course adding to the latter's self-complacency and ease of mind, —or, when tired of this, to assist them in their exercise ; forcing a Freshman by means of various "encouragements," to dance upon the spring-board, or swing a club, or climb a rope or ladder, and so on. The favorite song of the Sophs is called "Bingo," and winds up with a wild yell of, "B! I! N! G! O!—*My!* Poor!! FRESH!!!!" These practices which have been mentioned are confined almost exclusively to the first term of the year, and in great part to the first half of that term.

Within a week from the opening day, notices, devised

by "leading men," are circulated through the freshman division rooms, announcing that "there is to be a rush on Library street to-night at seven o'clock and every man must be there to defend the honor of the class." Sometimes the Fresh assemble and find no Sophs to meet them, sometimes the reverse is the case; but supposing both parties to be in readiness at the appointed time, each forms in solid mass, with its heaviest men in the front rank, and rushes towards its opponent, endeavouring to sweep it from the walk and street, go through it, break it up and disorganize it generally. As a preliminary, there are of course defiant songs, outcries and a general interchange of compliments. But the rush: a seething, struggling mass of men, shoving, crushing, trampling one another, snatching caps and tearing clothes, fighting for dear life to work their way through with some show of unbroken ranks. The force of the first attack having spent itself, the parties draw off and reorganize for another onset, and the process is again gone through with. The result is apt to be a drawn battle in which each side claims the victory. The Freshmen generally have the advantage in numbers, the Sophomores in experience and discipline; there are Juniors to marshal the former, and perhaps Seniors may help the latter, though sometimes Juniors and Seniors may both join the Freshmen if they are unequally matched with their opponents. The interference of the college authorities quickly breaks up a Library street rush, and with a few cries of "Faculty! faculty!" the combatants scatter before many can be identified, since those who are caught are heavily "marked" or even "suspended." There is in fact so much danger of this, that it is getting common to appoint as a place for the "trial of strength" Hamilton Park, the ball ground outside the city, where, at the close of some match-game of ball, which serves as an excuse for assembling, the parties can draw up their ranks and "rush" one another without fear of interruption. After one or two "square rushes," at the Park or elsewhere, every one's "honor" is for the time satisfied, and no more formal trials of the kind are attempted for the term. A party of Sophs, marching up from a regatta, or from a visit to the post-office, or in any way chancing to be together, will usually make any Freshman they may meet "clear the track," or be brushed off the sidewalk; and if the latter are in sufficient force to resist, there may be some scuffling and confusion. But these ex-tempore rencounters are not called rushes.

Freshmen are not "allowed" by the Sophomores to carry bangers, nor yet to wear the style of hat variously known as beaver, stove-pipe, and plug, until the last Sunday of the second term. About the middle of that term, however, they open hostilities upon a certain day, usually a Wednesday or Saturday afternoon, by a grand display of bangers ;—a large crowd of Fresh marching about the principal streets of the town, ringing these clubs upon the pavement by way of defiance, and perhaps displaying a beaver hat or two besides. This challenge is accepted by the Sophomores, and in the evening a "banger rush" takes place. Most of the bangers which were swung so valiantly in the afternoon have been laid aside, and only one or two are brought out in the evening by the Freshmen who are to act as champions. The others flock about those to form a body-guard against the expected attacks of the Sophomores, since the rush is begun by the latter for the purpose of wresting away the bangers and thereby vindicating their authority. Perhaps it takes place at the post-office, directly after supper, or on Chapel street, or in some obscure locality, at a later hour of the evening. If on

Saturday night, it happens at a very late hour. The freshman societies, adjourning at about the same time, join one another in front of Delta Kap hall, near the corner of Church street, and march up Chapel in close array, perhaps singing some defiant song. The Sophomores may await them at some crossing and there pounce upon them, or march along up Chapel street, on the opposite side of the way. Finally, an onset is made: Freshmen and Sophomores struggle and twist together, roll each other in the mud and slush, lose and regain the all-important banger, and are at last dispersed by the policemen or faculty or both. If an arrest is made, both classes raise the cry of "Yale! Yale!" and try to rescue the unfortunate from the clutches of the peelers, in which they often succeed. Force failing, they may attempt to bargain for his release by the promise to quietly disperse. There is always money enough in a crowd to "bail out" any who may be arrested, so that a student seldom passes a night in the lock-up, and the subsequent fines do not much trouble him, for if a poor man his comrades make up the amount. The worst feature of his arrest is the bringing his name to the ears of the faculty, whose mandates are more to be dreaded than those of the courts. It is a habit of the New Haven policemen, at the time of a rush, to arrest some upper-class man who may be quietly watching the sport ;—this being an easier procedure than the seizure of one of the actual combatants, and serving quite as well, in the eyes of the general public, for a proof of official vigilance. Banger rushes, after the first, are of a rather intermittent character, happening, off and on, for the rest of the term. When a solitary Fresh, carelessly swinging his banger, is pounced upon by several Sophs, and cannot escape by flight, he clings to the sacred cane, and shouts with all his might the numeral of his class. This generally brings both friends and enemies, and he becomes the central figure of a rush, in very short order. "Beaver rushes" are of the same general character, except that the Sophs, even though they fail to get possession of the hat, are quite certain to smash it, which is almost as gratifying. For this reason the wearing of beavers in advance of the traditional time is too expensive a sport to be indulged in by more than a few individuals. Sometimes a banger or beaver rush takes place on the ice of Lake Saltonstall, four miles from the city, when crowds have assembled there for the nominal purpose of skating. Rushes here, as at Hamilton Park, are free from the reproach of disturbing anyone but the participants ; but for the past two years these banger rushes of the second term have been abandoned altogether. A Freshman never defies a Sophomore on Sunday, by displaying either banger or beaver, nor does the latter make depredations on that day, though at any other time he will confiscate a Freshman's club or hat wherever he finds them.

The rush seems to be a sort of substitute for the old foot-ball game,—abolished by the faculty in 1857,— though perhaps it also flourished at the same time with it. About a month after the opening of the term, a notice was posted at the Lyceum door, challenging the Sophomores to meet the Freshmen in the annual game of foot-ball, and signed by three of the latter, in behalf of the entire class. A notice, accepting the challenge, appointing the green as the place, and half-past two of a particular Wednesday or Saturday afternoon as the time for the trial, was in turn nailed up at the Athenæum door, attested by the signatures of three sophomore committee men, and usually headed by some poetical quotation welcoming the Fresh to destruction. The Freshmen supplied the ball ; umpires were chosen from among graduates or upper-class men ; spectators from the upper classes and the town covered the State House steps and other convenient places for looking on ; and the game began. Better than any possible account from one who has never seen it, is this description of the sport, written, after graduation, by a man who regretted its abolishment,—a member of the class of '58, who was killed at the head of his regiment :

" Off with your coat, man, if you don't want it torn. Don't you hear the 'warning'? That is Jones, the best player in the sophomore class. He steps back, runs forward, and up goes the ball, way over the heads of our side. Lucky you were back there by the steps to catch it. Good! well done! Stop! don't kick it ; this is Rushing game ; give Brown your hat and let him run one way hiding it in his bosom ; and while he makes that diversion you run the other. Now then! Run! Never mind those fellows who run out to head you off ; dodge them if you can, and if you are caught, hang on to the ball like grim death. *" Hi ! 'Fifty-four ! 'Fifty-five ! Stop him ! Quick ! this way ! Hold him ! Push ! Get the ball !"* But you can no longer distinguish separate sounds. You are now the center of a dense mass of men, shouting, shoving, dragging, struggling, swaying to and fro toward either side of the field. You know that you have one man by the throat who is trying to seize the ball, and in the exultation of conscious power you don't see that he has you by the hair. There is an unsatisfactory sensation in your legs which you afterwards conclude must have been produced by the stamping and kicking of a hundred boot-heels ; but you don't mind that, for one of your battered limbs is twined round your adversary's, so that the next move of the crowd must bring him down. Ah ! there it goes, but the sway is in the wrong direction, and brings you down under him; and what is worse, under that forest of boots! But the ball! your sacred trust! He lets it go—we are close to the fence—and whistle—away it flies just as some big heel comes crushing against your head. ...

"'Do you feel better now?'

"'Oh yes! stunned a little, that's all. But the ball, is it over?'

"'Over! I should think so. But you must go home now, you are hurt.'

"'Hurt! I am *not* hurt. I hope you don't think I mind a little blood. Pshaw! come and join the next game!'"

The class of '61 was the last to post a challenge. It was accepted by '60, and everything was appointed in due order, when the faculty voted that the game should not take place, and it has never been heard of since. From the fact that it had been dispensed with by some classes before that, the custom seems to have been somewhat on the wane, or it might not have died so quietly. The Sophomores, being experts, were of course almost inevitably the victors. Sometimes, however, both parties claimed the victory, as in 1853, when a fierce dispute arose between the Fresh of '57 and the Sophs of '56, and a four-page sheet called the *Arbiter* was issued, " in the interest of impartial justice," to defend the claims of the Freshmen. " Songs of the Ball," too, were every year written, printed, and sung by the victors, and doubtless by the vanquished also ; and the leader of the victorious class was usually rewarded with a boquet or similar token of approval, sent by the lady witnesses of the spectacle, the reception whereof he publicly acknowledged. Foot-ball had been a popular college pastime for full half a century at the time of the abolishment of the trial of strength between the two lower classes which annually happened in its name. Two years later, a municipal law forbade the students to use the green as a play ground, and so the sport itself, as well as the annual struggle which was its outgrowth, became obsolete.   In the fall of 1870 the custom of kicking ball was revived somewhat,—the freedom of the college yard being granted for the purpose,—and there were two or three match games played at Hamilton Park between the Juniors and Sophomores.

A disgraceful practice—which originated in the class of '70, and which bids fair to become a settled "custom," if indeed it has not become one already—is the painting upon the fences and walks in the vicinity of the colleges, and even upon the buildings themselves, the numeral of the freshman class, in gigantic characters, with perhaps an "Oh, Soph!" added. This unspeakably childish procedure is presumably intended as a defiance to the class above.   The Freshmen who are thus guilty of sneaking out at midnight with brush and paint-pot to perpetrate this imbecile barbarism are not known to their classmates, who condemn the practice as heartily as do all the rest of college.   This is one of the occasions where a few individual fools are able to act in the name of and disgrace an entire class and college. The men in '70 who begun the business are most of all to blame, for the traces of their bad work remained next year, to suggest the idea to their freshman successors.   The worst of these accordingly felt called upon to mark "'71" in still larger characters, and in still more prominent places, than "'70" had been marked. The next year Freshmen thought it a brave deed to improve on *their* predecessors.   And so it has gone on. The worst thing about it being that the deed is done before a freshman class is well enough organized to make its opinion condemning it felt by each individual; and when done the infamy is practically indelible.   A few of the '69 Sophs whose doors and windows were daubed in this way, seized upon the first Freshmen who came to hand, and forced them in broad daylight to scrub off the work of their classmates. The Freshman who climbed up the Lyceum lightning rod and painted " '64 " upon the white face of the college clock, did a thing whose difficulty somewhat atoned for its foolishness ; but in this cowardly disfigurement of the college buildings there is absolutely no redeeming feature. A somewhat analagous, though far less disreputable, practice, occasionally in vogue among the Freshmen, is the issuing of printed handbills in ridicule of their superiors. Though the sarcasm is often weak, there is at least an attempt to say something, and the bills even if pasted up can be torn down again. " Give me that banger, Freshie, or I'll tell the faculty," were the words upon a '69 poster, which was issued to acquaint college with the fact that a Sophomore, by the use of this threat, had forced a Fresh to surrender a banger which he had stolen from the former's room. Similarly, " '69 below par ;, Sophs selling at a discount at the Hamilton Park stock exchange," was the bill issued by the '70 Freshmen, when no Sophomores went to the Park to rush them at the time expected. To pull off one of the pointers of the clock upon the Lyceum tower is often an object of freshman or even sophomore ambition. The '70 Freshmen once, in the night time, placed a white flag bearing the numeral of their class upon the highest pinnacle of the Library.

Another disreputable practice of the Freshmen, which fortunately was put an end to before the painting nuisance commenced, was known as "gate-lifting." On the night before Thanksgiving day, crowds of Freshmen were wont to range about the city, unshipping the gates of the citizens, carrying them off for some dis-

tance, or making a pile of them in the college yard. Thither the next morning would assemble the irate owners, in search for their property, at whom the Fresh would shout, "Lift up your gates!" as they carried them away.   It happened that the gate stealing Freshmen of '69 came to grief in this wise : A pair of them were arrested by the police, shut up over night with the common criminals, heavily fined by the judge next day, and suspended by the faculty for the space of a term.   Since then, few traces of the "custom" have been made manifest.   On the night in question, two innocent Freshmen who chanced to be upon the street were seized upon by the peelers and locked up with the others, in spite of their protestations.   They of course escaped conviction, though held by the newspapers to be equally guilty with the others, and to owe their release to good luck,—instead of to the real fact, that they had no possible connection with the matter.

The street lamps are among the things which suffer at the hands of students.   Several '69 Freshmen had a habit of "collecting" from inside the lamps the little strips of glass on which the names of the streets were painted.   The "value" of one of these signs was proportionate to the difficulty of obtaining it,—the central streets being of course the most dangerous localities in which to "work," and the signs nearest the police headquarters the ones most eagerly desired.   Lamps are oftener smashed by Sophomores or other upper-class men than by Freshmen.   Those in the vicinity of the colleges, especially, are apt to be broken pretty constantly by snow balls in the winter time, and do not fare much better at other seasons.   Blowing them to pieces with fire-crackers is a common diversion as Fourth of July approaches.   One particular lamp, on High street, back of the Library, is notably unfortunate.   The glass is seldom allowed to remain in it whole for twenty-four successive hours. Frequenters of the gymnasium practice upon it as a target. Not content with smashing the glass, its enemies have at times lugged off the lamp frame bodily, and suspended it in the college yard, at the same time breaking off the burner, and setting fire to the direct stream of gas. Several years ago, the post itself was blown up with gunpowder, and the gas from the main pipe ignited, thereby raising an alarm of fire. It was a year or two before the post was replaced, but as the same old practices have been renewed, the powers-that-be would probably consult their own interest if they again discontinued it, and left that unrighteous locality again in the dark. The present plan of having the lamp guarded constantly by a policeman only aggravates its misfortunes.

Freshmen, though they do not institute, at least take part in and pay for the " Thanksgiving Jubilee," which celebration may therefore appropriately find a place in this chapter. It is managed by a committee of sixteen, —four from each class, half of whom are appointed by Linonia and half by Brothers,—and is held first in the hall of one society and then in that of the other in alternate years. .The freshman committee-men solicit subscriptions—a dollar or less being the amount ordinarily expected—to defray the expenses of the exhibition, and when these are paid in to the upper-class committee-men the Freshmen receive in return admission tickets to the show. Armed with these they assemble in front of Alumni Hall on the night appointed, some time before half-past seven, when it is announced that the doors will be open, each one eager to have a first chance at the seats. Perhaps while clamoring for admission they notice that no upper-class men are to be seen about the entrance, and wonder that the "managers" within are able to produce such an uproar. Half-past seven. The doors fly open; there are no ticket-takers; up rush the Freshmen to the hall. Dismay fills them as they enter it, for it is crowded already! Across one end is stretched a stage, with drop-curtain and footlights. Close to this, on comfortable settees, are ranged the Seniors with their invited guests from among the recent alumni; behind them are the Juniors; then the Sophomores, upon wooden benches, or standing; and close to the furthest wall the few empty benches left for the Freshmen! These are filled in an instant, and still the crowd surges up from below. The rear men, not understanding the state of the case, press resistlessly upward, and the jam becomes terrific. Freshmen cling to the window-sills, hang from the door-casings, stick in some way to every inch of projecting surface that can be made to furnish a foothold, and sway to and fro under the impetus of new arrivals. Nor is the rabble made up altogether [of Freshmen. Sophomores or other upper-class men, ignorant of the approved way of gaining access to the hall, or coming too late to profit by it, members of the professional schools and other outsiders, struggle and pant with the rest, or desperately attempt to work their way through the solid mass of humanity, and join their friends at the front. A private staircase in the rear of the hall is the portal through which the Seniors, and the initiated generally, are always admitted,—to the surprise and confusion of the rabble. Awaiting the rise of the curtain, the seated portion of the audience smoke, sing, yell at the Fresh to make less noise, suddenly rise up to see what the matter is in the rear, and sit down without finding out, discuss the programme,—which is distributed by being flung in handfuls about the hall, thereby adding to the confusion of the rabble, who fight desperately to secure the copies as they fall,—and otherwise divert themselves.

At last the rising curtain reveals several Seniors upon the stage, and one of the committee announces that the first thing in order is the election of officers from among the Freshmen,—their shortest man to be the president, and their longest the secretary, of the meeting,—and calls upon the audience to present the candidates. The crowd at once springs to its feet, with a wild shriek of "Pass him up!" and two or three short Freshmen are rolled over the heads of the audience, on to the stage, where they are stretched out upon their backs, and a gigantic measuring stick, fifteen or twenty feet long, applied to them. "The shortest" is then announced by name as president, and his "hight" is mentioned in some absurd way as being so many "barleycorns," or "degrees," or cubit inches"; then the long men are passed up and measured in the same manner, and the one chosen is said to be so many "millimetres" or "square miles" long; after which both "officers" are put off the stage and left to shift for themselves in finding seats or standing places again. As a matter of fact, the shortest Freshman and the longest one, hearing of this practice beforehand, often stay away from the meetings, at least till after the officers are chosen; so that the men really measured upon the stage are often about of the average size. The main thing, however, is to "keep up the custom," and so long as this is done in theory, the practice makes little difference. The Freshmen who are "passed along" with such an appearance of roughness, are not injured in the process, save perhaps as to their wearing apparel, which may thereby become soiled and torn, and accept their fate in its true light, simply as a joke, in which nothing serious or degrading is intended by any one.

After the "overture by the orchestra,"—a half dozen professionals hired for the purpose, or an amateur band

of college musicians,—the first thing on the programme
is the "opening load," which is often "necessarily
omitted" for some assigned reason, such as, "on account
of the lateness of the hour the load could not be
opened," or "because the faculty ordered it unloaded."
Then come two or three plays, between which are sand-
wiched a comic oration and a comic poem, both relating
to college life, and perhaps a display of negro minstrelsy
ends up the show. The names of the committee-men
figure upon the first page of the programme, which, for
the rest, is expressed in the form of a burlesque, as
absurd and ludicrous as the ingenuity and wit of the
committee can devise. Thus we have the "sanguino-
lently and demoniacally loquacious pantomimic representation" ; "the spamodically pharmaceutical tragedy" ;
the "mysterious, Milesian, mediæval, moral-play" ; the
"savory, side-splitting farce" ; and so on. The minstrels, likewise, are "tenebriously umbrageous Stygio-
Ethiopian," or "dulcifluously incanting ingrescent,"
ones, or "American citizens of (corked) African
descent." The "oration," or "sermon," or "address,"
is about "the ignitious combustibility of all corroso-in-
flammable matter," or "analytical mathematics as a
means of religious instruction." The poem is an
"epic-ac ode," or a "dorggerel," or a "jocular, jingling
jumble, joining jovial jests in juxtaposition with jubilant
jokes," or is made up of "'class'ical (l)odes." The
music is by the "'first nine' Yale muses," or the "Med-
dlesome society," or the "dulce strainers," or the "Yale
tooters." The "finale" is omitted because a certain
"old clo'" man "has stolen the 'close' of the performance," or is "to be had at Moriarty's [a well known ale
seller's] after the show is concluded." "Gentlemen are
requested to wipe their boots before entering the hall,
and are *particularly* requested not to spit on the backs

of those who sit in front of them." "Freshmen accompanied by their mothers or nurses, $1. Theologues, Law students and other children admitted gratis." "Students taking seats are expected to occupy them for the remainder of the year, unless released by the proper authority." "No two students of different classes can occupy the same seat, unless they take a seat of the lower grade ; but if a student has a brother, the two can sit on the floor together, provided they don't let their legs hang down." " As the faculty request that all the students (Theologues included) shall be present at the exercises, church papers, certifying their presence will be required. The papers may be handed to the college carpenter." " Members of the *incoming* class will find seats as soon as possible." " No one allowed to be high except the secretary." " Photographs of the leading artists can be obtained at 303 Chapel street. Price $2.50 per dozen." The "point" of many of these titles and " notices" of course lies in their fatuousness, and utter want of connection with the things to which they are joined. The show takes place the Tuesday before Thanksgiving, and is three hours or more in length.

Thus, the Jubilee as it existed during '69's " four years at Yale." Now, as to its earlier and later history. Originally it was called " Thanksgiving *Eve,*" and always took place upon that Wednesday night. In the old times, when Linonia and Brothers were something more than " institutions," the attendance upon their meetings of that evening was smaller than usual, owing to the absence of those who had gone home to celebrate Thanksgiving. Hence the custom arose of giving a burlesque character to the proceedings. The shortest Freshman was put in the president's chair, and the longest one at the secretary's table, and the meeting proceeded under their auspices, instead of those of the regular upper-class officials. In place of a formal debate, was held a " raffle": a number of "questions," mostly of a bombastic or nonsensical character, were thrown together in one hat ; the names of those in attendance in another ; and each man was obliged to speak upon the question drawn out with his name. The speakers were expected to be "funny," and were usually only foolish,—each man consenting to make a silly display of himself for the sake of witnessing a similar discomfiture of the others. Of course, once in a while a really good thing would be said or a really ludicrous event take place, but the meetings as a whole, were described as being dreary enough, spite of the cheers and applause of those who had made up their minds to appear amused, under any circumstances.

It was in 1855 that the attempt was first made to vary this traditional celebration. A committee from that society was appointed to make preparations in Linonia, and Brothers was invited to attend the show. "When the eventful night came, we had Linonia hall filled. Our stage was the vacant space west of the president's desk, our green room was Calliope hall, our wardrobe, some old hats, shawls, and coats gathered in college, and a skirt, cap, veil, etc., from some garret in town. The performance consisted of such personations as Widow Bedott's ''Kiah, we're all poor creeters.' The man with forty ailments, who was 'pooty well, thank'ee, heow deu yeou deu.' ✳ The trial of the case 'Bullum vs. Boatem.' 'The Suppression of the Press.' The Yankee that was courtin' Betsy Jane, but was 'as well as usual.' We had, too, the Yankee Orator, one to speak, one to gesture ; and if anyone had a good song or act, was known to have hit off any good point in play or charade, he was called for with cries of immense encouragement and prevailing force, after the manner of college audiences, and then he was applauded, as you would expect by a company bound to make the best and most of everything. The performances had almost entirely an extemporaneous cast, some parts were entirely off-hand, and for that very reason all charity was extended to the actors, and the three hours were closed with the feeling that we had succeeded and redeemed the evening."

The next year a joint committee was appointed from each society, and the show was held in Brothers hall; and so it has since gone on, first in one hall, then in the other. A shortest and a longest Freshman from each society were chosen presidents and secretaries and seated in the president's desk. Then there were two presidents and one secretary. Finally, as now, a single one of each, without distinction of societies, although seats were always provided for them. Negro minstrels exhibited for the first time at this Eve of '56, and among other things was a "living bass-viol" impersonated by the largest man in the senior class. "'Somebody's' clothes-line, run three or four times from his neck to his feet, made the strings; a cigar box made the bridge; his own ears, the keys. The performer walked in his instrument, tuned it up, and beginning to play, the huge yet flexible voice of the 'machine' produced the sounds which were supposed to be the tones of the viol. This was a success, especially when, in the midst of a brilliant passage, the instrument collapsed and was carried out. Another thing was the Hutchinson family intensified. Another was the celebrated lecture on the wonderful Gyascutus from the Rocky Mountains, which wound up with a leap which overwhelmed in utter confusion all the audience nearest the stage." In '57 the stage for the first time reached across the end of the hall. The "scenery" was made of strips of blue cambric, and the different localities were represented by placards hung upon the same, as "Forest Scene," "Inside the Castle," and so on. "One of the most striking performances of the evening was a solo by prima donna 'Bob' Stiles. His magnificent bust and arms, the pride of the gymnasium, were powdered and cosmeticated, and set off by a low-necked, short-sleeved concert dress. This dress — black cambric, shining like satin, over hoops eighteen feet in circumference—was engineered through the door, when 'Bob,' the biggest man in the class, was led in by Watkins, the littlest man. His solo began with a delicately-trilled falsetto, set off with the most languishing attitudes, and wound up suddenly with a stentorian double bass, which woke the most enthusiastic responsive cheer. The performance of that night held the audience in well-nigh continuous laughter for four hours." In 1860, mention is first made of a printed programme, of the "opening load," of the "censor's report," and of the name Thanksgiving Jubilee, which has since been applied to the show. The "censor" was a Senior, appointed by the committee, whose duty it was to get off personal "hits" at the expense of his auditors, somewhat after the manner of the class historians on Presentation Day, and decree the infliction of absurd "fines" for real or pretended offences. He was wont to "touch up" a good many Seniors, quite a number of Juniors, some Sophomores, and the few Freshmen who had chanced in the space of a term to make a college reputation of some sort. His "report" was read from an immense roll, a good many feet in length, "and in time came to be considered *the* feature of the entertainment."

Thus the silly inanities of "Thanksgiving Eve," invented for the amusement of the unfortunates who lingered about the college, grew, in the ten years' interval, to be the " Jubilee " known to '69 men, held in season to be enjoyed by those who spent Thanksgiving abroad equally with the ones who stayed behind. Thus, little by little, it lost its impromptu character, and became more formal. The tendency to introduce smut and vulgarity also grew apace, until it culminated in 1865 in the production of an indecent farce,—the "parts" of which were all sustained by Sophomores,—and a censor's report that was little better. The faculty, hearing of the matter, suspended the offenders, and next year decreed that no female characters should be represented upon the stage at the Jubilee. They offered the committee, under certain restrictions, the use of Alumni Hall, but the offer was not accepted, and for the first time since the custom was inaugurated the Jubilee was abandoned. The money obtained from the Freshmen for defraying the expenses went to pay for a supper for the upper-class committee-men. Next year, the prohibition of woman's apparel being still insisted on, the " female " characters evaded the rule by the employment of a sort of Turkish costume that served equally well to distinguish them. Since then the restrictions have been disregarded altogether ; but the censor's report has never been revived.

At the Thanksgiving of 1869 a new policy was adopted in regard to the celebration. An elaborate stage was erected in the south end of Alumni Hall, and fitted up with scenery and "properties" from the city theater. Raised seats and settees were at the opposite end, and the usual benches filled the intermediate space. On these sat the classes in order, Seniors nearest the stage, Freshmen in the rear, while the reserved seats behind were occupied by ladies and their attendants,—the admission of the former being the novel feature of the show. A regular admission fee of

a quarter dollar was charged each person, and double
that amount was required for a reserved seat. The
specially-engraved tickets bore a representation of a
turkey. Formal steel-plate invitations to the entertainment were also issued. The hall, of more than twice
the capacity of the society-halls, was crowded, without
being jammed as in days agone,—all but the latest
comers securing seats of some sort. Save for the
absence of tobacco smoke and freshman wranglings,
the character of the show was like that of its predecessors. The opening load, entitled "the perfect stick,"
represented a gigantic glue bottle. The cost of the entertainment was $300, and the receipts fell $50 short
of that sum. The expenses of any previous Jubilee had
never exceeded a third the first named amount.

Last year the Jubilee was for a second time omitted,
—the appointed committee being unwilling to engage
in the work on the conditions offered by the faculty:
that the exhibition should be held in one of the society
halls, that there should be no "female" characters in the
plays, and that the committee should be held individually responsible for any violations of order or decorum.
The fate of the institution in the future seems uncertain, but if revived at all it will probably be in its older
rather than latest form; for, though that experiment
was in its way an admitted success, there is a general
sentiment against opening the exhibition to outsiders,
especially to ladies, as a process tending to make the
show more formal and expensive, and to deprive it of
its characteristic and peculiar flavor, as a jolly gathering where the undergraduate sense of fun is allowed
free vent, in the presence of those alone who comprehend and appreciate it. If the general public be admitted, stiffness and formality will come with them;
their tastes will have to be catered to; their presence

will put the college men on their good behavior; and the old heartiness and abandon, the careless mingling of all the classes in an evening's joviality, which made the Jubilee unique among college celebrations, will soon disappear altogether. So say the opponents of reform, and their case seems a strong one. Alumni Hall may wisely be retained as the place of meeting hereafter, and all undergraduates taxed equally in support of the exhibition. But it is a gratuitous assumption to suppose that the students, left to themselves, will act disgracefully, or that a repetition of the indecencies of 1865 can only be prevented by the presence of ladies at the Jubilee.

With Presentation Day the Seniors close their active connection with the college, and at chapel prayers the following morning the Juniors occupy their vacated seats; the Sophomores take those of the Juniors, and the Freshmen those of the Sophomores, where in old times the latter were wont to leave upright pins, chalk dust, bits of pitch, and things of that sort, for the benefit and improvement of their successors. About the year 1850, the custom arose among the Freshmen of celebrating their accession to sophomoric dignity by a performance called a "Pow-wow," upon the night of Presentation Day. It was held upon the State House steps, and consisted of burlesque speeches, songs and poems, in glorification of the performers and ridicule of the class above them, and the unpopular tutors from whose reign they were soon to be set free. The Sophomores attended and endeavored—by mock applause, cheers and outcries—to drown the voices of the speakers; and the Freshmen in turn, by a deafening blast of tin horns, would overwhelm these sophomoric interruptions. Between the two, little could be heard of the speakers' remarks, which, like the printed programmes, were

intended to be sharp and witty, but were oftener vulgar
and indecent.   Among the "subjects" and "speakers"
at one of the best of the Pow-wows were: "Salute-a-tory,
by a Big W(h)ig," " Poem, 'Pipes,' by a Broken Reed,"
"Stump Speech, by a Wood-be DeForest," and "*Expect*
Oration, by one who chews-es."   This description of the
Pow-wow in 1857 will apply well enough to them all:
" About nine o'clock, blasts from sundry tin horns in
the freshman quarters reminded the weary and sleeping
that Presentation Day 'was n't dead yet.'   As it grew
later and darker, Freshmen, covered as to their faces
with burnt-cork, Freshmen with striped pants, Freshmen
with hooped skirts, Freshmen with hoofs and tails, mild
Freshmen with coats turned inside out, fierce Freshmen
with big beards and bob-tailed trainer-coats, Freshmen
with bears' heads, and Freshmen with bare heads—in
fine, Freshmen with all sorts of conceivable and practi-
cable disguises, each one armed with a banger as big as
he could lift, and a tin horn as big as he could blow,
issued from their rooms, and marching sternly across the
college-yard, assembled at the State House steps, for
the purpose of celebrating their entrance into sophomore year.   After orating, in spite of the noisy Sophomores, who kept up a continual shouting of ' Hear ! '
' Hear ! ' 'Good ! ' 'Time for you, Fresh, to be in bed !'
and sundry other equally entertaining and witty remarks,
they sang a Greek song that looked quite natural, and
then formed the procession.   The boarding schools
were serenaded as usual, only one, however, acknowledg-
ing the compliment.   At half past two in the morning
squads of muddy Freshmen crossed the college-green,
and disappeared among the brick buildings, there to
dream for an hour or two of hobgoblins, Greek songs,
mud-puddles, serenades, fair faces, morning flunk, and
dunning Pow-wow committees."

Like other things of the sort, the ceremony became year by year more elaborate. A band of music was engaged, the place of meeting was lit up by blue lights and fireworks, transparencies were carried in the procession, and more grotesque and costly disguises made use of. But the excesses of Pow-wow brought it under the ban of the faculty, and that of the class of '66, the last one ever projected, had to be given up. Next year the threat to expel two thirds of the class prevented even the attempt at its revival, and it has never since been heard of at the college. In 1864, however, the Freshmen "celebrated," at a certain hour of Presentation Day, by "marching up and down Chapel street as a body-guard to 'Hannibal,' the college candy-man, who, attired in a scholar's habit, a huge book under his arm, a pair of eye-glasses over his nose, one of the new red biennial caps of the Sophomores upon his head, and a sporting cane in his hand, was personating the high feelings of the newly fledged Juniors as well as any negro could."

As the " Biennial" was superseded by the " Annual" examinations, so the " Biennial caps" gave way to " Annual caps," and the " Biennial Jubilee" found a successor in the " Annual Dinner." On the morning of Presentation Day the Freshmen now assume their Annual hats. These are of the well known " Oxford" pattern—a head-piece fitting close to the skull, surmounted by a stiff square, with a tassel depending from the corner on the left side. Each class varies the color. The cap of '69 was blue with white tassel, that of '70 was white, that of '68 mouse-color, and the red cap of '66 has been already noted ; before that, a sort of wicker-work had been sometimes employed. The nine committee-men wear hats of velvet with tassels of gilt, and so bargain with the hatter that these cost them nothing, their price being made up to him by his charging a higher rate for the common kind sold to the class. The members of the committe also wear, as a badge of office, tiny forks of gold, inscribed "Annual" with the numeral of the class. For these they are themselves supposed to pay. A freshman committee-man of the class of '69 has the credit of making this addition to collegiate insignia. The hats are worn from the time of assuming them until the close of the examinations, especially during the progress of the latter; though of late the examinations open within a few days of Presentation, instead of after a three weeks' interval, as was the case in the time when "Biennials" and Biennial hats were in vogue.

The last session of freshman "Annual" closes at noon of the Thursday before Commencement. An hour or two later, the emancipted Fresh assemble in the college yard, and led off by a band of music,—after serenading and cheering their division officers, or the most popular ones,—file down Chapel street to the railway station or steamboat dock, and there embark on car or boat for some one of the many sea-side resorts—like Savin Rock, or Branford Point, or Charles Island—which lie about New Haven; singing on the way the songs of jubilation which have been written and printed for the occasion, or giving forth the old-time melodies with which they are more familiar. Arrived at the appointed locality, while the committee bustle about to see that nothing be lacking to the "perfect feast" for which they had previously made the arrangements, and the band plays a lively strain, and the denizens of the hotel gaze in wonder at the new comers, one of the chief actors of the day—"the historian of the first division"—is arranging his manuscripts and clearing his throat, in readiness for the fulfilment of his duty.

At length a table is set up under the trees, the Freshmen lie upon the ground in a circle around it, the historian doffs his hat and mounts his improvised rostrum, and the reading begins. A "class history" is nothing unless "funny." The committee select from each division the one whom they consider its wittiest man (latterly the division itself elects him), and he compiles a "history" of his fellows, wherein he attempts the rather dificult task of "touching up" their individual peculiarities, "in a way to afford amusement to all, and offense to none." Ludicrous blunders in the recitation room, absurd translations from Greek or Latin authors, impossible demonstrations of Euclid's problems, all the laughable mishaps of a year of a hundred and fifty Freshmen, are carefully collected by the historians, and "set off" in as "taking" a style as they chance to be masters of. Everything depends upon the manner of telling a comic story, and if the historian is fit for his place, he keeps his auditors in a constant roar of laughter to the very last word of his narrative. At its close, whether good or bad, "three times three" cheers are given for the historian, and as many more for the division he represents. The history devotes particular attention to the exploits of those who have been dropped or suspended from the class, and these former members who are present,—and there usually are some such—are forced, after their "histories" have been read, to mount the table and "make a speech" in response, which speech is always vociferously applauded by the others. The same process is also gone through with in the case of any one in regard to whom anything particularly "good" (which may often mean "bad") happens to be related, or from whom "something funny" is likely to be elicited.

The reading of one or more histories having been finished, the crowd sit down to the dinner. There are special bills-of-fare, adorned with the names of the class and its committee, and the fare itself is something wonderful. Course succeeds course, and is partaken of with a relish and gusto never before experienced. The joyous feeling of relief from the long-dreaded bugbear of examination gives a zest to the entertainment that nothing else could afford. All sorts of "sentiments" are offered and accepted with the greatest enthusiasm, and "cheers" are given for every body and every thing that can be imagined. Lemonade, with or without the claret, is the strongest potable usually upon the bill, and those in want of something more ardent order it at their own expense. Quite a number become exhilarated thereby, but only a few, and sometimes none, get so much the worse for liquor as to lose their self-command, and require the attention of their comrades on the homeward way. During or after the repast the remaining histories are read, and then come singing, and music and dancing—in which last the maidens from the hotel may be induced to take part, or a "stag party" of students alone enter into it. Finally the class ride back to the city on their special train or steamboat, and arriving there at midnight or later, perhaps serenade and cheer their tutors once more, and elicit "speeches" in acknowledgment, or sing a final song or two, and then, dismissing the band, join in one loud cheer for the class and the day, and retire to rest. So ends the first year of the four.

The last Biennial Jubilee—that of the class of '67; and the first Annual Dinner—that of the class of '68—took place upon the same year, 1865, and within a day or two of each other. Except that it was held at the end of sophomore instead of freshmen year, the Jubilee was in all respects like the Dinner that has been described—though the reading of class histories was a feature first introduced by the latter. It was said to be a custom to invite to each Jubilee the committee who who had served the class above on a like occasion, but the '69 men distinctly voted that the '68 committee be not invited to their Dinner, and the old practice has not since been revived. As already stated, politics usually interfere in this celebration. Unless all the actual and possible societies have what they consider "their share" of the committee-men and historians, there is hard feeling, and perhaps a " split" also. In the class of '67 the members and adherents of one junior society held the Jubilee in one place, those of the other two in another. The Freshmen of '70, though having no junior politics, were nevertheless able, by the exclusion of Gamma Nu men from the committee, to arouse ill-will enough to keep all members of that society, and a good many others, from the Dinner. Their successors of '71, over a curious wrangle in which all the societies of the first three years were in some way concerned, divided, like the men of '67, and went half one way and half the other. Each of the two factions also adopted its own style of Annual cap. Before setting out for their different destinations, on the day of the Dinner, they joined together in giving their instructors the customary serenades and cheers. Next year, the Freshmen gave up the Dinner entirely, and not more than half of them procured Annual hats. Last year, though a committee was appointed, it was decided to indulge in neither hats nor Dinner ; but the present year, the latter institution will be revived in all its glory, by the Fresh of '74. Its omission by the two preceding classes was due in some measure to the freshman boat races against Harvard in which they engaged, as many thought themselves unable to support the expenses of both enterprises. As Presentation will hereafter come close upon Commencement, and follow rather than precede the Annual examinations, it is likely that Annual hats will be seen no more. The wearing of them had been growing less and less popular, as Freshmen came to realize better the foolish expensiveness of paying two or three dollars for what was of practical service for but a single afternoon ; and with the sole remaining pretext for the "custom" removed, there will probably be no longer even the pretense of observing it. The Dinner itself, however, deserves to be perpetuated, for when well managed it may be made the jolliest celebration of the college course.

It is easy to see, in all the contemptuous and abusive treatment of Freshmen, mentioned in the present chapter and elsewhere, an illustration of the tenacity with which an old tradition clings to a college, and keeps alive there the relics of a code which has itself long been obsolete and forgotten. The following quotations from the laws which were enforced as early as 1760 show the servitude to which the Freshmen of a century ago were obliged to submit : "It being the duty of the Seniors to teach Freshmen the laws, usages and customs of the college, to this end they are empowered to order the whole freshman class, or any particular member of it, to appear, in order to be instructed and reproved, at such time and place as they shall appoint ; when and where every Freshman shall attend, answer all proper questions, and behave decently." "The Freshmen are forbidden to wear their hats in the college-yard until May vacation ; nor shall they afterwards wear them in college or chapel. No Freshman shall wear a gown, or walk with a cane, or appear out of his room without being completely dressed, and with his hat ; and whenever a Freshmen either speaks to a superior or is spoken to by one, he shall keep his hat off until he is bidden to put it on." "A Freshman shall not play with any members of an upper class, without being asked ; nor is he permitted to use any acts of familiarity with them, even in study time. In case of personal insult a Junior may call up a Freshman and reprehend him. A Sophimore in like case may obtain leave from a Senior, and then he may discipline a Freshman, not detaining him more than five minutes, after which the Freshman may retire, even without being dismissed, but must retire in a respectful manner." "Freshmen are obliged to perform all reasonable errands for any superior, always returning an account of the same to the persons who send them. When called, they shall attend and give a respectful answer ; and when attending on their superior they are not to depart until regularly dismissed. They are responsible for all damage done to anything put in their hands by way of errand. They are not obliged to go for the undergraduates in study-time without permission obtained from the authority ; nor are they obliged to go for a graduate out of the yard in study-time. A Senior may take a Freshman from a Sophimore, a Bachelor from a Junior, and a master from a Senior. None may order a Freshman in one play-time to do an errand in another." "Freshmen shall not run in the college yard, nor up and down stairs, nor call to anyone through a college window," and so on.

As early as 1775 attempts were made to abolish these regulations, but "in 1800 we still find it laid down as the Senior's duty to inspect the manners and customs of the lower classes and especially of the Freshmen ; and as the duty of the latter to do any proper errand, not only for the authorities of the college, but also, within the limits of one mile, for resident graduates and the two upper classes." It was not until 1804 that the Freshmen were formally exempted from the duty of running

the Chapel and dining hall before the Seniors ; the dangerous tendency of which irregularities he set forth, purely, as he said, out of regard for my good. And so it went on, until—owing to the taciturnity, which, in accordance with the previous direction of a friend, I persisted in maintaining—the sport grew tiresome to the Seniors, and I was dismissed, with a parting admonition to be more careful with my clothing ; as my cap—which they had purposely secreted—was only brought to light after considerable searching." A man named Kane, in the same class, was also " brought before the Sanhedrim, and solemnly warned not to follow the course of his Old Testament namesake, who was doubtless his ancestor ; " and all the proceedings of the " lectures " bear a strong family resemblance to those of the modern " smokings out," already described, into which they seem to have degenerated.

CHAPTER II.

SOPHOMORE YEAR.

ooming in College—Drawing and Choosing the Rooms—Trading of Choices—Rooming Alone—Packing an Entry—Moving—Rent—Buying and Selling Furniture—Fuel, Water and Light—Sweeps, Regular and Private—Paraphernalia of a Student's Room—Its Self-Invited Visitors—Candy Sam, Hannibal, Fine Day, and the Rest—The Tricks Sometimes Played upon Them—The College Police, and the Extent of their Interference—The Charm of Dormitory Life—Sitting on the Fence—Unsuccessful Attempt to Break up the Practice—Cause of the Failure—Out-door Singing—Origin of the Practice, and of the Songs—Glee Clubs, Cecilia, and Beethoven—The Latter's connection with the College Choir—R. S. Willis's Account of it—And its First Concert—Its Recent Character and Membership—Concerts and their Profits—Sophomoric Abuse of Freshmen—Public Sentiment concerning It—Areopagus—Nu Tau Phi—Omega Lambda Chi — A Mock Initiation — Compromises with the Faculty—Burning the Coal Yard—Base Ball—Yale against Harvard—The Record with other College and Professional Clubs—Places and Times Devoted to the Sport—Entertainment of Visitors—The Burial of Euclid—As Described in 1843—Fifteen Years Later—Davenport's Lithograph—The Last Celebration of the Rite—Similar Ceremonies Elsewhere.

It is in sophomore year that the undergraduates in considerable numbers begin to occupy the college dormitories : the mode of gaining and holding rooms therein may therefore appropriately be described at this place. The case of the class of '69 will probably serve as a fair index of the comparative proportion of each class rooming in college during the four successive years. Of 160 Freshmen in that class, 17 roomed in college ; of 132 Sophomores, 54 ; of 128 Juniors, 93 ; and of 119

Seniors, 107. The rooms are allotted toward the close of the third term, the "choices" of course being in the order of the classes. Each applicant signs his name to a printed blank, which states that he "on honor" intends to occupy a college room during the next year, with a particular person whom he names as his chum. These blanks are perhaps distributed, signed, and handed in during a session of the annual examination, and the announcement made by the senior tutor of the hour when he will preside over the drawing, in some designated recitation room. At the time and place appointed the interested parties assemble; the names of each pair of chums are thrown into a hat and well shaken up; then the first pair drawn have the first choice, the second the next, and so on, until all the names or choices are exhausted. The senior tutor makes out an official list of the drawings, pastes it upon a board, and hands it to the pair at the head of the list. As soon as they have chosen their room they mark its number opposite their names, and hand the list to the ones next in order; and so it goes on till the last pair have made their selection, and handed the shingle back to the senior tutor. These are all to be Seniors next term, and so have had the pick of all the rooms in college, without limitation. Next, the senior tutor presides over a drawing for the prospective Juniors. The number of rooms allowed their class is limited, and so a certain number of unlucky applicants fail to secure any rooms at all. A list of the drawings is again made out, and on it are indicated the rooms already chosen by the Seniors. The Juniors having made their selections, the proceedings in the case of the to-be Sophomores are exactly similar, except that fewer rooms are allotted to their class, and the number of disappointed applicants is therefore greater.

There is always more or less "trading of choices" in every class, after the drawing; usually, of course, before the rooms are actually chosen, though sometimes afterwards. The owners of the first or second choice may receive a bonus of $75 or even $100 by exchanging it for one of the poorer choices, and proportionate prices are given for exchanges of choices less unequal. Choices, however, cannot be directly bought and sold. A man who has drawn no room at all cannot "buy out" one more fortunate, since the latter has pledged himself in advance to "occupy a college room." Except for this rule, men with no intention of occupying them could draw college rooms, and by their speculations and traffic in the same raise the price of rent. No exchanging or trading of rooms is allowed between members of different classes. If an upper-class man rooms with a member of a class below him,—as a brother, a cousin, or an old acquaintance,—he must draw his room with the class to which his chum belongs. After a man has drawn a room, his withdrawal into a lower class does not deprive him of it; neither, when one of a pair who have drawn a room withdraws from college altogether, is a new chum saddled upon the one who remains. The latter can now have the room to himself, or can even take in a lower-class chum without causing complaint. When '69 was in college, the only other way of holding a college room alone—except in special cases—was for a man to practise a greater or less amount of deception, in support of the pretense that he had a chum,—using for this purpose the name of some accommodating class-mate who occupied a room in town. The latter was accredited with a college room, in the official catalogue, and charged with the rent of the same upon his term bill; with the money to pay which rent the real occupant of course supplied him. The number who engaged in this species of fraud, however, was not large, and those who insisted on rooming alone generally kept clear of the college buildings. Now, however, in the senior class at least, quite a number are allowed to occupy rooms by themselves.

Of late years South College has been the "first choice" of the Seniors, and its three upper floors are entirely taken up by them, as are also the two upper ones of North, which used to be the favorite. North Middle is the headquarters of the Juniors, and in South Middle may be found representatives of all four classes, the Freshmen upon the ground floor. Sophomores usually occupy nearly all the ground floor rooms of the other three colleges mentioned, and some of the rooms on the fourth floors also. A front is commonly preferred to a back, a middle to a corner room ; likewise one on the second story to one on the third, on the third to one on the fourth, on the fourth to one on the first. The proximity of a tutor's or professor's room is only a slight drawback in making a choice. Of course a room's eligibility depends largely on the character of the crowd who are to inhabit a particular entry. In the last two years, especially, the attempt is always made to "pack" an entry, or at least a floor or two of it, with a congenial and harmonious crowd. Hence the large sums often given to effect exchanges of rooms which are in themselves equally desirable. It sometimes happens that the owners of a packed entry combine to get rid of the few disagreeable men quartered among them by helping make up the bonus whereby more desirable comrades may be enabled to buy them out. Members of a particular society often agree to keep together in choosing their rooms. In North or South Middle you may perhaps find one or more floors of an entry peopled entirely with Psi U or with DKE Juniors; and similarly, in South or North, you may observe a half-dozen or more Bones men or Keys men rooming in close proximity.

After once occupying a college room a man seldom goes back to the town again; though a Sophomore, not lucky enough to draw a junior room, is sometimes forced to do it. This is a hardship which should be provided against by a rule allowing such a one to occupy his old room for a second year. It is not often the case that a man holds the same college room for two successive years. He can usually do it if he chooses, provided of course he has a right to any room at all, but the advantages to be gained by removal more than compensate for the trouble of making the change. After drawing his new room, he has only to sign a blank, ordering the transfer of his furniture and effects from the old room to the new, and hand it in to the proper authority before his departure. The work is done during vacation, under the direction of the faculty, and the cost of the same charged upon the individual's term-bill. If he chooses, he himself can directly bargain for and superintend the removal,—at greater cost of time and money. The annual rent of a college room varies from $12.50 to $50, according to location,—a man who occupies a room alone of course paying double,—but as all the furniture and equipment has to be purchased, the actual disparity between its cost and that of a room in town is not so great as appears. Still, everything taken into account, college rooms are, on the average, undoubtedly less expensive than those in town. Each individual consults his own taste and purse in the fitting up of his apartments, some being very plainly, others luxuriously furnished. The amount spent by a pair of chums in this way varies from $200 to four or, in rare cases, even five times that amount. As already remarked, none but poor Freshmen room in college, and the Sophomores rarely lay out much upon their college rooms ; so that it is only during the last two years that the rich men much affect the dormitories and exert themselves to make them attractive and comfortable. Much new furniture is every year brought into the buildings, but much remains there, year after year. A Senior seldom carries much away with him, on his departure, but sells his goods to under-class men, or his washerwoman and her "friends," or, as a last resort, to the second-hand dealers. For the latter half of the third.term, the trees in the yard are white with notices of furniture sales at this or that Senior's room ; in the manufacture of which notices all the artistic, literary and humorous talent of each individual owner is made use of. Every notice attempts in some way to be better than every other, and the result is sometimes quite amusing. "Furniture for sale," is also the legend displayed from many a Senior's window, and perhaps left dangling there, long after Presentation Day, when everything has been " sold " and the owner has disappeared forever.

As the real expense of the furniture is the difference between the buying and selling price, it may happen that a very well furnished room may in the end cost little more than one fitted up in much inferior style. Chums in college almost always occupy separate beds and bed-rooms ; in town, they as invariably sleep together. Each room is heated by a separate stove, and coal is the fuel employed. This is supplied by the college authorities at cost prices. A student, whether rooming in college or town, orders at the treasurer's office a quarter or half ton or more of coal, paying for it at the time of ordering, and it is shortly afterwards delivered at his room. The price varies somewhat with the number of flights of stairs up which it has to be carried. No coal carts, save those belonging to the college, are allowed to enter the college yard; and fuel purchased of the dealers has to be carried by hand from the nearest gateway. There is usually little reason for witholding patronage from the college coal-yard, but when for any cause an inhabitant of college chooses to buy his fuel elsewhere, it seems poor policy to hinder him by any such petty inconvenience. Open grates, though in the minority, are not uncommon; and large Franklin stoves, with open wood-fires, are sometimes discovered in the rooms of the luxurious. Each man must build his own fires, trim his own lamps, and draw his own water at the college pump, or hydrant, or cistern, or basement sink. A large, jug-like pitcher of stone was long used for the latter purpose, though the ordinary tin water-pail is gradually superseding it. The are no stoves in the new Farnam College, which is heated by steam, and lighted by gas, and supplied with water sinks and faucets on every floor.

To each college is allotted a negro "sweep," who must make the beds, sweep the rooms once a week, and keep them in order generally. He of course has a key to every room in the college to which he is assigned. As too much is expected of these sweeps their work is not very thoroughly done, and many are in the habit of presenting them with a quarter or half-dollar a week as a means of securing special attention to themselves. This is of course demoralizing, and leads to the special neglect of those who offer no fees. Another plan is the employment of a "private sweep," that is, a negro who, besides making the beds and doing the ordinary chamber work, builds the fires, draws the water, blacks boots, buys the oil, fills and trims the lamps, and runs on miscellaneous errands. For these services he receives a salary of something like a dollar a week. Lodgers in town, in rare instances, are also able to boast of employing private sweeps. Since '69's time, the faculty have forbidden the occupants of college rooms either to fee the regular sweeps or to employ private ones, but of course the former prohibition is evaded.

In a student's room, beside some one of the innumerable varieties of the inevitable, book-case, lounge, table, and easy-chair, will often be found a melodeon or piano-forte. The walls are adorned with all kinds of pictures, society posters, and knick knackery of every sort. Hats stolen from Freshmen by Sophomores, or from Sophomores by Freshmen, in some historic rush ; Annual caps ; bangers and other canes ; oars, swords and boxing gloves ; ball clubs and badges ; flags and streamers ; masks with tin horns, pipes or cigars in their mouths ; policemen's caps and "billies" (rare) ; signs from the street lamps or from traders' windows ; gilt eagles, mortars, watches, and other mercantile symbols ; figures cut from theatrical show-bills ; names of college, class, open societies and boat clubs ; wooden spoons, society monograms and groups of society pins anything and everything in the way of a memento of past experience, whether gained by gift, purchase or theft ; all are displayed here. Pipes, tobacco and cigars, playing cards, bottles, glasses and decanters, lie in sight amid the books and papers, or readily at hand in drawer or closet. And branded on the inner side of closet doors are the names and initials of former occupants ; or regular manuscript lists of them carefully compiled from old catalogues by some antiquarian, and running back for nearly a century.

Many are the uninvited and usually unwelcome guests who knock at the college doors. First, there is "Candy Sam," the blind negro who for the past dozen years has "helped hold up the Athenæum tower," and exhorted the Freshmen to patronize the only legitimate candy seller recognized by the institution. Each day he finds his way to every college room, with his apples and confectionery, and soon learns to recognize by their voices, his individual patrons. The Freshmen usually take up a collection for him at Thanksgiving time, and the other classes "remember" him before the opening of the long vacation. He gets all his clothes from college men, and is never tired of sounding the praises of the good fellows in past classes who liberally patronized him. "Sam" is good natured, garrulous, and often amusing. His true name, which he rarely mentions, is Theodore Ferris. Aside from the intermittent "Trade Wind," whose energies are mostly confined to the hawking of "fresh vanilla 'n' lemonice," "Sam"'s chief rival is a crafty black man called "Hannibal," whose entrance into the room is always accompanied by some such formula as, "Not wishing to interrupt the gentlemen in their studies I called to see if either of the gentlemen would like to invest in purchasing from me a package of my nice superior old-fashioned home-made molasses candy." This rigmarole, like all the rest of "Hannibal's" speeches, is delivered with the greatest appearance of gravity, and without pause of any sort save that supplied by the peculiar intonation. Then there is the Jew, ready in all seasons and weathers with his inevitable greeting, " Fine day ! any old clothes for me to-day, my dears?" There is "Old Matches," the tireless. There is " Ajax," and the " Father of Ajax." There is Daniel Pratt, Jr., impecunious but undaunted. There are the street Arabs, ready to "clean a spittoon" or " wash their faces in the mud" for five cents ; the little girls who want a penny wherewith to purchase crackers for a sick mother, or to buy a new dress ; the widow of large family whose husband was killed in the war ; the beggars of all sorts and sizes ; the pedlers of subscription books, of pictures, of patent medicines and patent blacking-boxes and patent lamp-shades ; the owners of every possible device likely to attract a student's money. All these range through the college buildings, without let or hindrance, following one another in endless succession, day after day.

Of course doors are often locked against them, but this is inconvenient, and likely, besides, to keep out more acceptable visitors. The small fry seldom venture above the first floor of the building, unless specially ordered, having a wholesome fear of the upstair rooms, induced by the tricks often practised upon those of their number who have been caught there. A wandering organ-grinder or harpist is sometimes hired, by the men who are to recite there, to play under the window of a recitation room, thus calling down upon himself the rebuke of the tutor, who sternly orders him from the yard. Another trick is for a student to personate a college official, in warning away these and similar stragglers, with many admonitions of mock solemnity.

Two tutors or professors are allotted to each dormitory, and occupy separate rooms. These, with a single exception, are all on the second floor front. In South and South Middle they are the two corner rooms ; in North Middle and North the two middle rooms. In the latter college the two corner rooms of the second floor front are also occupied at certain hours of the day by professors who reside in town ; and the third floor front corner room of the south entry of that college is the exception referred to, being occupied by a tutor or professor. These resident officials never act as spies, and seldom interfere in any way with the inhabitants of the entries, with whom, it usually happens, they are not personally acquainted. If an unusual uproar and disturbance, late at night, proceeds from a room in a tutor's vicinity, he calls there and requests that less noise be made ; and if the racket is unabated, perhaps after a second warning, he reports the case at the next meeting of the faculty. So, too, if a party of carousers insist upon smashing one another's windows, crockery, and furniture, or rolling dumb-bells and coal-scuttles down the stairs, or firing off cannon-crackers in the entries, the tutor is obliged to take 'cognizance thereof, and report to his superiors. So long, however, as a man behaves himself with tolerably decency, and doesn't greatly disturb his neighbors, he is free from all inter-ference, and can do what he likes in his own room. It is this peculiar independence, afforded by no other mode of living, that gives the life in dormitories its greatest charm. A man dwelling there can come and go whenever he will, at any hour of the day or night, and no one need be any the wiser. By himself, or with a jolly company of invited comrades, he can "sport his oak," and while away a pleasant evening, in for-getfulness of the outside world. No irate landlady up-braids him for his late hours, or his want of neatness, or his destructive proclivities. He is his own master. His room is his castle. And if he can't "wallop his own nigger," he can at least swear at his private sweep. The man who fails to room for at least a single year in the dormitories, loses one of the most distinctive expe-riences of college life. So well is this truth recognized, that, spite of all the inconveniences of the present "shells," "brick barracks," "factories,"—as, with too good reason,, the old colleges are often called,—they are always crowded, and are then unable to accommodate a large portion of the applicants. It is, therefore, likely, that in the good time which all Yale men hope is coming, when the college yard shall be surrounded by commodious and elegant edifices like the new stone dormitory, that all the undergraduates will be only too happy to improve the opportunity of living together within the walls.　Many items in the foregoing description will of course have no application to the denizens of the new Farnam College, who are obliged to conduct themselves more discreetly, in return for receiving its luxuries, and who are chaffed at as " aristocrats," " nabobs," and so on, by those who prefer to put up with the inconveniences of the old buildings, rather than submit to the prim regulations of the new.

" Sitting on the fence " is a privilege that no Freshman may enjoy ; at least until Presentation Day, when by courtesy he becomes a Sophomore.　Each of the three upper classes lays claim to a particular portion of the fence as a roosting place.　The Seniors affect the neighborhood of the South College gateways, occupying the space between and a length or two each side of the same.　The Juniors take up the rest of the Chapel street front, toward the east ; and the Sophomores extend on College street, from the corner of Chapel to the Athenæum gateway.　Here, on pleasant days, for an hour or two after dinner and supper, crowds of undergraduates perch themselves, and smoke, chat, laugh and sing together.　The Sophomores naturally improve the opportunity thus afforded to howl and shriek at the Freshmen who may be obliged to pass near them. under pretext of doing away with this, and silencing the complaints of the townspeople against the blocking up of the sidewalks, the faculty decreed, in the autumn of '66, when the class of '69 were Sophomores, that there should be no more sitting upon the fence, or gathering of groups in its vicinity, under penalty of five marks for each offender.　The rule was exceedingly unpopular ; and it could not be enforced.　Crowds perched upon the fence as usual, scattered on the approach of an official, and then came back to their roost again. The fence was repeatedly torn up, hacked to pieces, and set on fire, and the college carpenter's repairs of the day were destroyed on the approach of night, until watchmen had to be employed to protect the fence from its relentless foes. Next spring, plank benches were set up under the trees, in various parts of the yard, and use was made of them by the students; but they were no substitute for the fence, which was as attractive as ever, and as ever the most popular rendezvous. Little by little, the faculty left off marking, and at the end of the year they abandoned definitely the attempt to enforce the obnoxious rule,—not however thinking it necessary to make any public announcement of their defeat. The benches were removed, a year and a half after their erection.

The result of the conflict showed the inability of the faculty to enforce an unfair rule which the common sense of college unanimously condemned. Without question, it is somewhat unpleasant for travelers afoot to run the gauntlet of hundreds of students' eyes, and they may at times suffer other annoyance because of the assembled crowd; but, after all, their inconvenience is but trifling when compared with the solid, substantial comfort which undergraduates take in sitting on the fence. There is nothing wicked or disreputable about the practice, and as it is one of the most cherished relaxations of every college man, its attempted abolishment was impolitic and foolish. Each victim of the decree felt this prohibition of an innocent amusement to be an unreasonable infringement of his personal liberty, and spite of marks, warnings, and suspensions, all joined in asserting their rights and forcing the faculty from an untenable position. It may be doubted if any large number of townspeople seriously object to the practice, for it is not difficult for the timid to walk upon the further side of the street when passing the colleges; and, for a good natured man, the sight of a fence full of merry faces must be a pleasant one. To sit there of a pleasant afternoon, watching the passing pedestrians; listening to the tirades of the "great American traveler," or the music of an itinerant harpist, or banjo-player, or organ-grinder; applauding the songs and stories of "Crazy Charley," or some other strolling vagabond; pitching pennies into the mud, for the encouragement of impromptu prize-fights among the street ragamuffins; chaffing with Candy Sam or Hannibal; "listlessly loafing the hours away;" seems, to many a one, happiness supreme.

Singing, too, is never entered into or enjoyed so heartily as when sitting on the fence; the subtle fascination of that locality—seeming to accord well with the spirit of melody. One of the pleasantest recollections of a graduate is the memory of moonlight evenings under the elms, enlivened by the inspiring sounds of grand old college tunes. While "on the fence," each class sings by itself, though two crowds sometimes alternate with each other. The musical talent varies in different classes, but usually the Seniors do the most outdoor singing, the Juniors a little less, and the Sophomores least; while the Freshmen, having no place on the fence, cannot be said to sing at all. Often a party will sing for an hour or more, — changing from grave to gay, from lively to severe—while the windows and balconies of the New Haven Hotel testify their appreciation of the music. The collection of Yale songs published in 1867 numbered about 100, assigned to half that number of distinct airs. Many of them of course are in vogue elsewhere, but a great majority undoubtedly originated at the institution or were first adopted by it as distinctively college songs. In the collection of American college songs, published a year later by a member of Hamilton College, Yale is assigned 38 pages out of the 245, or 14 more than Harvard, which has the next largest number, and about four times as many as the average of the 21 colleges represented. Certain it is that at no other institution is this sort of music so extensively indulged in. Of late years, with the dying out of certain old customs whose celebration demanded original songs, fewer such melodies have been produced than formerly, yet about every class leaves behind it two or three new ones—in possession of a society or the general college public—with vitality enough to keep them for a long time afloat. What the popularity of a college song depends upon it would be hard to say. The operatic choruses and—the negro minstrels supply many new ones, which are held in high favor for a short time and then for the most part are forgotten. A few, however, manage to outlive the ephemeral popularity of the others, and finally become incorporated with the regular songs of the college. Next to a really meritorious piece, one which is outrageously absurd seems to stand the best chance of adoption ; and it is very desirable, if not indispensable, for a tune that would find favor in college, that it should not be often heard outside it, especially upon the street. Yale men, except professional singers, rarely know more than the first verse or two of any one song, so that, if given to the end, all but the chorus becomes a solo. Usually, instead of this, the tune is changed and a new song started, and so on till the crowd's collection of "first verses" has been exhausted. Even so old a melody as "Lauriger" is seldom rendered entire, and probably not one man in a dozen could give the last verse correctly without previous cramming.

This custom of singing is a comparatively modern one, and the secret societies have the credit of introducing it,—several of the college melodies having been originally their own private property. The first collection of Yale songs was issued in 1853,—N. W. T. Root of '52 and J. K. Lombard of '54 being the editors,—and comprised an octavo pamphlet of 56 pages. A second edition, of the same number of pages, was put forth by the same editors in 1855. Three years later, Edward C. Porter of '58 edited the third edition, enlarged to 72 pages, and again in 1860 the fourth, of 88 pages. The first edition was printed by L. M. Guernsey of Springfield, and published by E. Richardson ; of the others, J. H. Benham was the printer and T. H. Pease the publisher. The next collection of Yale songs was " Carmina Yalensia,"—large 8vo, muslin cover, 88 pages,—issued in 1867 by Taintor Brothers of New York, F. V. Garretson of '66 being the compiler. The collection now current is " Songs of Yale," 12mo, 126 pages, compiled by C. S. Elliot of '67, and published by C. C. Chatfield & Co. in 1870. Few of the songs now sung, and few indeed of those in the earliest collection were written much before 1850. " Gaudeamus " and " Integer Vitæ " were introduced in 1848, by Richard S. Willis of '41, who brought them from the German universities. " Lauriger " was similarly derived, and more recently "Abschied," "Edite" and "Lathery." " Benny Havens " was first brought from West Point by the Cochleaureati of '54. " It's a way we have at Old Yale, Sir," is an original Yale song which has been adapted to almost every college in the country. The air—" We won't go home till morning "—to which it is sung is an old one, which, like many others once popular with the general public, is now rarely heard outside of college walls. It is a curious fact that many of those now recognized as distinctively college tunes, were formerly public property, which, after enjoying for a brief season, the outside world abandoned and forgot.

"Glee clubs" are often organized, sometimes as class, sometimes as college affairs. A club of the latter sort is quite certain to give public exhibitions, "for the entertainment of the audience and the emolument of the members;" and a class club may do the same, or it may practise for its own amusement simply. The two may exist at the same time and be in part made up of the same individuals. A class glee-club is never organized before sophomore year; neither is a Freshman, unless a remarkably good singer, admitted to one of the other sort. The most famous of strictly class glee-clubs was that of '63; but the present club, which is mostly made up of '71 men, is said to be the best ever organized, has given several very successful concerts, and proposes to devote a month of the next vacation to an extended tour on land and water,—singing in public often enough to pay for the expenses of the trip. Like most clubs of the sort, it comprises about a dozen members. Of more formal character is the aged institution known as the "Beethoven Society," which was originated in 1812, by some members of the class which graduated the following year, among whom was Professor Olmsted, the second president of the society. It always formed the college choir until 1855, when, on account of some difference with the faculty, it ceased to perform that office, and its place was supplied by a rival organization of still greater antiquity called "Cecilia." At the end of two years this society became absorbed in Beethoven, and the latter again controlled the choir until about 1860, when the present arrangement, elsewhere described, was effected. It naturally happens, however, that nearly all the members of the choir are still claimed by the society. When the name "Beethoven" came to be applied to what was at first known only as "the singing club" is uncertain, but by the time it was 25 years old, its ordinary number of members was about 30,—two thirds of whom were singers, and the rest composed the "grand orchestra."

"We had every unique instrument from the piccolo fife to the big drum. Of course our music in its grand *ensemble* of voices and instruments was often what might be termed *rousing:*—and whenever we put forth our musical energies we kept the attention of our auditors from the beginning to the end. The instrument greatly predominating in our orchestra was the flute. 'The inevitable flute' had, indeed, ever to be repressed and discouraged. Every second fellow who wanted to join the choir played a flute. We grew, indeed, to be relentless on the flute question. Having secured several of the most accomplished upon that pastoral instrument, we turned our backs resolutely upon all other piping shepherds. Strange to say, however, the instrument best played of all was the violin. We actually had violin playing rather than that fiddling naturally (of students) to be expected. We were also supplied with the viola, 'cello and double-bass, so that the quartette of the 'strings' was complete. Of the 'brasses' we had but a single representative,—a big ophicleide. It was our great gun, that ophicleide. We based a good deal of our musical reputation upon the fundamental notes of that deep-mouthed orator. We had now and then a guitar, a triangle, a piccolo flute, etc. Such instruments as were *not* heard, by reason of the general din—like the tinkling guitar—were supposed to be heard. They *looked* pretty when the fellows played them—and a great many serenaded misses in town could testify that (when heard at all) they also sounded pretty.

"Up to 1841, each graduating class had gone to the no inconsiderable expense of hiring a New York orchestra to play at Center Church during the Commencement exercises, as is still the practice. But that year we determined to save all expense and do the melodious thing ourselves. Nor this alone. We resolved to attempt the as yet unheard-of enterprise, and give a concert on the evening preceding Commencement. It was held in a church on Church street, the pulpit being removed for the occasion and a staging constructed. The number of tickets issued was unlimited, and—unfortunately for the accommodations of the church—the sale was unlimited : so that when the evening of performance arrived, one-third of the audience had to listen from the street, we putting up the windows, and the audience complacently submitting to such unprecedented concert-arrangements. Between the parts of the programme an address on Music was delivered by the president [R. S. Willis, whose words are being quoted], he feeling safe from any expressions of disapproval, from the fact that precautions had wisely been taken, early in the evening, to request the audience to refrain from any tokens of satisfaction or dissatisfaction—if for no other reason, out of regard for the character of the place."

Since then, the character of Beethoven has materially changed. The orchestra was long ago abandoned, and the " big ophicleide" and other instruments are things of memory only, though perhaps instrumental clubs like "Tyrolea," and the "Yale String Band," and "Yale Tooters," in turn inherited them. There was also a "Musical Band" organized as early as 1827, which raised money enough to make extensive purchases, but which came to an early end. Its instruments were bequeathed to the president of the college, who afterwards on special occasions used to loan the band's big bass drum to the students. There are periods of suspended animation in the Beethoven society's existence, followed by vigorous revivals and displays of unwonted vitality. When in good working trim, it aims to give two or three concerts a year in New Haven, and, with the faculty's permission, as many more at such places as New York, Brooklyn, Jersey City, Hartford, Providence, and even Boston. On these occasions the best singers among the late graduates, who are members of the professional schools or otherwise residents, usually lend their assistance. One of them is sometimes chosen leader of the society, and employed on a salary as a director of the rehearsals. Otherwise, if necessary, a professional is elected to the position. Regular weekly rehearsals are held on Wednesday evenings and are an hour in length ; while in preparation for a concert the practice meetings are of course more frequent and prolonged. Posters on the trees request the attendance of members. Calliope hall is sometimes used as a place of meeting ; or an apartment in town is rented for the purpose. While '69 was in college, the membership varied from 40 to 70,— 50 being the average. The Seniors usually outnumber the others, though the last published list exhibits : Seniors 20, Juniors 20, Sophomores 9 and Scientifics 8. In the old times, there doubtless was fierce rivalry between Cecilia and Beethoven in electioneering for new members, and " likely" Freshmen were called upon and made to display their vocal abilities, by partisans of the two clubs on the look-out for the best singers among the new comers. Now-a-days, an under-class man is elected on the recommendation of those who know him to be a " good singer," and any Senior, possessed of sufficient musical sense to keep time to an ordinary chorus, finds no difficulty in becoming a " Beethovenite." There is therefore no particular " honor" about an election to, or an " office" in, the society, and consequently there is little wrangling on those points. The " constitution," "archives," and " properties," are not very extensive or valuable.

Students are dragged to Beethoven rehearsals, as to all others, with great difficulty. Even with a concert in preparation, attendance is by no means general. Only a small portion of the members take the prominent parts in the concerts,—the remaining voices being used to help on the choruses,—and the complaints of partiality and injustice, so common among musical people elsewhere, are not always wanting. As every member of a class or college glee club is almost certain to belong to the society also, a " grand concert" is usually advertised in the name of the " Beethoven Society and Yale Glee Club." In such cases " the society" gets the credit for the elaborate, " scientific" pieces, and " the club" for the hearty college songs, which the audience most expect and relish. The profits of the concerts are not usually large, for the cost of transporting so large a company is considerable, and the money made by a successful show may be offset by that lost in an unlucky one. Students are not distinguished as shrewd business managers. Still, enough is usually made to pay the running expenses of the society without a resort to taxation ; and a respectable surplus is often left to present to the Yale Navy, or some similar needy "institution."

The number of Sophomores in any class who amuse themselves by abusing the Freshmen, in the ways described in the last chapter, is not very large. A dozen ringleaders, and as many more who occasionally lend their presence to such proceedings would probable include them all. The rest of the class, with self-respect enough not to favor such things themselves, are yet indifferent as regards the others, or at best but passively hostile to them. It is a rare thing for a Sophomore of influence to utter a bold protest against the excesses of his classmates. The common remark that "a few bullies and cowards in every sophomore class are able to disgrace it and the college, in spite of an all but unanimous sentiment againt them," is not true, as a matter of fact. The number of evil doers, as stated at the opening of the paragraph, is certainly few, but there is no strong public sentiment against them. They do not lose their social standing and importance. They are still accounted good fellows. They are chosen to the highest offices and receive elections to the best societies. Class and college look upon their sins as venial ones, and, while disapproving of the same, do not inflict any sort of punishment on account thereof.

In the classes of '66 and '67 the Sophomores who specially engaged in the duty of "disciplining" the Freshmen called themselves the " Court of Areopagus," and published under that title in the *Banner* the names of two "judices," three "accusatores," four "lictors" and four "carnifices." Each name was formed by an odd-looking combination of letters, like " Nchokotsa," " Mochoasele," " Kantankruss," or " Phreshietaugh," followed by the small Greek letters corresponding to the initials of each man's real name. The whole was printed in heavy black type and surmounted by mourning rules, to make more plausible the included motto, " Nos timeunt Freshmanes." In the " Bingo" song, then as now shouted at the Fresh, " A-re-op-a-gus ! Freshmen stand in fear of us," supplied the place of " Here's to good old Yale, She's so hearty and so hale." The two classes who successively supported the "court" also published "personal" lists in regard to the peculiarities of their own "fellows." The long, short, fat, thin, big, little, hard, soft, odd, good, gay, and strong, "fellows" of the Sophomores, each had their initials indicated by the small Greek letters. This is mentioned because of its exceptional character, for the practice, though common at other colleges, is rarely indulged in at Yale. It should not be inferred that "Areopagus" was peculiar to the classes mentioned. It had existed for ten or a dozen years before their time, as a sort of freshman bugbear, but it had not previously published the fact of its existence so boldly. The Easthampton boys are said to have introduced it, as an institution of similar name and object had long been kept up at their academy. Everything about it was shrouded in mystery, and its very indefiniteness added terror to its name among the Freshmen. When one of them was hazed, "the Areopagus" was believed to be at the bottom of it, even though the victim was punished without a formal trial and sentence under the peculiar and awe-inspiring forms belonging to that august tribunal. Since its disappearance from the *Banner* the name has become obsolete. "Turdetani" was the title of a somewhat similar affair devised by the Sophs of '63.

Sophomores and also Juniors occasionally form make-believe "societies" among themselves, possessed of certain letters or symbols, whose signification is usually a joke or "sell" of some kind. A thing of the sort in '68 became well known on account of the popularity of a jingling chorus, originated by it, which was mostly made up of a repetition of the name, "Nu Tau Phi." When the '68 men came to be Juniors, they thought a transfer of the joke to a half-dozen Sophomores might be productive of cigars and potables, and accordingly announced that those expecting elections to the "society" should be in their rooms on a certain night. At the appointed time, several roguish Sophs thought fit to impose on their classmates who had made any preparations for "election," by pretending to be Juniors, offering the elections to "Nu Tau Phi," and helping themselves to their wine and cigars. The fraud was carried out successfully in two or three cases. In others, the chief actors of the joke were discovered in the midst of it. When the real Juniors finally appeared, they brought, as "election cards," large pasteboards on which were scrawled the names of the "elected." That was the end of "Nu Tau Phi," but the success of these spurious elections to this mock "society," suggested to the Sophomores the idea of playing a similar game upon ambitious Freshmen. Accordingly a number of them devised the "Omega Lambda Chi,"—adapting the latter part of the title to the "nu-tau-phi chorus." On an appointed evening Freshmen were visited by individual Sophomores, pledged to secrecy, and then electioneered for a mysterious society whose name was not divulged. If they consented to join it, they were to be prepared to receive their elections at midnight. As many of these visitors belonged to the regular sophomore societies, which at that time had agreed to give no pledges, the Freshmen connected the offer with a secret attempt to get around this agreement, and readily swallowed the bait. So "Lambda Chi" gave out its elections, and was well "treated" by the humbugged Freshmen who "accepted the honor." They in turn were thus inspired to practice a somewhat similar trick upon one of their own number, who, having entered the class late in the year, had by foolish actions rendered himself obnoxious to them. As the time for giving out the regular sophomore society elections approached, he was accordingly waited upon by some classmates, who played the part of Sophomores, and offered him an election to "Phi Beta Chi," or some similar variation of the real name of a sophomore society. Accepting this "with pleasure," he was blindfolded, taken to a hall in town and tossed in a blanket, make to speak a piece, answer a series of nonsensical questions, and so on, and finally given the "grip" invented for the occasion, and left standing in the street near his lodging-house, under a pledge not to open his eyes until his attendants had made good their escape. So, pleased with his "election" was the victim of this transparent humbug, that he firmly believed in the fraud up to the night when the real elections were actually conferred upon his classmates. The Freshmen, too, kept their secret well, and the trick was known to but few save the participants. Their dupe shortly afterwards bade adieu to the class and college. As for "Lambda Chi," the name at least is still current in college, and perhaps the sell connected with it has become traditional.

The faculty of course attempt to shield the Freshmen from abuse and imposition at the hands of the Sophomores, but in the nature of things their control over such matters is small. Their most effective means of action is in the nature of a bargain or compromise. Suppose that several Freshmen are caught in a rush, and suspended indefinitely, or even dropped from the class altogether. Their classmates sign a petition to the authorities, praying that the verdict be reversed, and promising, if their classmates be restored, to take part in no more rushes, and in sophomore year to refrain from all interference with their inferiors. The Freshmen of '68 took a pledge of this sort, in behalf of some Sophomores who had hazed one of their number, but afterwards broke it; and there are doubtless similar cases of bad faith on record. The Sophomores of '72, however, preserved in all its strictness a pledge of non-interference, and scrupulously refrained from the least abuse of the Freshmen, who, in turn, though bound by no pledge, gave but little trouble to *their* successors; and perhaps it is possible that a better state of things is henceforth to prevail. It was suggestive to notice, during the period of unexampled harmony between '72 and '73, the frequency of the newspaper item, " Hazing has been revived at Yale College."

The Sophs of '69 have the discredit of introducing the practice of burning the college " coal-yard "; or at all events the trick, which seems to be almost becoming a "custom," had not been known of for several years before their time, if ever. It was on the night of November 13–14, 1866, that the first conflagration happened. At that time, an extraordinary meteoric display was looked for by the scientific men of the country, and the college professors specially interested in the matter made considerable preparations for taking accurate observations of the expected shower, from the top of the south tower of Alumni Hall. It was arranged to have several relays of Sophomores and Juniors join them there in watching out the night and counting the meteors as they fell. All college was excited upon the subject of the heavenly pyrotechnics, and kept wide awake till midnight, awaiting them: then in disgust went to bed, content to rely upon the fire alarm which was to arouse all the city in case the expected display really appeared. At about two o'clock in the morning the alarm did ring, rousing out the citizens to behold— not a meteoric shower, but a conflagration in the college yard, whereof the north coal-yard furnished the material, sending forth a sheet of flame which brought into bold relief the figures of the star gazers perched upon the top of the tower. This was a practical joke which, though exasperating to many, yet from the peculiar circumstances of the case, had some reason for being; but the later attempts of the same sort have been without anything to recommend them. The south yard was made a bonfire of in celebration of Grant's election to the presidency, and was then rebuilt of brick. A year later the north was again fired, and it was burnt for the third time at the opening of the summer term of 1870, on which occasion tutors' windows were smashed, the Bible was removed from the chapel, the handle was broken from the college organ, and the chapel cushions of the college officers were thrown into the fire. The outrage thoroughly exasperated all college, and when a few days later the faculty detected the three drunken Sophomores who were guilty of perpetrating it, and promptly expelled them, every one joined in approving the verdict. The yard was fired for the fourth time, in the midst of a driving rain storm, on the night before last Thanksgiving day, supposably to signify dissatisfaction at the omission of the Jubilee. As the coal-yard proper is quite a large structure, the exertions of the fire department have thus far prevented the destruction of more than one side or corner of it, though their engine hose has sometimes been cut and disabled by the incendiaries or their abettors, by whom also the peelers have been yelled at and insulted. The cost of rebuilding is assessed in the shape of "extra damages" upon the students' term bills ; and so, in money as well as reputation, all college suffers from the vandalism of a few cowardly sneaks.

Though the organization of a base-ball club is one of the first things accomplished by Freshmen, yet it is usually in sophomore year that a class nine attains its greatest efficiency. After that, its best men are drawn into the University club, and though the separate organization may be kept up for the first part of junior year, it is almost certain to be abandoned before the fourth year opens.   The game first assumed its present importance as a leading sport of college at about the time when '69 entered the institution, in the autumn of 1865,—though clubs had at times figured in the *Banner* for a half-dozen years preceding.   In the University nine, then for the first time organized, there were three Freshmen.   The class club, at the close of freshman year, beat the corresponding club of Harvard, 36 to 33 ; and again, a year later, 23 to 22.   It then became absorbed in the University nine, which for the three following years suffered defeat at the hands of Harvard : July 25, 1868,—17 to 25 ; July 5, 1869,—24 to 41 ; July 4, 1870,—22 to 24.   There have been four other matches between as many successive freshman classes in the two colleges : '70's, in 1867,—38 to 18 ; 71's, in 1868,—18 to 36 ; 72's, in 1869,—28 to 19 ; and '73's, in 1870,— 21 to 18.   Yale, therefore, has won five out of the six Class matches with Harvard, but has lost all three of the University contests.   In 1869, the University match was played at Brooklyn, and the freshman match at Providence ; in 1870, the corresponding localities were New Haven and Springfield ; all previous games had been played at Worcester during the week of the regatta.

Up to the exit of '69,—which class was represented in every game,—the University had played with and defeated the University nines of Wesleyan, Columbia, Princeton, and Williams ; and had engaged in 24 games with 11 different non-collegiate clubs, in half of which it was victorious, with a total score of 547 to 427. From that time till the close of 1870, it played and was defeated in two college matches,—by St. John's, June 1,—19 to 13 ; by Princeton, July 6,—26 to 15 ; was victorious in four games played with two amateur clubs of Connecticut, by a score of 136 to 56 ; and was defeated in all but one of six games played with five professional clubs, by a score of 63 to 176,—the successful game being that with the Lowells, June 17,—14 to 8. The first two trials of 1871, which are the only ones that can be recorded here, were: with the Mutuals, May 6,—10 to 20; with the Eckfords, May 13,—17 to 14. Two previous (1870) games with the former club had resulted: 12 to 49; 9 to 31; and one (1869) with the latter: 8 to 24. The other professionals included in the previous summary were: the Athletics, 12 to 29, and the White Stockings, 8 to 35. Probably as large a number of matches as those here recorded have been played in the interval by the various class clubs, but the only college contests of the sort, aside from those with Harvard, were the 1867 games of the '69 Sophomores against Princeton: May 4,—52 to 58; June 27,—40 to 30 (?); and the 1870 game of the '71 Juniors against the University nine of Trinity: June 1,—26 to 19. Matches between the different classes, or between Class and University, have also been quite common. At the opening of the season of 1870 a member of the graduating class offered for competition a champion flag, the first possession of which was decided in this wise: the Seniors played with the Sophomores, the Juniors with the Freshmen, and the victors in these two trials—Juniors and Sophomores—fought for the championship, which was won by the former, but afterwards taken by the latter ('72), by whom, spite of several contests, it has since been retained. A single game decides the matter, and the holders are constantly open to challenge, and, if Seniors, must, upon graduation, surrender the flag to the incoming senior class. Matches for the championship are rather discouraged by the captain of the University, as tending to impair the efficiency of his nine, by absorbing a half holiday which had better be spent in a University match of some sort. Excepting the trials with Harvard, the first '69 sophomore match with Princeton, and the '71 junior match against the University nine of Trinity, all the college games have been played at New Haven, as have also a great majority of the others. It is expected, however, that during the next long vacation the University nine will make arrangements for an extended tour and trial of skill with the best local clubs in various parts of the country. The enthusiasm over base-ball was never as high at Yale as now, and the nine is confessedly superior to any other that has yet represented the college. In the victory of May 17, its members were: four Juniors, three Freshmen, one Senior, and one Sophomore.

The ball-ground, where all of the matches and most of the practice games are played, is at Hamilton Park, situated about two miles from the colleges, on the line of the horse railway. When the reputation of the contestants will warrant it, an admission fee is charged ; and the receipts obtained in this way are often considerable, as an important "match game" is quite certain to attract a good many spectators, both from town and college. A professional club stipulates in advance for a certain share of the gate money, as a half, or two thirds ; otherwise it is kept by the Yale men to help pay for the necessary expenses. These are, in one way and another, considerable ; 'and when a class club is to be fitted out with new uniforms and equipments for a contest with Harvard, or is to entertain guests from another college, it has to ask pecuniary aid from those who are willing to support a class " institution " in which they themselves have no personal interest. So, too, in similar cases, subscription papers for the benefit of the University club are circulated through all the classes,— especially in those which have no separate clubs of their own to demand their assistance. Self-appointed Sophomores of '68 had a trick, early in the year, of collecting subscriptions for this and other "causes" from verdant Freshmen, and "going on a bum" with the money thus extorted; but they are believed to have been without successors in their rascality.

Wednesday and Saturday afternoons are the times specially set apart for the sport by its votaries, and are the only times when the faculty allow the playing of matches with outside clubs, though class matches are for reason sometimes played upon other days. An open lot within a half mile of college is to some extent made to do duty as a practice ground, though possessed of little save its proximity to recommend it. " Muffins," or clubs which make no pretence to good playing, are its chief patrons. "Pass ball" was considerably practised in the gymnasium yard, and to some extent on the college or city green, where, in these latter cases, players were exposed to fine by the college authorities, or arrest by the city police. But recently, as the faculty have sanctioned the tossing of ball within certain limits of the college yard, the other places are deserted, and the practice in the yard is constant. The faculty consent rather grudgingly to a club's playing outside of New Haven, in term time, and occasionally forbid it altogether, though recently they have adopted the rule of allowing three such games each term. Sometimes when they permit a game, for which the arrangements have been made, they allow no friends and backers to accompany the actual players on the journey; the time of the game is usually so fixed that the absentees need lose but one or at the most two recitations. But there are always stragglers, and those who return promptly are not apt to " rush," when called up the morning after a ball match.

The vanquished party in a ball match always yields

up its ball as a token of defeat; and a Junior of '69, who was an officer of the University ball club, collected these emblems of victory that had been won from outsiders by the college clubs, had them gilded and inscribed with the time and place of the match, the names of the contesting clubs, and the score, and placed them in an ornamental case, in which they were displayed for a year or two, in Hoadley's window. But the custom was not kept up, on account of its expensiveness, and the case with its original contents has now been banished to the room of the club president. Relations with an amateur or professional club usually extend no further than the game itself, and the same holds good of the annual contests with Harvard, which are held on neutral ground (though the University match of 1870 was necessarily played at New Haven). But when another college club is invited to Yale, or a Yale club is invited to another college, for a friendly trial of skill, there is usually an expressed or implied understanding that the club shall bring along its friends, and all take part in a general jollification. Thus the Yale club, after beating the Columbia men, treated them to a good supper, which the latter reciprocated by instituting an elaborate banquet on the occasion of the proposed " return match" which the weather prevented from being played. The '69 Sophomores were likewise most hospitably entertained by the Princeton Sophs who defeated them, and were loud in their promises of a complimentary return. Yet for some unknown reason neither they, nor their University club, when they came to New Haven, were shown any special attention by the Yale men, and they naturally felt aggrieved in consequence. Whatever the cause of this cavalier treatment, it seems to have been inexcusable, and it certainly was regretted. That it was entirely exceptional is perhaps the best that can be said of the discourtesy. At these inter-collegiate suppers, perhaps there is more wine disposed of than is absolutely neces-sary, yet the rule is honest hilarity rather than drunken-ness. Such gatherings, next to secret-society conven-tions, furnish the chief medium through which under-graduates of different colleges can become acquainted, and, if kept free from excesses, are manifestly advanta-geous to all concerned in them.

Nothing has thus far been described in this chapter which could not with almost equal reason be included in those which follow ; yet up to a recent period Sopho-more Year was possessed of one distinctive custom,— the ceremony known as the " Burial of Euclid." As long ago as 1843 the custom was said to have been " handed down from time immemorial"; and with this preface a writer of the period thus goes on to describe it : " This book [Euclid], the terror of the dilatory and unapt, having at length been completely mastered, the class, as their acquaintance with the Greek mathema-tician is about to close, assemble [by divisions ?] in their respective places of meeting, and prepare (secretly for fear of the faculty) for the anniversary. The necessary committee having been appointed, and the regular prep-arations ordered, a ceremony has sometimes taken place like the following : The huge poker is heated in the old stove and driven through the smoking volume, and the division, marshalled in line, for once at least 'see through' the whole affair. They then 'understand' it, as it is passed above their heads ; and they finally march over it in solemn procession, and are enabled, as they step firmly on its covers, to assert with truth that they have ' gone over' it—poor jokes, indeed, but sufficient to afford abundant laughter. And then follow speeches, comical and pathetic, and shouting and merriment. The night assigned having arrived, how carefully they assemble, all silent, at the place appointed! Laid on its bier, covered with sable pall, and borne in solemn state, the corpse (*i. e.*, the book) is carried with slow procession, with the moaning music of flutes and fifes, the screaming of fiddles, and thumping and mumbling of a cracked drum, to the opened grave or the funeral pyre. A gleaming line of blazing torches and twinkling lanterns, moves along the quiet streets and through the open fields, and the snow creaks hoarsely under the tread of a hundred men. They reach the scene, and a circle formed around the consecrated spot; if the ceremony is a burial, the defunct is laid all carefully in his grave, and then his friends celebrate in prose or verse his memory, his virtues, and his untimely end: and three *oboli* are tossed into his tomb to satisfy the surly boatman of the Styx. Lingeringly is the last look taken of the familiar countenance, as the procession passes slowly around the tomb; and a moaning is made—a sound of groans going up to the seventh heaven—and the earth is thrown in, and the headstone with epitaph placed duly to hallow the grave of the dead. Or if, according to the custom of his native land, the pyre, duly prepared with combustibles, is make the center of the ring; a ponderous jar of turpentine or whisky is the fragrant incense, and as the lighted fire mounts up in the still night, and the alarm sounds dim in the distance, the eulogium is spoken, and the memory of the illustrious dead honored; the urn receives the sacred ashes, which, borne in solemn procession, are placed on some conspicuous situation, or solemnly deposited in some fitting sarcophagus. So the sport ends; a song, a loud hurrah, and the last jovial roysterer seek short and profound slumber."

A member of the class of '38 writes that during his college career the Burial "was talked of as a thing once practised"; though it is probable that the ceremonies had been less elaborate than those which were in vogue in 1843. When the study of Euclid was restricted to freshman year, the ceremony was not abandoned, nor the time of holding it changed. The preliminary meeting in the division rooms, for the purpose of "understanding," "going over" and "seeing through" the book, was naturally given up, but the custom was held on to by the Sophomores, instead of being transferred to the Freshmen and celebrated by them at the actual time of finishing the study. It is possible that the Burial was omitted by some classes, but it seems to have been observed pretty regularly by most, for the *Lit.* speaks of it in 1857 as "the annual disgrace," and a year later Davenport's well-known lithographic sketch of the ceremony was published, accompanied by a description,— to be quoted from hereafter. The Masonic "Temple," on the corner of Court and Orange streets, was the place where the opening rites used to be held, the crowd marching thither from the rendezvous on the State House steps. The building was also in those days often used by collegians for other celebrations,—Freshman Initiation, and the Wooden Spoon Exhibition, at times being held there. The Burial took place about the middle of the first term, though the mention of snow in the account already quoted would imply a later date as customary in those earlier years. Many and perhaps all in the two upper classes were made acquainted with the password that would admit them to the exhibition, but the few townsmen who managed to slip in were there by sufferance rather than invitation. The town rabble of course followed the procession from the hall to the funeral pile, perhaps with a few upper-class men among them, though most of these no doubt kept away from the burning. The printed programmes, and the various original songs, poems, orations and speeches, aimed to be witty, but, like those of the freshman Pow-wow, too often succeeded in being simply vulgar and obscene. Indecent jokes at the expense of unpopular tutors and professors, as well as of Euclid himself, were all too common, and these, combined with other excesses, finally brought the custom to its downfall. In one class only ('53), the oration, speeches, songs, and the rest, were all published, in a covered pamphlet, of which—fortunately for the credit of all concerned—but few copies were printed. The account accompanying the lithograph of 1858, already noted, says :

"Late on some dark October evening, mysterious forms, under cover of fiendish masks and satanic habiliments, are seen pointing in silence and with solemn tread toward the 'Temple.' Repeating the Homeric password, they file up the winding staircase, guarded by the gleaming swords of the 'force committee,' and enter the hall, already echoing with the shouts and songs of the assembled multitude. On the stage in front lies an effigy ; and the likeness thereof is of an aged man ; and the name thereof is Euclid. Around the effigy are innumerable Sophomores, dancing and singing in solemn measure :

> " 'In the arms of death old Euclid sleepeth,
>   Sleepeth calmly now ;
> And corruption's ghastly dampness creepeth
>   O'er his pallid brow. ·
> His *triangles*, which so often floored us,
>   Soon shall find their grave ;
> He'll *try angling* with the *lines* that bored us,
>   In the Stygian wave.
>
> " His accounts all *squared*, he hath departed
>   From his earthly *sphere ;*
> On a narrow *bier* his *body's* carted,
>   Not a *la(r)ger bier*.

> We've *described* the *space* of his existence,
>   In these *given lines*,
> And we'll burn old Euclid in the distance,
>   'Neath the waving pines.'

. "The wild, grotesque hilarity of these midnight songs, when once experienced, can never be forgotten. Oration, poem, and funeral oration follow, interrupted with songs and music from the band: 'Old Grimes is dead,' 'Music from the Spheres,' and other choice and solemn masterpieces. Then are torches lighted, and two-by-two the long train of torch bearers defile through the silent midnight streets, to the swell of solemn music, and passing by the dark cemetery of the real dead, bear through 'Tutor's Lane' the wrapt coffin of Father Euclid. They climb the hill, and in the neighboring field commit it to the flames of the funeral pyre, invoking Pluto in Latin prayers, and chanting a final dirge ; while the flare of torches, the wild grotesqueness of each uncouthly-disguised wight, and the background of cold, starlit sky, and dark encircling forest, makes the wild merriment seem almost solemn."

In the lithograph, "the scene represented is the ceremony at the funeral pyre, when the flames are already kindled, and the priest is dooming the shade of the departed to the endless pains of the bottomless pit. On the left is seen a band of jolly students—Euclid haters—mounting the hill of science with the aid of ponies and wings, all in a state of great hilarity, with the exception of one, whose refractory steed gives a downward tendency to his movements. On the right are seen the infernals bearing away the body of Euclid in triumph, and in the foreground a weeping crocodile is represented as shedding significant tears. In the left hand corner, the sad effects of overmuch study are faithfully represented by the wan features and forlorn